God Loves **YOU** !
John 3: 16

GREATEST KENTUCKY DERBY UPSETS

GREATEST KENTUCKY DERBY UPSETS

BY THE STAFF OF BLOOD-HORSE PUBLICATIONS

ECLIPSE
PRESS

Lexington, Kentucky

Library of Congress Control Number: 2006909020

ISBN: 978-1-58150-156-8

Printed in the United States
First Edition: 2007

Race charts are copyrighted © 2007 Equibase Company LLC

a division of
Blood-Horse Publications
PUBLISHERS SINCE 1916

Contents

Introduction 7

Chapter 1   *A Homegrown Classic* 11

Chapter 2   *The Longest Odds* 29

Chapter 3   *The Work Horse* 41

Chapter 4   *Destined To Win* 57

Chapter 5   *The Spoiler* 75

Chapter 6   *Defeating the Dancer* 89

Chapter 7   *The Second-Stringer* 103

Chapter 8   *Viva Canonero!* 121

Chapter 9   *Risk and Reward* 141

Chapter 10   *Lil E. Who?* 161

Chapter 11   *Small But Mighty* 175

Chapter 12   *Decreed By the Derby Gods* 189

Photo Credits 205

About the Authors 206

Introduction

THE KENTUCKY DERBY occupies the hopes, thoughts, and dreams of the collective American Thoroughbred world from late autumn until the following May. Under such prolonged scrutiny, everything about the Derby takes on sizeable proportions:

• A three-year-old allowance race in February with a well-bred winner generates far more interest and analysis than would be true in, say, July or August.

• The debut of the previous year's two-year-old champion is awaited with high interest, although across the decades these youthful champions rarely prevail in the Derby's test of intermediate maturity.

• Major spring prep races are subject to myriad interpretation as backers of the winner exult and backers of the beaten apply their alchemy of exculpatory explanation.

Finally, the Derby arrives on the first Saturday in May, and in about two minutes the months are compressed into an explosive expression of reality. In this atmosphere a mere surprise might be seen as a shock and a highly anticipated result accepted as a coronation, although the extreme emotions of the moment are sometimes tempered with the passage of time.

In addressing which Derby upsets are the most memorable, the editorial staff of Eclipse Press, *The Blood-Horse*, and selected authors recognized that there is more to the subject than which winner had the longest odds or which loser the shortest.

In the pari-mutuel system, a horse can have the short odds generally associated with a "sure thing" and can still be regarded as something less. Since race charts began posting odds in the modern format, in 1903, the shortest-priced horses to lose the Derby were Bimelech in 1940 and Honest Pleasure in 1976. Each went off at 2-5.

On a Richter scale of upsets, however, the impact of these results would be considerably different. Bimelech was an unbeaten hero of the beloved Idle Hour Stock Farm of Colonel E.R. Bradley. He had prepped in Kentucky, and Kentuckians could hardly imagine his defeat, but he was deposed by the 35-1 Gallahadion.

In contrast, Honest Pleasure came to the Derby off a Blue Grass Stakes victory that was less impressive than his earlier wins, and he was beaten in the Derby not by an abject longshot, but by the logical second choice, Bold Forbes. The latter was coming off a victory in the Wood Memorial and went off at 3-1. In that case the defeat of a 2-5 shot had little of the stunning qualities of Bimelech's defeat. Prior to the race, one of two things seemed likely to happen, and one of them did.

Similarly, the longest odds do not always equate with the greatest upset. A truly stunning upset requires a heavy favorite, a Derby colt being hailed as potentially an exceptional champion. In the case of 50-1 Giacomo's victory in 2005, yes, it was a surprise that he won, but it was not particularly sensational that any of the others lost. The favorite, at 5-2, was Bellamy Road, whose status was based largely on a single performance rather than consistent achievement. Much the same circumstance had prevailed when Thunder Gulch won at nearly 25-1 in 1995. An oddity of that 1995 Derby was that a highly accomplished Florida Derby winner was dismissed at such odds at Churchill Downs. Contrasting to these was the victory of Dark Star in 1953, which was a more amazing result, although his odds were only half as long as Giacomo's. What made Dark Star's 25-1 victory so stunning was that he defeated Native Dancer. The Dancer was a previously unbeaten champion who already was being accorded legendary status.

As each Kentucky Derby has a unique flavor, it follows that so, too, does each Derby upset. The victory of Donerail at 91-1 survives as the greatest upset from a purely mathematical (longest odds) viewpoint. The 1971 victory of Canonero II, on the other hand, might in many minds have been one of the most shocking results in Derby history, but owing to his being part of a six-horse mutuel field, the odds were a modest 8.70-1. (Only Canonero II confounded the oddsmakers; the five others in the mutuel field occupied the final five places in an overall field of twenty.)

Lil E. Tee's 1992 Derby victory was stunning in the context of the exalted status handed Arazi from the previous year's Breeders' Cup Juvenile. When their careers were over, Arazi was seen as a prodigy unable to carry his brilliance at three and Lil E. Tee a highly accomplished horse who might have been a champion at four had he stayed sound.

The upsets by Exterminator (1918) and Iron Liege (1957) were given additional spice by the fact that, prior to Derby Day, they had not even been regarded as the prime contenders in their own stables, while the 1904 Derby win by Elwood took character in part from the gypsy aspects of his pre-race campaigning.

Genuine Risk pulled off a unique upset. This was a Derby won by a highly accomplished racer from a prominent stable and with a proven Derby-winning trainer. What made the race so special was that Genuine Risk was a filly, and no filly had won the race since Regret sixty-five years earlier.

What we have at hand, then, is a selection of a dozen Kentucky Derby upsets. Each of these Derby Days was prefaced by core assumptions, but in each case, by the time night fell, the whims of the Turf had enjoyed an uproarious laugh.

Edward L. Bowen
Lexington, Kentucky 2007

A Homegrown Classic

THE KENTUCKY DERBY had achieved some measure of importance by 1904, having become for Kentuckians, at least, a source of pride and sporting identity. That year's running, though, did little to advance the race's national reputation as a gangly former plater with long, awkward strides — disparaged by many pundits as a "Missouri mule" — crossed the finish line first.

Elwood won the 1904 Kentucky Derby. That much is sure. But the stories surrounding the horse vary, even as to the day's weather and the condition of the track.

Elwood's victory came during an era that might be called a crisis point in the race's history. Only two years earlier Matt Winn had been cajoled into transferring his acumen from a successful tailoring business to address the serious economic issues confronting Churchill Downs.

Winn had witnessed every running of the Kentucky Derby since its inception in 1875, when he watched the race with his father from a wagon in the infield. He had seen the Derby rise in prestige with victories of horses well known outside the region, such as Hindoo in 1881 and Ben Brush in 1896. He had seen, too, however, the doldrums, when the financial straits of the racetrack were thought to have added to the despair of Merriwether Lewis Clark, the race's founder. Clark was also in poor health when he took his own life in 1899.

In *The Kentucky Derby: The First Hundred Years* (Houghton Mifflin Co., 1974) author Peter Chew relies on the perspective of Joe A. Estes, former editor of *The Blood-Horse*: "Estes divided Derby history into three general periods — 1875 to 1898, 1899 to 1914, and 1915 onward [the victory of Eastern star Regret sealing the race's status as a nationally important event]. During the first period, purses were not high, but the race attracted crack horses, both Eastern and local, who were to leave their stamps on the breed and succeeding Derby winners. From Manuel in 1899 through Donerail in 1913, mediocrity characterized the Derby fields. The race had become a local affair, getting by on its tradition, in Estes' view."

Certainly an appreciation for its history prompted Winn to form an organization to save the race and its home track. Elwood's upset was not of sufficient dimension to create national headlines such as Donerail's 91-1 victory would in 1913. *(See Chapter 2.)* Nor was Elwood himself of an ilk to boost the prestige of the race. His very participation, though, might be taken as evidence that the race exerted a strong hold on Kentuckians and those with a personal association with racing in the state.

****

Charles E. "Boots" Durnell, who campaigned Elwood in his wife's name, had been born across the Ohio River from Louisville on June 13, 1876, in New Albany, Indiana. His father was a horse dealer. The young Durnell got his nickname and his first job at the same time. When he was twelve, he walked into the Churchill Downs stable of the Scoggan brothers and found the trainer, Enoch Wishard, whom he asked for a job. Wishard was said to have looked over the pint-sized lad and noticed the boy's brass-toed boots that had red tops and were several sizes larger than necessary. Wishard asked what the lad could do, and Durnell replied simply "ride horses." Wishard said, "Okay, Boots, you can go to work right away."

The Scoggan brothers, local businessmen and breeders, took in Sam Bryant as a partner, and they won the first Belmont Futurity that year with Proctor Knott. The winner's purse was $40,900. The following spring the Scoggans–Bryant partnership was back at Churchill Downs with Proctor Knott, who was beaten a nose in the Derby by the 17-1 shot Spokane.

Young Boots proved a capable exercise rider but when moved into actual race riding had only moderate success. He once recalled of his first race, "The flying mud was so thick I finished with my eyes shut." Durnell went back to breezing but saw no way from his position to move up to owning his own horses, which was his ambition. In a career move that mirrored that of Hall of Fame trainer Sam Hildreth, Durnell figured the regular fees earned by blacksmiths could be managed frugally enough to generate a useful stake. He was plying this trade at the Emeryville track in California when he gathered $300, enough for a down payment on a horse he had noticed. The purchase price was $1,500 for Dr. Shepard, with the rest to come from the horse's earnings — or bets on him.

Durnell left behind numerous quotes and recollections of his career. Of this tentative entry into equine ownership, he was quoted by J.H. Ransom, compiler and publisher of *Who's Who and Where in Horsedom*, as follows: "I entered him in a claiming race with some very good horses. It was for a purse of $1,500 with $800 to the winner. I was full of confidence ... Dr. Shepard got away on top and led from wire to wire. With the $800 and a little money that I won because I thought the horse could win, I paid off the note and owned Dr. Shepard in full."

Initially, Durnell did not make it on his own, however, and went back to work for Wishard. In the 1890s he is believed to have gone with Wishard to England. Wishard hooked up with John (Bet-a-Million) Gates and James Duke, highrollers unfettered by respect for the rules of the game, and they landed some big scores. Their successes reinforced the idea on the British Turf that the Americans who ventured over to the birthplace of the sport were a suspicious lot. The story of Royal Flush has come down through the years as the biggest coup, landing Gates some $360,000, and has been pinpointed as an example of Wishard's use of cocaine to hop horses.

The well-known equine researcher Dr. Tom Tobin wrote of Wishard in his 1981 book *Drugs and the Performance Horse* (Charles C. Thomas Publisher): "Royal Flush was six years old and appeared to be well over the hill when he came up for sale. Wishard bid 450 guineas for him and took him home to his Red House Stable in Newmarket. Following in the medicated footsteps of his predecessors (other Wishard runners), Royal Flush finished first in the Royal Hunt Cup at Ascot and, with a slightly increased dose, won the Stewards' Cup at Goodwood a couple of months later."

Trainer George Lambton convinced England's Jockey Club that the doping of horses had become a threat to English racing, and Wishard, Gates, and their associates departed.

In his book on jockey Tod Sloan titled *Yankee Doodle Dandy* (Yale University Press, 2000), John Dizikes also spoke of Wishard's reputation as a doper. He recalled that in 1899 Wishard won fifty-four races in England to lead the trainers' list. According to Dizikes, Wishard in 1902 granted an interview to a racing journalist to whom he said he had never found any hop that "did any good. I have heard of lots of things, and tried, I think, all of them," but only in the past, and back home in America.

Sloan himself recalled Boots Durnell in his book, *Tod Sloan, by Himself* (Brentano's, New York). The expatriate American jockey, himself denied a license in various European countries by that time, was functioning as a sort of adviser and unofficial trainer, by his telling. He claimed to have brought Durnell over to France, where Durnell developed an amusing reputation for his pidgin French.

Durnell "was about the funniest guy I ever saw or heard when he first attempted to make himself understood in France ... When he got one or two French words in his head, he would shrug his shoulders every other moment ... One day Baron Leonino came to the stable and Boots started in on him. I saw the Baron's face begin to broaden into a smile when Boots said, 'Ze gallop your cheval has done zis matin is ze fastest by ze watch we 'ave 'ad for quelques jours. 'E 'as eat up and 'e is as fit as a violin.' "

Sloan added that Durnell became so confident in his version of French that when shopkeepers failed to comprehend his comments, Boots dismissed them as "fools who didn't understand their own language."

Sloan recalled Durnell's getting ruled off, but for nothing more nefarious than insisting on trying to be a jockey and getting left at the start so ineptly that he could not be allowed to continue.

****

Durnell returned to America and launched out on his own again. By 1903 he was racing during the summer in Chicago and heading to California for the autumn and winter. He was stabled in San Francisco that year when he heard one day that a horse sale was to be held at a local boxing ring. He and some friends decided to attend, but not with the idea of buying anything. According to Ransom, "the stock was ragged and the breeding rather poor, but finally, out came a slender colt, a bay yearling son of Free Knight out of Petticoat, by Alarm. Petticoat was a granddaughter of the great American Eclipse and her dam was a daughter of Leamington. Something about the youngster fascinated Boots, although it was not his looks, and he bid $100 on him. After three more bids, he was knocked down to him for $300, and he led the little fellow to his barn."

Mrs. J.B. Prather of Faustiana Stud in Maryville, Missouri, had bred Elwood. The horse was not named at the time of the sale, and Durnell be-

15

stowed his mother's maiden name — also his own middle name — on the colt. Elwood raced in the name of Boots' wife, Mrs. C.E. (Lasca) Durnell.

At two, Elwood raced in some $300 claiming races, but he was not successful enough to attract a claim. He made seventeen starts and won only once, although he finished second in two little stakes, the Youngster Stakes and Competition Stakes.

Elwood's sixteenth start at two came on October 7, 1903, at the Worth Jockey Club track in Chicago. He finished fifth on a sloppy track. Durnell gave the colt nearly three months off. On December 29, Elwood made what was technically his last start at two but in a sense was his debut at three. Elwood finished last of six in an all-age race of about three-quarters of a mile at Los Angeles.

Elwood's campaign from January through April bore little resemblance to anything that might be regarded as preparation for a classic colt today. The same could be said, however, of the other four horses that eventually contested the Kentucky Derby with him. The routes taken to the race were not as well established as they would become, with certain prep races being on the pre-Derby schedules of most modern contenders.

Between January 12 and April 6, Durnell sent Elwood out seventeen times, all in California. The races were a motley collection including selling races, various sprints against older horses, and the $1,250 Coronado Beach Selling Stakes.

Elwood was unplaced more often than he won. As we shall see, Durnell was something of a lightning rod insofar as his standing on the Turf was concerned, and he was destined to spend most of his career ruled off in New York while scrapping to get a license in other states. This would invite the thought that Elwood's in-and-out running was geared toward landing bets at good odds, but the charts of the day indicate no particularly attractive payoffs.

The highlight of that California campaign came when three-year-olds were asked to go a mile and a half as early as February 27 in the Ascot Derby. Most of Elwood's races had carried purses of $400 or less, but the Derby had a purse of $2,000. He finished second to Bill Curtis, beaten by four lengths on a muddy track.

Despite the pedestrian aspects of Elwood's status at that time, the Ascot Derby was an occasion that generated some attention from a national trade publication, *The Thoroughbred Record*. The *Record*'s correspondents at the time included Captain Thomas Merry, who adopted the name Hidalgo and submitted from Los Angeles frequent commentary presented under the heading "Hidalgo's Prattle."

In one column Hidalgo recalled the following about Ascot Derby Day:

"I got out there [Ascot Park] just before noon and one of the first that I met was Mr. Durnell. 'How about your colt, today? This track is hardly to his liking, is it?'

" 'Well, he certainly does not like a muddy track,' answered his owner, 'and at the same time, he is in good shape and will run a good race if there is no more rain … I don't expect him to win or any other horse but Bill Curtis.'

"By 1:30 o'clock, it was pouring down and all hopes of Elwood's chances were extinguished."

Bill Curtis won easily from Elwood, and, Hidalgo continued, "As they were leading Elwood back to the barn, Mr. Durnell said to me: 'I can beat that colt on a fast track any day in the world, and do it quite as easily as he beat me here today. My colt never was any part of a mud horse, but if it is a dry track at Louisville on the second day of May I'll win that Kentucky Derby as sure as you've got a hat on your head.' "

Well, this story prompts questioning. The records show that on February 16, Elwood had won a seven-furlong race over a muddy track. This was but two races before the Ascot Derby. (In between, he had finished last of five against older horses in a mile and one-sixteenth selling race over a fast track.) Hidalgo's commentary was written after the eventual Kentucky Derby triumph. If accurate, it underscores that to a horseman whose early days had been centered around Churchill Downs, the Kentucky Derby even then was not far from the center of ambition.

At any rate, the campaign proceeded in its desultory fashion. Elwood's last race of the spring in California came on April 12, when he finished seventh in an eight-horse field on a fast track at Los Angeles, in a one-mile race with a $500 purse.

His next start came nearly a month later, on May 2, in the Kentucky Derby.

Several elements of the lore of Elwood's Derby tend to be questionable and contradictory but charming. A story recorded by Ransom was that "One day in … 1904, Boots' brother-in-law phoned him from Kentucky and said 'if you have any kind of a three-year-old handicap horse, put him in a car and ship him to the Derby. It has been raining for days and the track's a quagmire. No one here has been able to train their horses.' Boots hung up the phone, disconsolate, for he had no such horse in his barn. He yearned for that far-goal of glory, the mecca of every breeder and race horse man [obviously a statement assigning the Derby's later status retroactively]. He shrugged off the idea as an impossibility … However, when he walked back to his stable and ran speculative eyes over the awkward carcass of Elwood, his optimism rose. He suddenly remembered a workout when the horse was just flying in the mud, jumping and kicking like a bronc. He had a real mud horse."

So, according to various stories and the official record, we had a trainer who thought his horse disliked mud, although he had won in it, and now was excited by the prospects of off going for the Kentucky Derby.

A variety of stories also touched the Derby itself.

Ransom tells how Durnell, low in funds, traveled with Elwood, bedded down himself in a box car he shared with the horse. Elwood seemed stiff and sore after the long trip, and that, along with his origins, summoned snide reference to "the Missouri mule." Durnell had difficulty finding a rider, and Frankie Prior agreed to take the mount only because he wanted to ride in the Derby.

Whatever historians might conclude about the status of the Derby in 1904, *The Thoroughbred Record* addressed it grandly. From the issue of April 30, 1904:

"On Monday next, the thirty-first [it was actually the thirtieth running] Kentucky Derby will be run over the Churchill Downs course. Never in the history of this track has the prospect been brighter for a good contest ... The majority of the horses racing at Memphis and Nashville will stop off at Louisville, and from there they will divide up, some going to St. Louis, Kansas City, and Worth. With a good day the Derby crowd will be the largest seen at the Louisville track in years, as the Derby this year has attracted a great deal of attention owing to the extreme doubtfulness of the winner."

A *Record* note on the race's prospective line-up described it as "Kentucky's great classic," and Hidalgo, after the fact, called it "the great three-year-old race on the historical Churchill Downs."

In those days, before the Kentucky Derby was linked to East Coast races (the Preakness and Belmont), horsemen looking for likely "Derby timber" were thinking not just of one race but of a series of races in the upper South and Midwest with the name "Derby". These included the Tennessee Derby, Latonia Derby, and Chicago Derby, in addition to the Kentucky Derby. The climax, raced in mid-June, was the American Derby in Chicago. Inaugurated in 1884, or nine years after the Kentucky Derby, the American Derby offered a far richer prize. In 1904, for example, the winner of the American Derby received $26,325, compared to the Kentucky Derby winner's take of $4,850. (Matt Winn was making progress with his local institution, but 1904 was almost a dozen years before the breakthrough triumph of Regret.)

Illustrative of the high prestige of the American Derby, that same issue of the *Record* devoted considerable space to pre-race prices on the Chicago race. Again, reflecting differences in racing of a century ago with today's Turf, the early nominations to the American Derby had closed, and the intent of the operators of the Washington Park (Chicago) track was to keep them confidential until closer to the race. However, sufficient word had slipped out that a future betting book was being operated, so the track officials felt compelled to reveal the official list. Of 115 nominees, English Lad was offered at the shortest odds, 8-1, while Elwood was listed at 50-1. Fifty-two horses were offered at 100-1 odds or higher, with the top prices being 500-1.

****

As for the 1904 Kentucky Derby, one of the most prominent contenders was owned by Captain S.S. Brown, and as the race approached, much of the pre-race press commentary centered on that owner's stable, which was among the more successful outfits in the Midwest at that time. When the Brown stable was transferred from Memphis, Proceeds was well regarded as a challenger for the Derby. As it turned out, American Derby early favorite English Lad was not in the Kentucky Derby field, his stable choosing to enter him in a purse race that same day in Chicago as part of his preparation for the American Derby. Proceeds was the Kentucky Derby favorite in his stead.

Proceeds, who went off at even money, was the only runner in the field of five coming off a win. He had captured the $4,730 winner's purse in the Tennessee Derby at Memphis on April 4. He had also won his three-year-old debut, so he had a four-race winning streak dating to his final two-year-old races the previous October.

Proceeds clearly had been considered a good prospect as an early two-year-old. Almost a year before the Derby, he had made his debut in the Bashford Manor Stakes at Churchill Downs. He was not ready for that level so soon, however, as he finished sixth of seven. Thereafter, Proceeds had been a consistent winner, his victories including the Lake View Handicap ($2,930 to the winner) and Competition Stakes ($2,240). Proceeds was trained by Robert Tucker, who would win the Derby with Agile for Brown in 1905.

A close second choice to Proceeds at 6-5 was Fay and Wehmhoff's Ed Tierney, who had finished third in his only start at three. Ed Tierney had been an early bloomer, winning the Memphis Stakes ($2,190) in April of his two-year-old year, but the juvenile had been tried without success in various other stakes in Chicago and New York. He did, however, win his final race at two, at Latonia Park in northern Kentucky.

Third choice in the 1904 Kentucky Derby at 5-2 was William Gerst's Brancas, who went into the race off a second in a handicap race after having finished last in the Cumberland Derby at Nashville. Those were his only races since he had won four races in fourteen days at St. Louis to conclude his two-year-old season the previous October. The fourth choice for the 1904 Derby was the Talbot brothers' Prince Silverwings. He was 7-1 while making his debut at three. He had not raced since finishing third in a sprint at Worth in Chicago the previous October. Prince Silverwings had been another that bloomed early. He had won the Kenwood Stakes ($2,000) at Washington Park in Chicago the previous June and was also second in two other Chicago stakes, the Maywood and Junior handicaps.

Elwood, at 15-1, was the longest shot in the field, such as it was.

****

Author Chew, for his history of the Derby, found the charming story of matrimonial strife. By Derby Day, Durnell had decided not to run Elwood. The trainer had a spat over the subject with his wife, who wanted Elwood to run, and Boots "didn't bother to show up for the race ... [Mrs. Durnell], of course, won the argument and had someone else saddle him."

However, Mrs. Durnell should have been appreciative of the fact that her husband won an allowance race on the Derby undercard with Lady Lasca, a two-year-old filly he owned, trained, and obviously had named in her honor.

This tale is silent on the question of how Mrs. Durnell afforded the trip from California to Kentucky and is at odds with the melodramatic recollections of Boots that Ransom quoted years later. The version attributed to Durnell is full of emotion, detail, and bravado:

"They finally got away in the deep slop and as they swung into (the) backstretch, I could see nothing of my awkward plater and I knew then the real heights of my folly. But wait. As the flying pack plowed into the gooey stretch, from far back came a mudplastered woeful sight, a horse eating up ground in great surging strides, and up there on his back was a ludicrous Ichabod Crane. Down through the long and boggy stretch the strange apparition continued his long furious jumps, simply running over horses at the end and coming out to open daylight at the wire. Somewhere along the line and with stunned disbelief, I might have sensed the real meaning of that long, awkward stride and who it was, with hoarse bellows of encouragement, I shouted the unknown horse home."

This is a dramatic story, but the race chart makes no mention of mud. In fact, the track was listed as fast!

The 1904 Kentucky Derby chart shows Prior keeping Elwood in fourth position most of the way, then dropping to last in the upper stretch. Elwood rallied to outgun Ed Tierney at the wire by a half-length, with Brancas three lengths farther back in third and Prince Silverwings fourth. Proceeds, who carried 122 pounds to the others' 117, led for a half-mile and gradually dropped back, finishing last.

The time of 2:08 1/2 was competitive with other Derbys of the era, faster than six of the others among the first ten runnings of the young twentieth century. The value of the race was $6,000, with $4,850 going to the winner. Elwood was the first Derby starter raced in the name of a female as owner and, therefore, of course, the first winner for a female. He was also the first Derby winner to have been bred by a woman.

The quality of the field was easily criticized, but dismissal of Elwood seemed premature when he came out two and a half weeks later to win the Latonia Derby. Contested at one and a half miles, the Latonia race found him rallying to catch Ed Tierney and win by a nose. Jockey Prior had to battle Elwood, who kept swerving behind the leader, and it was a determined ride that straightened the horse in time to earn the win. The front pair finished fifteen lengths clear of the two other runners.

However, Elwood's days as a leader among three-year-olds were numbered. Either worn out or overmatched in the American Derby, he was last of sixteen most of the way and was only able to pass one horse as W.M. Scheftel's Highball won the big prize. English Lad was fourth and Proceeds, twelfth.

The St. Louis Derby, in which he finished third, was Elwood's last race at three. He had run twenty-three times that year, winning six races, and earning $13,580.

At four, he won once in twelve starts and at five failed to win in three races. Illustrative that his was a different era, the Derby winner by then had been gelded. In his last start for Durnell, Elwood finished ninth and last, twenty lengths behind the eighth horse, over a sloppy track at Oakland, California, on December 11, 1906. One year later Elwood reappeared racing for Burlingame Stable. From December 3 to December 10, 1907, he was entered in three selling races at Oakland, running last in two of them and ninth of ten in the other. The chart of his last race noted that he was "pulled up" by jockey Eddie Dugan. Elwood's career record showed fifty-eight races, eight wins, seven seconds, five thirds, and earnings of $15,590.

****

Elwood thus faded into obscurity after his Kentucky Derby triumph, but Boots Durnell was just getting started as one of the unique characters of the Turf. It was in the aftermath of winning the Derby that Durnell hopped over to France at Sloan's request, only to be ruled off and then reinstated. In Durnell's obituary years later, *The Blood-Horse* conceded that "the circumstances of this episode are not clear." The same might be said for his being ruled off and then reinstated back in California after his return from Europe.

Later Durnell hooked up with Bet-a-Million Gates, who had been Enoch Wishard's man years before, and another highroller in John Drake. Durnell hit New York. He was a big spender, hung out with Ziegfeld girls, and was a dashing figure of sorts. Photos indicate he favored a flat straw boater, which was hardly avant garde, but Durnell's version sported an exceptionally deep cloth band that had wide alternating stripes.

In 1907 Durnell was down as the owner of Nealon for the great Suburban Handicap in New York. W.A. McKinney was listed as trainer. It is assumed that Gates was the actual owner, perhaps with Drake as partner. Nealon was 20-1 in a field headed by favorite Electioneer and also including other high-class horses such as Superman and Dandelion.

Willie Dugan was on Nealon and his brother Eddie was on Faust, also owned by Durnell and, therefore, running as an entry. The favorite broke in a tangle and did not seem able to run freely thereafter. Faust led into the stretch but was exhausted. Whether by intent or not, Eddie Dugan left an opening on the rail as his mount grew weary, and Willie shot Nealon through to score at big odds. Gates was said to have made more than $300,000 on the race, and 25 percent of the booty went to Durnell.

Soon thereafter Gates and Drake went to Europe on oil business. With his big buddies an ocean away, Durnell was denied stalls at Saratoga. In the manner of The Jockey Club of the time, there was no explanation, but Boots Durnell was effectively ruled off in New York. Perhaps suspicion about the Nealon score prompted the action. There was also implication that one of Durnell's girlfriends was being wooed by one of racing's swells who was in a position to retaliate.

At any rate, Durnell went back to Europe, where for some seventeen years he wandered from France to Romania. Given his apparently fanciful description of Elwood's Kentucky Derby, Durnell and his version of his exploits should be approached with caution, but he came home eventually with stories of having trained for such owners as the Aga Khan, Lord Carnarvon, and Queen Marie of Romania. In the latter country, he recalled having won the Derby, St. Leger, "all the major stakes." Jockey Eddie Dugan was with him through many of these exploits. (Dugan's ride on Elwood in his last race was apparently coincidental.)

Durnell spoke of looking out of his hotel window one morning and seeing dead bodies, as the Germans had invaded Romania. He also claimed to have been in Moscow when the revolution began. He asserted that Minoru, an English Derby winner, was beheaded by the Bolsheviks because his very existence represented aristocracy.

Durnell said he and Dugan made their way to Manchuria, where "I attended a race meet, bought a horse, saddled a winner, and won a bet." The final version of his modern tale of Ulysses involved "a boat from China to 'Frisco ... Was I glad to be home!"

Press stories of Durnell also indicate that somewhere along the way he took on another wife although there seems no explanation about what became of the first one. (If the Ziegfeld stories are true, she likely just left him.) The second wife, Deede, had been a French stage star, and Boots managed her career for a time in New York. Durnell was still not able to train in that state, but Phil T. Chinn, an old acquaintance who also knew the tastes of both wealth and penury, was said to have helped get him a license in Kentucky.

Durnell hooked up with W.T. Waggoner, said to be the wealthiest oilman in Texas. Waggoner was building a racetrack at Arlington, Texas, and establishing a racing stable. Durnell was involved in purchasing high-priced horses for Waggoner. The Jockey Club accepted the arrangement that Waggoner could race in New York with Durnell as manager. Durnell, however, resigned the job in 1929, by which time he had acquired an excellent training center in Louisville. He also had a pair of important clients.

The next year, however, the Kentucky Racing Commission denied him a license. Thomas Cromwell, then editor of *The Blood-Horse*, strongly criticized The Jockey Club's denying Durnell a license in its own jurisdiction and encouraging other states to follow suit. The ruling body pursued the practice of denial without putting anything in writing, and the Kentucky Racing Commission's action came after a representative traveled to New York for a face-to-face meeting with The Jockey Club. Cromwell described it as the "persecution" of Durnell.

In 1935, racing authorities in Illinois suddenly, and without comment, issued Durnell a license, and he was back in business. The Jockey Club never changed its stance, but other states allowed Durnell to train. He prospered anew.

In 1940 Durnell won his third Arlington Futurity, with Cleaveland Putnam's Swain. The horse's breeder, Henry Knight, earned both cash and a gold cup for the event, and he gave Durnell the choice of which one he would like as a gift. The cup stayed with Knight.

The final chapter of Boots Durnell's career found him back in California. He and Deede had a home on Baldwin Avenue, very near Santa Anita, and with his colorful and questionable past receding in the distance, Durnell was accorded status as a respectable citizen.

Boots Durnell died of a heart attack on February 16, 1949. Four days earlier Red Tape, whom he trained and whom he owned in partnership with his brother Jesse, had become his last winner, paying $17.70.

Ten years later Phyllis M. O'Brien, assistant to the general manager of Santa Anita, wrote a note in response to an inquiry. The note was something of a forgiving benediction: "The Durnells lived for many years in

Kentucky Derby
Purse: $6,000 Added

Churchill Downs - May 2, 1904. Thirtieth running Kentucky Derby.
Purse $6,000 added. Three-year-olds. 1 1-4 Miles. Main Track. Track: Fast.
Gross value $6,000. Net value to winner, $4,850; second, $700; third, $300.

Horse	A	Wgt	Eqp	Odds	PP	St	1/2	3/4	1	Str	Fin	Jockey
Elwood	3	117	b	15.00	3	4	4^1	4^{hd}	4^x	5^x	1^x	F Prior
Ed Tierney	3	117		1.10	5	3	3^1	3^{1x}	3^1	3^2	2^3	J Dominick
Brancas	3	117		2.50	4	5	5	5	5	2^x	3^{2x}	L Lyne
Prince Silverwings	3	117		7.00	1	2	2^2	1^1	1^1	1^{hd}	4^1	D Austin
Proceeds	3	122	b	1.00	2	1	1^{1x}	2^x	2nd	4^x	5	G Helgeson

Off Time: 4:19 **Time Of Race:** :25 :49¼ 1:15¼ 1:42 2:08½
Start: Good For All **Track:** Fast
Equipment: b for blinkers

Winner: Elwood, b. c. by Free Knight—Petticoat, by Alarm (Trained by C. E. Durnell).
Bred by Mrs. J. B. Prather in Missouri.

Start good. Won driving; second easily.
ELWOOD, was well ridden. Prior rated him along for the first seven furlongs and never made a move until rounding the turn into the homestretch, where he moved up on the outside and fought it out with BRANCAS, PRINCE SILVERWINGS and ED TIERNEY in the last quarter, and outstayed the latter in the final drive. Dominick nursed ED TIERNEY along for the first half mile and made a determined effort in the stretch run, tiring the last fifty yards. BRANCAS stumbled at the start and Lyne kept taking him back in the first half-mile, moved him up fast at the home turn and was in front for a few strides, but tired. PRINCE SILVERWINGS showed much early speed, but tired after a mile. PROCEEDS stumbled at the start but this cut no figure in the result.

Owners: (1) Mrs C E Durnell; (2) Fay & Wehmhoff; (3) William Gerst; (4) Talbot Brothers; (5) S S Brown

©EQUIBASE

Arcadia ... a dirt road divided their place and the back gates of the race track ... They were fine people and helped the infant stages of racing here in California."

Being among the "fine people" would not have been a comment frequently made of Durnell through much of his life, but, as Elwood's Derby had illustrated, Boots was never constrained by prevailing opinion.

By Edward L. Bowen

The Longest Odds

IN THE AFTERMATH of the 1913 Kentucky Derby, a glossy bay colt stood in the winner's circle, flanks heaving and roses draped over his sweat-slick withers. This was pretty much as expected. The only hitch was that it wasn't the bay colt everyone had expected to be there. Instead of heavy favorite Ten Point, the winner was Donerail, who had just pulled off the biggest shocker in Derby history and rewarded his few backers with a payoff of $184.90 on a two-dollar bet, the largest in Derby history.

Had breeder-owner-trainer Thomas P. Hayes stuck by his original plans, Donerail wouldn't even have been in the race. Accounts vary as to whether it was jockey Roscoe Goose or close friend William J. Treacy who talked Hayes into entering the colt. According to Treacy's son, J.R. "Buddy" Treacy, it was his father, not Hayes, who actually paid the entry fees — and then plopped down a $100 bet with a local bookmaker when Hayes reluctantly agreed to go along with the entry. Why Treacy was so enthusiastic about the colt is something of a mystery, for Hayes had his reasons to doubt. After all, he had known the colt since the animal's birth at John S. Barbee's Glen Helen Farm near Lexington, where Hayes boarded his mares. Neither sire nor dam was of any great repute; the mare, Algie M., was well enough bred, being by the great runner and sire Hanover out of a mare by the good stayer Bramble, but Algie M. had been neither a good runner nor had she produced one to that time. McGee, the sire, stood at nearby Mere Hill Stud. He would become known as the sire of the great gelding Exterminator and would lead the American general sire list in 1922, but when Donerail was conceived in 1909, McGee was just a hard-knocking sprinter who had never won a stakes and his first foals had yet to hit the racetrack.

Hayes was no novice when it came to evaluating a horse's merits, either. A former tobacco grower whose red silks featured a green tobacco leaf on the back of the jacket, the Augusta, Kentucky, native had gotten into the Thoroughbred business back in 1894, when he bought a draft of yearlings at the Lexington sales and shipped them to Little Rock, Arkansas, with the intent of beginning their training there. Misfortune intervened in the form of a railway accident that killed four of the year-lings and injured another four, but Hayes persevered as both owner and trainer as well as getting into the breeding side of the business.

Hayes named the big-boned, sturdy colt Donerail after a local flag station on the Queen & Crescent Railway and, when the time came, put him into training. The colt had apparently drawn some attention in his early training, for when he won at first asking on September 9, 1912, in a five and a half-furlong maiden race at the old Kentucky Association track in Lexington, the *Daily Racing Form* chart read, "Donerail, a sup-posed good one, wore Prince Hermis down after going three-eighths and won as his rider pleased."

If Donerail was supposed to be a good one, he did not show it in his next two starts, both at five and a half furlongs. He was well beaten when he tried to step up to allowance company at the old Douglas Park track near Louisville on September 16, running fifth of six. He fared no better in the Beechmont Stakes five days later, also at Douglas Park, in which he finished seventh of eleven. The latter race was won by the filly Gowell, a rival Donerail would meet on several occasions.

The colt showed better form in his next three starts — all within a three-week period. On October 5, he closed well after a slow break to finish fourth in an allowance at Douglas Park; came on again near the wire after dropping back mid-race to be third to Gowell in the six-furlong Golden Rod Selling Stakes on October 16 at Churchill Downs while beaten only about three-quarters of a length for the win; and was third again to Gowell in the five and a half-furlong Rosedale Stakes on October 23 at Latonia Park in northern Kentucky while "coming fast at the end."

After these promising runs, Donerail threw in a clunker in a six-furlong allowance at Latonia on October 28. Although he did finish third, the race chart indicates that he "quit badly" in the stretch after racing forwardly in the early going and lost a race he apparently had a good chance to win, considering he was only beaten slightly more than a length for the victory. But stretched out to a mile over the same track three days later, the colt showed good speed throughout and finished fast to win by one and a half lengths. Donerail closed out his season with two lackluster performances in six-furlong races at Latonia, running unplaced both times, and went into winter quarters having won two of ten starts with three third-place finishes.

Donerail did not come out for his sophomore debut until April 26, 1913, when he went to the post for the mile and one-sixteenth Phoenix Hotel Spring Handicap at Lexington. He did not exactly cover himself with glory; after unseating his rider at the post and bolting for a good quarter-mile, he was caught and remounted but showed only brief speed in the actual race before fading to finish fourth and last behind the good older filly Flora Fina.

Donerail actually ran a good race in his next start, the nine-furlong Blue Grass Stakes on May 3 at Lexington, but was overshadowed by Foundation, who ran a still better one in his 1913 debut. The flashy chestnut son of 1901 champion juvenile Nasturtium grabbed a one-length advantage at the break and never looked back, widening his lead throughout the stretch to win by five lengths. Donerail, who had chased him in second throughout, "stood the final drive resolutely," according to the chart, but could not overhaul the winner, who was described as having been under mild restraint at the end.

Still, it had been a tenacious performance over the longest distance Donerail had yet tried, a fact that perhaps should not have been over-looked in the Derby betting by those who saw the race. It was also the colt's first race with local hero Roscoe Goose in the saddle — again, perhaps, something that should not have been overlooked.

Born in a Louisville suburb in 1891, Goose began riding in fair races near the city in his teens. He soon moved up to the larger, better-es-tablished tracks and had his first winner at Churchill Downs in 1908. Within a few years he had become one of the leading riders at the track, and his opinion of Donerail would prove crucial to the colt's Derby entry. There was little question that Donerail had liked him and run well for him during the Blue Grass — better than he had run for any of his other jockeys. The point was underscored three days later in the ten-furlong Camden Handicap at Lexington, when Donerail, ridden by another jockey, finished a weary fifth behind Flora Fina after tiring in the final eighth.

At this point Hayes could hardly be blamed for his reluctance to put Donerail in the Derby. Up to that time the colt had won only two of thir-teen starts and had never won a stakes. He had been thoroughly beaten in two of his three races at three and in the other had run well but still not well enough to win; further, the colt that had defeated him with such apparent ease, Foundation, was among the Derby favorites.

As good as Foundation had looked in the Blue Grass, even he took second billing to Ten Point, who was the talk of the town as Derby Day grew closer. Winner of the Walden Stakes as a two-year-old, the bay son of Jack Point had done nothing wrong in the spring of 1913. He was coming up to the big race off three straight wins, all at Havre de Grace in Maryland and all against older horses: the six-furlong Belair Handicap, the Philadelphia Handicap over the same distance, and the Susquehanna Handicap over a mile and seventy yards. He had actually been the first choice of Roscoe Goose, who tried and failed to get the Derby mount on him. It is a measure of the high esteem in which Ten Point and Foundation were held that Gowell, who had defeated males repeatedly in stakes events as a juvenile and who had won the Ashland Oaks that spring as well as running third in the Blue Grass and the Camden, ended up going off at Derby odds of 87-1.

Whether it was Goose, hunting for a Derby mount, who persuaded Hayes to enter the colt with the promise that he "would get part of the purse" as recorded in Goose's *Blood-Horse* obituary of June 21, 1971, or Treacy who did the trick with his willingness to put up the colt's entry money, Hayes finally decided to enter Donerail in the Kentucky Derby. How much faith he had in the colt is debatable, however. Records indicate he did not bet so much as a dime on Donerail in the pari-mutuel betting — he was said to have been disgusted that the horse was not getting odds of 100-1 or longer — but it was reported after the race that Hayes had put down a $100 bet at the 100-1 odds he wanted with the same bookmaker that had taken Treacy's bet.

****

An estimated crowd of 30,000 watched as eight three-year-olds went to the post for the thirty-ninth Kentucky Derby on May 10, 1913 — a small field by modern standards, but the Kentucky Derby in 1913 was not the marquee event it would later become. The best racing of the early part of the century was centered in New York and New Jersey, and Eastern elites usually viewed horses coming out of "the West" with a patronizing suspicion as to their true class.

The Kentucky Derby, first run in 1875, carried a good enough purse during its early years to attract both the best of the Western runners and some forays by Eastern-based horses, and the roster of its early winners was graced by such names as Hindoo and Ben Brush. By 1902, however, Churchill Downs had sunk deeply into debt and was no longer offering either the purses or the prestige to bring in much beyond local runners.

A syndicate headed by Colonel Matt Winn bought Churchill Downs in 1902, and a slow turnaround began. But single-digit Derby fields were the norm from 1887 to 1914, with only three runners contesting the race in 1892 and 1905. The 1913 field was the largest since 1909, when ten runners faced the starter, and one of its attractions was doubtless the purse: The largest in Derby history to that time, it had a gross value of $6,600, with $5,475 to the winner). New York had only just resumed racing following the shutdown created by anti-gambling legislation in 1911–12, and the Derby purse was one of the largest for three-year-olds anywhere in the country.

Churchill patrons made Ten Point a 6-5 favorite despite the fact he had never gone farther than an extended mile. Foundation was sent away at 23-10, while Yankee Notions, a son of Yankee who was coming into the Derby off a good race against the tough older horse Rudolfo, was the third choice at 49-10. Donerail was dismissed at 91.45-1, the second-longest price on the board; the only colt that the crowd held at longer odds was Lord Marshall, who would vindicate the bettors' 183-1 judgment of him by running an uninspired sixth.

The year 1913 predated the use of starting gates in North America, and the Derby field lined up at the starting line with only a frail elastic barrier between them and the opening run. Starts in those days were often marked by a certain degree of chaos. Fractious horses wheeled and plunged; jockeys broke their mounts out of line to keep rivals from getting an advantageous start or else tried to time the barrier's rise and get the jump on the field (though they had to be careful with both tactics at the risk of being fined or suspended); and some animals plunged through the barrier in false starts. Starters had their hands full trying to get all the horses lined up and standing quietly for a brief moment with all noses pointed in the correct direction; on one epic occasion, the American Derby of 1893, it took the starter a full hour and a half to get control of the field and get them off and running.

The 1913 Kentucky Derby was free of such dramatics, however; less than one minute after arrival at the starting post, the tape flew up and the field sprang forward to the roar of the crowd. Donerail, away smartly from the No. 5 post position, settled nicely into sixth, with Roscoe Goose restraining him about four and a half lengths off the early pace.

That pace was being set by Ten Point, who was cutting out solid fractions of :23 4/5, :47 4/5, and 1:12 3/5 with Foundation as his closest pursuer. He still had the lead following a mile in 1:39 3/5 but was starting to shorten stride. Foundation, too, was tiring, and fresh challengers were moving up.

Yankee Notions was first to close in, only to be repelled. But now Donerail was moving. As the horses raced through the stretch turn, Goose had turned him loose, and the colt was answering powerfully. Fifth at the stretch call, Donerail caught up with the game-but-exhausted leader at the sixteenth pole and, under the whip, surged past to win by a half-length. Ten Point, courageous to the last, turned back a final rally by Foundation and held on well enough to be second by a length and a half over Gowell, who had come on to take third by a head over the fading Foundation.

Despite the surprise, the crowd vigorously applauded Donerail as he came back to the winner's circle and applauded with all the more enthusiasm as the time was hung out: 2:04 4/5, a new track and stakes record. Through the pari-mutuels, Donerail paid $184.90 to win, $41.20 to place, and $13.20 to show.

Kentucky Governor James B. McCreary made the trophy presentation, telling Goose, "You were on a gallant horse, and you rode a brilliant race."

Goose replied, "While I rode him to the best of my ability, I was on a good horse today."

William Treacy surely must have agreed with that assessment, for after the race he collected $10,000 in winnings from his bookmaker (as did Hayes, assuming the report that he indeed did place a bet is true). According to Buddy Treacy, his father spent $5,500 of the bankroll Donerail had won for him on a two-story brick home near the University of Kentucky; as for the rest, as Treacy said, "I think the horses got it back."

Goose was indeed on a good horse in the 1913 Derby, but by the time the print rolled off the presses the following morning, speculation must have been already in the air. As the *Daily Racing Form* chart put it, Donerail had shown "astonishing improvement over his Lexington racing"; another writer expressed his opinion by noting "the miserable long shot ran the classic faster than it was ever run before." And the Louisville *Courier-Journal* headline summed it up thusly: "Despised Outsider Comes From Behind to Capture Thirty-Ninth Kentucky Derby in Grueling Stretch Drive." The long and the short of it was that Donerail's Derby form was vastly better than anything seen from him before, and people must surely have wanted to know why.

Roscoe Goose may have been part of the answer, for he was clearly a good fit for Donerail. During the remainder of the colt's three-year-old season, Goose rode him five times and came back with two wins, two seconds, and a third, including a victory in the Canadian Sportsman Handicap at Fort Erie; in six starts under other jockeys, Donerail hit the board only once, running third in a handicap at Douglas Park. All told, Donerail made seven starts with at three Goose up and had a record of three wins, three seconds, and a third in those races, while his third in the handicap at Louisville was his only in-the-money finish in eight sophomore starts with other riders.

Still, Donerail did most of his 1913 post-Derby racing in Canada, at the time generally considered a step down in class from the competition in Kentucky, and none of his post-Derby efforts were nearly as impressive as his Derby run, Goose or no Goose. So what else, if anything, had changed?

All conjectures are pure speculation now, of course, but the possibility exists that Donerail's sudden change in form had more to do with the medicine cabinet than with his jockey. "Hopping" of horses was a widespread practice in American racing in the early part of the twentieth century and, though illegal, had little chance of detection. Most American racetracks did not begin testing for drugs until the mid-1930s, even though the needed tests for the stimulants then used — primarily cocaine and the arsenic-strychnine mixture known as Fowler's solution — had existed two decades earlier. And even in the cases of certain horses and trainers in which drug use was an open secret, enforcement was often lax to nonexistent. Indeed, one old-time trainer at Latonia was supposedly called into the stewards' office regarding drug use and was told *not* to quit using stimulants, but to make sure his horses got the same dosage consistently after one of his animals displayed a dramatic reversal of form. As long as bettors did not have to worry about horses being run "hot and cold" — being run on or off drugs to manipulate performance and set up betting coups for the owner, trainer, or both — the American racing industry of the time was not really too concerned about drug use in racehorses.

In any event, Donerail never again touched the heights he reached in his Derby victory, and while stimulant use during the Derby is one hypothesis that might account for the difference between this race and his other starts, another is that the colt began experiencing injuries that kept him from ever again being able to deliver a performance close to his Derby run. Although he was nominated to the June 14 Latonia Derby and was optimistically proclaimed by Hayes to have a good chance in the twelve-furlong event, his name was not in the entry box when the time for the race actually came, and it can surely not have been for fear of the competition. In fact, Donerail did not appear under colors again until July 16, when he ran eighth of nine in the Frontier Handicap at Windsor.

Donerail finished 1913 having won five races from twenty-five lifetime starts. At four he won five of twenty-eight starts but did not collect his first victory until his ninth race of 1914, and his biggest win was in the ten-furlong Hamilton Cup at the old Hamilton track in Canada. Something apparently went wrong with the colt after that grueling season, for Donerail is recorded as having quit badly in his last 1914 start, the Latonia Cup on November 7, and did not start at all as a five-year-old.

At six, Donerail started only eight times and failed to win although he placed in three small stakes at Churchill Downs and Douglas Park, and he was again absent from the races at age seven. His attempt at a comeback at age eight ended miserably as he ran ninth of nine in his only start, a one-mile handicap at Belmont. He ended his racing career with ten wins, eleven seconds, and ten thirds from sixty-two starts. He does not appear to have ever stood at stud in the United States or Canada and so faded from the scene.

Roscoe Goose also left racing in 1918, though for different reasons. While he enjoyed another classic success when he rode Kathleen to a win in the 1916 Kentucky Oaks, he had already lost a brother to a racing accident in 1915, and in 1917 came close to losing his own life in a nasty three-horse spill at Latonia. Although he recovered from a fractured vertebra well enough to return to the saddle, he made the decision to retire from riding in 1918 and later became a respected trainer whose clients included Senator Johnson N. Camden and Colonel E.R. Bradley. He trained a number of good Midwestern stakes winners for John Marsch, including Lightspur, Kings Blue, and the future Calumet

Kentucky Derby
Purse: $5,000 Added

Churchill Downs - May 10, 1913. Thirty-ninth running Kentucky Derby.
Purse $5,000 added. Three-year-olds. 1 1-4 Miles. Main Track. Track: Fast.
Gross value $5,000. Net value to winner, $5,475; second, $700; third, $300.

Horse	A	Wgt	Eqp	Odds	PP	St	1/4	1/2	3/4	Str	Fin	Jockey
Donerail	3	117		91.45	5	6^1	6^1	$6^{1\frac{1}{2}}$	5^1	5^2	$1^\frac{1}{2}$	R Goose
Ten Point	3	117		1.20	4	1^1	1^2	1^3	1^2	$1^\frac{1}{2}$	$2^{1\frac{1}{2}}$	M Buxton
Gowell	3	112		87.00	3	5^1	5^2	4^{hd}	$4^{1\frac{1}{2}}$	4^1	3^{hd}	J McCabe
Foundation	3	117		2.30	8	2^1	2^1	$2^\frac{1}{2}$	2^{hd}	$3^\frac{1}{2}$	4^{nk}	J Loftus
Yankee Notions	3	117	b	4.90	6	3^1	$3^\frac{1}{2}$	3^{hd}	$3^\frac{1}{2}$	$2^\frac{1}{2}$	5^5	J Glass
Lord Marshall	3	117	b	183.00	1	7^1	7^1	7^1	6^2	6^1	6^8	T Steele
Jimmie Gill	3	110	b	36.00	2	8	8	8	8	7^{10}	7^{15}	C Borel
Leochares	3	114		14.00	7	$4^\frac{1}{2}$	4^{hd}	$5^\frac{1}{2}$	7^{hd}	8	8	C Peak

Off Time: 4:52   Time Of Race: :23½ :47½ 1:12½ 1:39½ 2:04½ (new track record)
Start: Good For All   Track: Fast
Equipment: b for blinkers

Mutuel Payoffs

9	Donerail	$184.90	$41.20	$13.20
8	Ten Point		3.50	3.30
5	Gowell			14.10

Winner: Donerail, b. c. by *McGee—Algie M., by Hanover (Trained by T. P. Hayes).
Bred by T. P. Hayes in Kentucky.

Start good and slow. Won driving; second and third the same.
DONERAIL, showing startling improvement over his Lexington racing, was restrained to the stretch turn, where he moved up with a rush and, under punishment, drew away in the last sixteenth. TEN POINT showed superior speed for the first half mile and raced FOUNDATION to defeat, then tired in the last eighth and was distressed at the finish. GOWELL ran a capital race, made a fast and game stretch effort. FOUNDATION raced with TEN POINT to the stretch and was slightly impeded by the latter in the last eighth but tired badly. YANKEE NOTIONS ran prominently to the homestretch and tired in the final drive. LEOCHARES was hopelessly beaten after going the first mile.
Scratched—Prince Hermis, Sam Hirsch, Flying Tom, Floral Park.

Owners: (1) T P Hayes; (2) A L Aste; (3) J T Weaver; (4) C W McKenna; (5) H K Knapp; (6) J O & G H Keene; (7) Doerhoefer & West; (8) J W Schorr

Farm foundation mare Blue Delight. He also became known for spotting and developing young talent in the jockey ranks; among the young riders whose skills he helped to hone were Charley Kurtsinger, who won the 1937 Triple Crown on War Admiral, and Eugene James, who rode Burgoo King to victory in the 1932 Kentucky Derby and Preakness. Goose died on June 11, 1971.

Thomas Hayes continued training long after Donerail, who had passed from his ownership to that of an R. Marsden by the time the horse made his final start. Universally respected by his peers on the Midwestern circuit, Hayes returned to the Kentucky Derby spotlight in 1933 when, as agent for Mrs. Silas B. Mason, he purchased Head Play the day before the Derby and thus became the colt's trainer following the Derby. (Head Play remained in the care of Willie Crump, whose wife had been the colt's previous owner, for the Derby itself.) Beaten a nose by Brokers Tip in the infamous "Fighting Finish" Derby, Head Play came back to win the Preakness by four easy lengths, placed in several other important races, and is generally regarded as the American champion three-year-old male of 1933. As for Hayes, while he failed to come up with a second Derby winner, he still holds a place in Derby history as only the second man to breed, own, and train a Kentucky Derby winner, following in the footsteps of Major Thomas R. McDowell with Alan-a-Dale in 1902. Hayes died of a heart attack on August 28, 1933, shortly after his resignation as Mrs. Mason's trainer.

To this day Donerail's Kentucky Derby performance remains a mystery. A modest performer at two and winless prior to the Derby at three, the colt had more than justified his long odds, the longest ever held on a Derby winner. Entered by a reluctant trainer and ridden by a jockey for whom he was a second choice at best, he seems to have had no one who believed in him except perhaps William Treacy, whose reasons for backing Donerail went to the grave with him in 1945. He was never a great horse, and aside for a couple of minor stakes wins in Canada, he faded into obscurity following his record-setting Derby win. But for one shining moment in May 1913, he was the best horse in what is now America's most coveted race, and as such he is remembered.

By Avalyn Hunter

The Work Horse

THE GROOM DROPPED HIS SPONGE into the puddle on the ground. Mouth open, he pushed the filly aside. With soap suds dripping off the filly's rib cage, the groom ducked down to get a better look at the commotion in the stable yard. He had to see this for himself.

A late-model, expensive French Panhard sedan had come to a stop in front of the barn and a chauffeur stepped quickly to open the rear door. The groom could tell by the high-collared starched shirt, waxed moustache, and piercing blue eyes that the man who stepped from the sedan was the owner. From the moment that Willis Sharpe Kilmer burst into the trainer's office waving a rolled-up foal certificate in his fist like a weapon, everybody in the barn could sense trouble.

With the element of surprise on his side, Kilmer stood squarely in the doorway and lashed out. "I gave you instructions to buy a decent work horse for me," the owner shouted. "This goddamn goat couldn't beat a fat man running uphill." Kilmer's neck became so red and puffed that he had to loosen his tie. Henry McDaniel had been mending a bridle. Surprised, the trainer came out from behind his desk. Neither man took off his hat. It was going to be that kind of argument.

If any friendship existed between the two men, it was deteriorating fast. Kilmer walked back and forth, shaking his head, arguing that his

41

trainer had thrown good money at a bad horse. McDaniel, on the defensive, knew that he had to watch his words carefully. Holding the mended bridle with a grip that was turning his knuckles white, the trainer explained that perfection was impossible to find this late in the game. The horse would have to do until things turned around.

Edging closer to the fracas, the stable grooms and exercise riders pretended to be busy raking and cleaning tack. Just as they got within earshot of the fierce exchange, Kilmer stormed out of the barn, kicking an empty bucket to punctuate his exit.

When the limousine drove off, the grooms eased over to look in on the cause of all the commotion. What a dismaying sight. The horse was in stall No. 9, sound asleep. Amidst all the noise and hollering, the rangy looking gelding, bony and thin in flesh, was taking a nap. With each rumbling snore, wisps of hay fluttered and settled around his damp nostrils. Unimpressed with the new boarder, the grooms huddled outside the stall. A few took off their caps and scratched their heads. "Good God Almighty. I see why boss is some mad," one said, leaning on his pitchfork. "That horse got to be the ugliest thing anywhere around these parts. Mr. McDaniel must've found him in somebody's backyard."

A decision had to be made. No matter how ugly the horse looked, somebody had to feed and water the damn thing. They drew straws to see whose task it would be to rub the muddy-colored reject. The Kentucky Derby was ten days away and Exterminator was a horse that nobody wanted. Especially his owner.

****

Invisible. Improbable. Foal Number 84588 in the *American Stud Book* of 1915 was nothing to write home about. On May 30, 1915, at Almahurst Farm near Nicholasville, Kentucky, a knobby-kneed chestnut Thoroughbred baby came into the world without fanfare or fuss. The lightning of luck or the faculty of genius — a breeder hopes for one or both. Who knows what combination of conscious method or creativity governed F.D. "Dixie" Knight to arrange the mating of the sire McGee and the broodmare Fair Empress.

McGee (a $125 yearling) stood at Mere Hill, a small farm north of Lexington. He had a reputation earned on the Illinois tracks for sprint speed. Although he had sired Donerail, winner of the 1913 Kentucky Derby, the fifteen-year-old stud was considered a basic "market stallion." Fair Empress was a daughter of Jim Gore. Unplaced in two starts, she had some suggestion of route blood in her ancestry but little proof. Despite being a son of Hindoo, the grandsire Jim Gore had shuddered at the sight of nine furlongs. In truth, the pedigree that had produced Exterminator was suspect for both soundness and stamina. It could easily have been interpreted as "Rice Paper Hoof out of Porcelain Ankles by Short of Breath."

In August 1916, Knight sent his lot of babies to the yearling sales in Saratoga Springs, New York. With an influx of imported horses escaping from the war in Europe, the sale was well attended. Newcomers to racing and established stables showed up at Saratoga looking for fresh bloodlines off the boat from England and France. Hopes were high, and the average sale price that year went up to $932.

Prospective buyers mostly ignored the lean and growthy yearling that would later be named Exterminator. But one man, J. Calvin Milam from Lexington, Kentucky, had been back and forth to the tent several times. When the son of McGee—Fair Empress came into the sales ring, Milam took the bidding up to $1,500, where the gavel dropped. A smooth operator with a keen eye that could look past a pedestrian pedigree, Milam must have seen some potential.

"His looks may not catch your fancy," the forty-five-year-old Milam explained to a reporter, "but his breeding is acceptable and, all things considered, I got him for a fair price." Milam loaded the yearling on a railroad boxcar for transport to his farm (Merrick Place) on Tates Creek Pike near Lexington. Milam's "sales stable" method was bottom-line simple: Break the babies, race them for a year or two, and then turn the animals over for a profit. Show me the money.

Milam trained his own horses. In the early spring of 1917, he sent his stable to the Kentucky Association track in Lexington. The feed, tack, and equipment were packed. The exercise riders and a string of two-year-olds were primed for action. The whole team was ready to go. All except Exterminator, who remained straggly, disinterested, run down, and generally fretful in nature. He was way behind in his training. Time was money. Milam was not a man to waste either. He instructed the vet to castrate the colt.

****

Exterminator's racing debut came on June 30, 1917, at Latonia in northern Kentucky across the Ohio River from Cincinnati. Very tall (16.3 hands) and awkward in manner, the gelded son of McGee was one of only two horses starting for the first time. Six furlongs. Fast track. Five to one. Expectations were few and far between, but Exterminator led the field of twelve at every call and won easily.

Shipped to Canada for his next start, Exterminator finished fourth, beaten ten lengths in an allowance race at Windsor Race Course in Ontario. He came back with three days rest and beat an allowance field handily, earning $650 as top prize money. On July 26 at Kenilworth Park in Ontario, Exterminator ran his final race as a two-year-old in an $800 allowance event. Flying at the end, Exterminator finished fourth in a field of eleven. The deep closing attack took its toll. Exterminator strained a muscle in his left rear and was put on the shelf for recuperation.

Nothing spectacular but not bad. One win at home, one win and two fourths on the road. In those days there was no purse distribution back to fourth place so the campaign across the border barely made expenses. Exterminator's record as a two-year-old did not attract a lot of attention. But what one man sees in a horse is often beyond analysis.

The 1920s was an era when horses could obtain hero status in America. Prominent stakes were attracting large crowds, hoping to see some blue-blooded colt that could stamp future progeny. It was a time when geldings were being ridiculed. Despite being the butt of jokes, Milam went ahead and nominated Exterminator to the Kentucky Derby. Maybe it was just wishful thinking. Maybe it was shrewd business. Maybe it was an investment in the idea that all things are possible.

****

Seventy horses were nominated to the Kentucky Derby in 1918. From Baltimore, Maryland, to Bay St. Louis, Mississippi; from banker to bricklayer, the name on everybody's lips was Sun Briar. It was a done deal.

Fashionably bred and having won five of nine starts on the stakes circuit, running his competition into the ground, Sun Briar emerged as the overwhelming favorite in the winter future book to win the Kentucky Derby. In the minds of horsemen and fans, no other horse in the country could hold a candle to the promising colt owned by Willis Sharpe Kilmer.

Kilmer had shelled out $6,000 for Sun Briar at the same sale that Exterminator had sold for $1,500. Kilmer's purchase of the French-bred yearling had paid off in spades. Infatuated with his success, Kilmer decided to show off his prized collector's item. On New Year's Day, Kilmer threw a birthday party for the reigning juvenile champion at his estate in Binghamton, New York. No expense was spared. Press clippings and prestige — the showcase affair included a brass band, caviar, banners, balloons, wine, and cheese. Guided tours of the covered paddock and walking ring ended at the electrically lighted and heated stall of Sun Briar.

Before the cutting of the giant birthday cake, reporters and visitors were ushered into the trophy room to witness the shelves groaning under the weight of silver cups and crystal trophies won by Kilmer's runners. Image and impression. Kilmer kept himself, his breeding operation, racing stable, and Sun Briar on prominent display. The Kentucky Derby was gaining national prominence, and Kilmer clearly wanted to add that prize to his collection.

It was too windy and cold for balloons and birthday candles where Exterminator spent New Year's Day. While the flash bulbs and champagne corks were popping in upstate New York for Sun Briar, Exterminator was shivering in his stall at Merrick Place outside of Lexington. Waiting his blue-collar turn, Exterminator got a fresh rack of timothy hay as part of morning rounds. For a special touch, his groom reached over the stall door webbing and punched a drinking hole through the ice that covered Exterminator's water.

****

One of the many intriguing mysteries of horse racing is how and why young horses change over the course of the winter months. A prince can turn into a peasant or vice versa. Opposites emerge. By March what was a two-year-old eagle begins to act like a caged canary. Come April what was an ugly duckling begins to look like a three-year-old swan. It can be a look in their eye, the way they move, or a change of attitude on the racetrack. Something inside begins to bubble.

Backstretch observers who had not seen Exterminator for months did not recognize the gelding in March 1918. He was going to the track on his toes, neck bowed. From time to time, dapples appeared on his flanks. He began to put meat on his frame. He became more inquisitive about his surroundings. It wasn't the stopwatch or the time of his workouts that told the story. Exterminator had made a decision. He was getting himself into condition on his own schedule.

Sun Briar's development from two to three was headed in another direction. His workouts were less than spectacular. Ringbones (bony growths on the pastern or fetlock) were becoming "ouchy" and worrisome. The usually robust and handsome superstar was showing signs of being ordinary. Things were beginning to unravel. The Kentucky Derby was no longer in the bag. After Sun Briar ran a dull third in an April 25 prep race at Lexington, a disappointed Kilmer was forced to bite into a reality sandwich. His pride was hurt. The anxious and ambitious owner insisted that what was needed most was a running mate that would push Sun Briar to his best effort.

****

Kilmer was used to having things his way. A newspaper publisher by trade, the dropout from Cornell University had amassed his fortune from the marketing and sales of a patent medicine called Swamp Root. The questionable elixir supposedly cured kidney and liver ailments. Valid or not, the concoction had made Kilmer a very wealthy man.

Money cannot buy a winner of the Kentucky Derby but it helps. Kilmer authorized his trainer to go up to $700 to buy a "work horse" for Sun Briar. He outlined the strategy. Find a horse with a decent turn of foot and a calm disposition that could serve as an antidote to the high-strung Sun Briar. Something cheap and disposable.

Henry McDaniel listened. Almost since infancy, he had been on the backstretch of racetracks and had developed an instinct for horses and for what they could do. Kilmer could go on talking and listing all the things he wanted, but McDaniel already had a particular horse in mind. He walked straight over to C.J. Milam's barn with a halter rope in his hand.

At first Milam was not at all anxious to sell Exterminator. He finally put up a number of $13,000 for the gelding. McDaniel swallowed hard and countered, pointing out that Exterminator's record wasn't anything to brag about. "That's true," Milam said, flicking the ashes off his cigar, "but I thought enough of him to nominate him to the Derby." Two gentlemen in tweed sport coats, sipping coffee, cutting the ritual deal. The dickering went back and forth. McDaniel refused to budge from his top offer: $9,000 in cash plus two fillies he had back at the barn estimated to be worth $500 apiece. The deal was done. After the two men shook hands, Exterminator and Sun Briar were stablemates.

****

Kilmer was not a happy man. His trainer had just busted his budget and purchased a nothing horse for a sparring partner. He even refused to look at Exterminator, watching the workouts through binoculars from his limousine. The first two workouts (four- and five-furlong breezes) didn't help McDaniel's popularity. Sun Briar was clear by several lengths on both occasions. It was a flat mile match-up that told the truth and suggested that Exterminator had just been playing the part.

It was only four days before the Derby and, like gravy on rice, Exterminator was hooked to Sun Briar every step of the way. At the end, Sun Briar was clear by a "neck" but came back breathing hard and trembling. Unsaddled, Exterminator kicked and bucked his way back to the barn as if he were saying, "What would you like me to do next?"

Watching Exterminator cool out, McDaniel began some serious thinking. His father had trained the winners of three consecutive Belmont Stakes, and McDaniel, over the course of time, had seen hundreds of horses come and go. He was beginning to think he had never seen a horse like Exterminator. Something about the gelding kept buzzing around in the back of his mind. He called Kilmer and requested they meet in the lobby of the Phoenix Hotel in downtown Lexington. Not tomorrow. Immediately.

"I think we have underestimated this horse's intelligence," McDaniel explained to Kilmer, over drinks at the bar. "He presses when he is supposed to and he lays back when necessary. All this time he has just been playing with Sun Briar," McDaniel said with all the emphasis he could muster. "He seems to know what his job is all about. I've never seen a horse like him. If it was me, Exterminator would be my Derby horse."

Kilmer, who was already not getting a good night's sleep, was mortified. Reluctant to praise Exterminator and protective of Sun Briar,

Kilmer was torn between disappointment and the need to save face. Needing a second opinion, he went back to the lobby and placed a phone call to Matt Winn.

General manager and vice-president of Churchill Downs, Winn was more than just a big cheese. He was a man of immense influence who had raised money to save the track from bankruptcy. Winn had witnessed every running of the Kentucky Derby and had a unique perspective of what kind of horse it took to win. The promoter in Winn knew that Kilmer would want to have his clubhouse day at the races and all the attention that goes with having a horse in the Derby.

It wasn't easy but, for once in his life, Kilmer kept his mouth shut and listened. "Regardless of how you feel about Sun Briar, the timing isn't right," Winn advised. "I have been watching both of those horses for the last two weeks. If the boy hadn't held him back, Exterminator would have run off and beat him each time. That gelding may not be pretty, but he's a whole sight better than an empty stall."

That did it. On Friday, May 10, Kilmer dropped the required $250 in the entry box. Exterminator would carry Kilmer's brown, green, and orange silks in the Kentucky Derby.

****

On the morning of the race nearly two and a half inches of rain fell on Louisville. Exterminator's groom put on three pairs of socks to help secure his feet in a pair of rubber boots and walked out to the track. Struggling to keep his balance in the ankle-deep mud, he passed a crew of maintenance workers carrying shovels and shuttling wheelbarrows of sand and soil. There was a washout under the rail on the far turn. "Lord have mercy," the groom muttered to himself when he arrived at the three-quarters gap. "You could drown a frog out there. How is my poor horse going to stand up in this?"

When the groom returned to the barn, he emptied his pockets of pennies and dropped them into Exterminator's water bucket. Secret or superstition — it was a ritual passed down from generations of black grooms. The belief held that copper wire or pennies were like vitamins and minerals to horse's bones. It couldn't hurt, and, anyway, his horse was going to need all the luck he could muster.

It was time to talk. Gut level the way grooms talk to horses. First the groom looked into Exterminator's eyes. He thanked the horse for not being finicky, flighty, and for never whimpering or whining like some poor horses. Exterminator liked the sound of the groom's voice and began bumping his nose into his jacket pocket for a slice of carrot. Behind and inside the white blaze on the horse's head, the groom wanted to believe what he thought he saw. There was an almost quizzical look in Exterminator's expression. Something close to a casual wink as if the horse were assuring the man that there was no need to worry. Whoever or whatever was going to face Exterminator that afternoon was going down.

Inside the stall, the groom lifted each of Exterminator's feet and picked the hoof clean. He stepped back for a better look. True what everybody said — the bones seemed to jut at all angles, but the well-shaped head and wide-set eyes hinted of intelligence. The groom thought about his luck. How he had drawn short straw for this outcast of a horse that he was about to walk over to the paddock for the Derby. "Go on over there, Old Bones," the groom said, referring to Exterminator's nickname, "but don't you listen to a word they say. And don't be getting all riled up either. Nothing to be mad about. Just get even. You go out there this afternoon and you make 'em like it."

****

The Churchill Downs paddock was packed. With elbows on top of the fence and glancing up from their racing papers, fans made their last-minute visual evaluation of the horses. American Eagle was "washy" and had his ears pinned back. Jockey Johnny Loftus was to ride the favorite War Cloud, who had set a ten-furlong training record at Churchill

Downs on May 7. Loftus, hands on his hips, stood next to owner A.K. Macomber talking strategy. Most of the attention in the saddling area was on second choice Escoba. Trained by John Ward, Escoba (large margin winner of the Derby Trial) carried the strut and look of a winner, especially with his shimmering coat.

As far as Exterminator was concerned, nobody was asking for autographs. In fact, things were getting mean. "I tried to bet your horse in the future book," a man hollered at Kilmer, "but his name wasn't even listed."

Laughter broke out, triggering others' confidence to poke more fun at Exterminator. "Hey you, McDaniel. You got this race confused with a circus? Your horse looks like he is put together with tent poles."

"What a bunch of dreamers," a man in a topcoat said loud enough for everyone to hear. "They might as well have entered a hamster. He would have had a better chance."

"How did the Jockey Club allow them to name this animal? What is he going to exterminate? Himself?" a man shouted from the back row.

McDaniel ignored the insults. He shut them out. Sliding his hand under the girth one last time for a safety check, McDaniel legged jockey Willie Knapp up in the saddle. One slap on Exterminator's butt for luck and the trainer headed for the nearest betting booth.

****

The eight horses walked up to the start and began the chaotic dance of assembling themselves in post-position order. Lucky B. wanted no part of the proceedings and reared up, almost unseating his rider. The chestnut Sewell Combs kept turning and twisting sideways, reluctant to go near the rail. An unruly Viva America — the only filly in the field — bumped into everything around her. In the pandemonium of handlers cracking whips, assistant starters hollering for help, and jockeys tensing up for the exact moment of release, Exterminator stood calm. Motionless as a turtle on a log, the gelding exuded a quiet presence that finally settled the horses inside and outside of him.

Nearly thirty to one. His jockey's first mount in a Kentucky Derby. A work horse whose breeding suggested he might stop when reaching the track kitchen. A gelding that had last raced ten months ago in a five and a half-furlong sprint. Mud up to his fetlocks. Exterminator had them right where he wanted them.

The web barrier snapped up, and they were off. Viva America and Sewell Combs shot out as a pair, leading the field past the stands filled with screaming fans. Exterminator lagged toward the rear, then positioned himself forward into fifth. There was considerable bumping as the horses sorted themselves out rounding the first turn. Jas. T. Clark was cut off. War Cloud stumbled momentarily.

There were few fans in the infield to witness the commotion because all along the inside of the rail and flowing into a massive rectangular patch on the first turn were rows and mounds of sacked potatoes. War Cloud may have lost a step, but there was a much bigger picture in May 1918. America was at war with Germany, and Churchill Downs grew more than a thousand bushels of potatoes a month to help feed the troops.

As the horses turned onto the backstretch, silks splattered by flying mud, it was impossible to spot any particular horse. McDaniel, along with the other trainers, squinted into the distance to see whether he could identify his runner. The awkwardness of the scene was another example of how the war in France touched all aspects of life and sport. Most of the Churchill Downs trainers had donated their binoculars and field glasses to the Army. They had been collected weeks ago and shipped overseas.

Down the backside, less than ten lengths separated the field and position remained unchanged. Knapp and Exterminator were fifth, trailing the pacesetters by about seven lengths and well off the rail. Born in Chicago, Knapp was a veteran on the Midwestern circuit. Like with most jockeys of his day, formal education had not been a priority. The thirty-year-old journeyman may not have read Emerson or Thoreau, but Knapp was a quick reactor in the irons and clever about taking advantage during the running of a race. More importantly, he knew horses like the back of his hand.

At the five-sixteenths pole Knapp was jolted by something he felt underneath him. Exterminator was gliding, taking one long smooth stride to the other horses' two. And he was doing it with a rhythm. Knapp, feeling the power underneath, dug his heels into the stirrups and lifted himself slightly, grabbing some mane and flattening himself on Exterminator's neck. "Holy shit," Knapp cursed to himself, "this damn horse thinks he can win it."

On the far turn, Exterminator, like a pit bull off his leash, went into frontal assault. As if the racetrack were the only place he wanted to be or were meant to be, the gelding took aim on the leaders with a sustained run on the outside. With War Cloud and Escoba still in front and fighting for the lead, Exterminator cut the corner at the quarter-pole like a seasoned professional. The deep and tiring track had taken its toll on the leg weary War Cloud. With choppy strides and his head coming up, the favorite sent up the white flag. He had had enough. Now only one horse with any fight remained — Escoba.

No surrender. Respect. Represent all geldings. Second string, huh? Watch this.

Approaching the eighth-pole, Exterminator came up along the inside of Escoba, closing the gap to one length, half a length, eyeball to eyeball Russian roulette. True to his profession, Knapp felt obligated to swat Exterminator a couple of times with a right-handed whip. But it was the horse that had timed his move to perfection and was now playing cat and mouse. With mud splattering in all directions and the crowd pressing the outer rail to witness the finish, Exterminator made Escoba "like it" for another hundred yards.

When they expect you to kneel, stand up and take it all. Give 'em something to talk about. Nearing the wire, Exterminator drew off with gusto, winning by a decisive length. Viva America held on for third after War Cloud faded in the stretch.

As Exterminator galloped past the wire, a stunned silence fell over the track. For a few moments pigeons fluttering in the rafters of the grandstand could be heard. Then the first of a series of screams came from the Jim Crow section. As a facility, Churchill Downs was segregated, and a young black man was waving his two-dollar win ticket like a battle flag.

Jogging back to the winner's circle, Exterminator stopped and posed for the cameras. Two attendants tiptoed through the mud to place a wreath of red roses around Exterminator's neck. "Do you see that?" said one of them. "He's not even breathing hard."

****

Sixty-one dollars and twenty cents to win. Never again. From that day forward, in a career that would span eight years and one hundred races (almost all stakes and handicaps and one in a timed exhibition), Exterminator's odds would not go over 12-1. Even the jokes stopped.

"Old Bones" would go on to win fifty races. He was the public's choice fifty-eight times and he won thirty-one of those for a winning 54 percent. Talk about a horse holding up his end of the bargain! Exterminator won twenty-seven of the thirty-seven races in which he was held at odds of even money or less.

Versatility? Stamina? The men around Exterminator came and went through revolving doors. He would have nine trainers and eighteen different jockeys. It didn't make any difference. From coast to coast, from Canada to Arkansas to Tijuana, Mexico, Exterminator sprinted or routed. Rest or no rest. He started seven times at the distance of two and a quarter miles and won five of them.

Courage? Durability? Exterminator could carry the mail. Track hand-

Kentucky Derby
Purse: $15,000 Added

Churchill Downs - May 11, 1918. Forty-fourth running Kentucky Derby.
Purse $15,000 added. Three-year-olds. 1 1-4 Miles. Main Track. Track: Muddy.
Gross value $15,000. Net value to winner, $14,700; second, $2,500; third, $1,000; fourth, $275.

Horse	A	Wgt	Eqp	Odds	PP	St	1/4	1/2	3/4	Str	Fin	Jockey
Exterminator	3	114		29.60	5	5	5¹	4ˣ	1ʰᵈ	2⁴	1¹	W Knapp
Escoba	3	117	b	4.25	1	2	3¹ˣ	2ʰᵈ	2¹	1ʰᵈ	2⁸	J Notter
Viva America	3	113		29.00	2	1	1¹ˣ	1¹ˣ	3⁴	3²	3⁴	W Warrington
*WarCloud	3	117		1.45	4	7	4ʰᵈ	5²	4⁴	4³	4²	J Loftus
Lucky B	3	117		6.15	6	4	6ʰᵈ	7⁸	5ˣ	5⁸	5⁶	J McCabe
Jas. T. Clark	3	117	b	8.90	8	8	7³	6³	7⁸	7³	6¹²	J Morys
Sewell Combs	3	117	b	8.75	3	3	2ⁿᵏ	3¹	6²	6ˣ	7¹	L Gentry
American Eagle	3	117	sb	19.25	7	6	8	8	8	8	8	E Sande

Off Time: 5:21   Time Of Race: :24¼   :49¼   1:16¼   1:43¾   2:10¾
Start: Good For All   Track: Muddy
Equipment: s for spur; b for blinkers

Mutuel Payoffs
5	Exterminator	$61.20	$23.10	$12.40
1	Escoba		4.90	4.60
2	Viva America			13.20

Winner: Exterminator, ch. g. by *McGee—Fair Empress, by Jim Gore (Trained by Henry McDaniel).
Bred by F. D. Knight in Kentucky.

Start good and slow. Won handily; second and third driving.
EXTERMINATOR, moved up fast after going three-quarters and, slipping through next to the inner rail, raced into the lead and outstayed ESCOBA in the final drive. ESCOBA raced forwardly from the start and made a resolute effort in the last eighth, but tired in the last sixteenth. VIVA AMERICA showed the most early speed but found the distance a trifle too far for her. *WAR CLOUD met with much interference on the first two turns, but remained close up to the last quarter, where he tired and dropped back. SEWELL COMBS raced well for three-quarters. JAS. T. CLARK was sharply cut off when he moved up fast at the half-mile ground.
Scratched—Aurum, Jim Heffering.
Overweight—Viva America, 1 pound.

Owners: (1) W S Kilmer; (2) K D Alexander; (3) C T Worthington; (4) A K Macomber; (5) O A Bianchi; (6) J W Schorr; (7) Gallaher Bros.; (8) T C McDowell
©EQUIBASE

icappers, attempting to bring Exterminator back to the field, assigned him 130 pounds or more on thirty-five occasions. He won twenty. Carrying 138 pounds, he beat Firebrand in the 1922 Kentucky Handicap. Burdened with 134 pounds, Exterminator in 1920 won the two and a quarter-mile Ontario Jockey Club Cup by daylight.

After Exterminator's sensational back-to-back seasons at five and six (thirty-three stakes or handicaps with eighteen wins, five seconds, and seven thirds) the track handicappers got ridiculous. It took 140 pounds in the Independence Handicap at Latonia to make him run sixth, which was the worst finish of his career. Assigned 135 pounds in the 1922 Brooklyn Handicap, Exterminator beat Grey Lag by a head at the wire.

It is a very short list of Thoroughbred names that can aspire to equaling Exterminator's honesty and consistency. That fire does not burn anymore. A gladiator under heavy weight and over long distances of ground, whenever "Old Bones" went into the arena he made them "like it."

By Gary McMillen

Destined To Win

"This generation of Americans has a rendezvous with destiny."

THOSE STIRRING WORDS, spoken by President Franklin Delano Roosevelt to wildly cheering delegates at the 1936 Democratic National Convention and to millions of radio listeners were intended to embolden a nation just beginning to peer out from under the rubble of the most severe economic recession in its history.

His listeners, regardless of their financial circumstances, were a bit less sanguine than their president, despite recent surges in employment, national income, and corporate profits. They were all too mindful of the shocks that had begun with the stock market crash in late 1929, followed by thousands of bank failures across the country, unemployment in excess of 25 percent, and sharp declines in farm prices and corporate earnings.

Confidence was hard to come by in 1936 America, even among the well-heeled sorts who typically bred and owned racehorses. New York businessman and real estate mogul Morton L. Schwartz, a native of Louisville, Kentucky, had enjoyed his share of success as an owner and breeder since his first venture into the business when he bought a horse named Bat Masterson from legendary horseman John E. Madden. But, by 1935, he was so discouraged with the depressed state of the racing industry that he gave up his lease on Elsmeade Farm near Lexington and made plans to sell his breeding stock, while retaining only a few racing prospects that he would lease to other owners for the balance of the 1935 season.

Schwartz had no idea that one of those leased homebreds, a tall, leggy chestnut two-year-old named Bold Venture, would eventually team up with a veteran trainer and a rookie jockey to give the owner his own "rendezvous with destiny" in the following year's Kentucky Derby.

Bold Venture was foaled at Elsmeade on March 4, 1933, the same day Franklin Roosevelt was inaugurated to serve his first term during the depths of the Great Depression. The colt's dam was named Possible, a daughter of the intensely inbred (to Domino) sire Ultimus, a major source of speed in the American Thoroughbred of the day. Bold Venture's sire was St. Germans, an English-bred son of the great racehorse and sire Swynford out of a granddaughter of the epic race mare Sceptre. St. Germans had demonstrated classic form prior to being purchased by prominent American breeder Payne Whitney, who was looking for a fashionable young stallion to stand at his Greentree Stud in Kentucky.

The pattern of crossing leading English bloodlines with successful (and speedy) American strains was well established by this time, having already produced numerous high-class horses in the 1920s and early '30s, among them a Greentree-bred and -owned son of St. Germans named Twenty Grand, who had won the Kentucky Derby and Belmont Stakes in 1931 and was almost certainly the catalyst for Schwartz' decision to breed Possible to his friend Whitney's stallion.

Schwartz had enjoyed exceptional success in 1932 with Gusto, winner of the American Derby, Arlington Classic, and Jockey Club Gold Cup that year, but by the time Bold Venture was a juvenile, his owner's aforementioned pessimism about racing's immediate prospects led Schwartz to shop around his racehorses.

On May 18, 1935, Bold Venture was entered into a horses of racing age sale at Belmont Park. Displeased with the bidding, Schwartz had his friend Isidor Bieber buy back the youngster at $7,100, not a bad price in the Depression-era market but nothing like the $20,000 or so Schwartz thought the colt was worth.

Although Bold Venture and some other Schwartz youngsters later would be leased to Admiral Cary Grayson, former physician to and confidante of the late President Woodrow Wilson, for the rest of the year, the colt would remain in the hands of Schwartz' trainer, Max Hirsch.

The latter was already, at age fifty-five, well established among the first rank of American trainers. A native of Fredericksburg, Texas, Hirsch would later tell racing scribes that he had "hopped a train to get to Baltimore to get a taste of big-time racing" at age twelve. There he apprenticed to noted Maryland horseman R. Wyndham Walden, trainer of seven Preakness winners and one of the leading breeders and trainers of his era.

Hirsch rode for about five years, then turned to training when control of his waistline became a problem. He soon acquired a reputation as an astute conditioner of horses and trained for many top owners of the post-World War I era, among them George Loft, Mrs. W.K. Vanderbilt, the Sage brothers, Herbert Pulitzer, Mrs. F. Ambrose Clark, and, of course, Schwartz. By the time Bold Venture was on the scene, Hirsch had already trained stars such as Grey Lag, Donnaconna, Sarazen, On Watch, and Gusto. He knew his way to the winner's circle, and he knew how to handle the "big" horse, but he had yet to train a classic winner. His "rendezvous with destiny" was a promising but green two-year-old on the Hirsch shed row.

On June 1, 1935, thirteen days after Schwartz failed to sell him, Bold Venture debuted in a maiden race over five furlongs at Belmont. He was the object of enough clockers' gossip based on his morning works to go off as the 6-5 favorite, helped undoubtedly by his partnership with jockey Sonny Workman, one of the most sought-after riders in America. Bold Venture broke slowly and "raced greenly," according to the race chart, but closed some ground late and was second by four lengths. He would break his maiden by a head a month later over five furlongs at Aqueduct.

Thinking they had a stakes horse on their hands, Schwartz and Hirsch sent their charge off to Arlington Park for the lucrative Arlington Futurity. They prepped him in a purse race five days beforehand, and he had the misfortune to trip and fall in the post parade, cutting himself and shaking himself up a bit. Today that would result in an automatic scratch, but such things were the exception in those days, and he went on to run competitively, staying close to a strong pace and finishing a good fourth in a fast-run race as the 2-1 favorite.

Schwartz raced Bold Venture for the colt's first three starts but then leased him to Grayson for the rest of the 1935 season. On August 3, apparently none the worse for his exertions, he went postward under new colors for the Futurity on a miserably rainy day in Chicago. The weather must have disagreed with him, for he put on a bucking display in the post parade that led to his dumping the jockey and running around most of Arlington's oval before being caught. Still allowed to participate, he broke belatedly and trailed the field all the way.

Shipped back east to Saratoga, he was entered in an allowance race on August 19 and ran a solid second behind a wire-to-wire winner as the even-money favorite.

The bettors still loved him despite his recent failures, and on August 22 he was back on track at the Spa, where he won as favorite over a field of eleven others, including a son of 1930 Triple Crown winner Gallant Fox named Granville, owned by William Woodward's Belair Stable and trained by Sunny Jim Fitzsimmons.

That earned Bold Venture a four-day break before he went out for a prep for Saratoga's most important two-year-old race, the Hopeful, where he would meet Arlington Futurity winner Grand Slam; Valevictorian, a stakes winner in Detroit; Jean Bart, a son of Man o' War; and a youngster from Wheatley Stable (and trainer Fitzsimmons) named Seabiscuit. Favored again, Bold Venture ran down Grand Slam in the stretch and won by a length and a half.

The Hopeful, run on August 31, featured seventeen starters and didn't go well for Bold Venture, who was favored at 4-1. The chart indicates he was stuck in a mob scene and never found room to run, eventually finishing ninth.

More misfortune befell Bold Venture. Shipped to Belmont for the fall meeting, he was in a train car that caught fire and had his head held out an open door to avoid suffocation from smoke that claimed the lives of two other horses belonging to his trainer. In spite of Bold Venture's misadventures, Hirsch thought highly of the colt and intended to aim him for the Futurity and other important fall two-year-old races, but Bold Venture fell victim to a virus sweeping the Belmont stable area and was put aside for the year with three wins in eight starts and only $2,500 in earnings but a reputation as one of the potential standouts in his class.

Meanwhile, Schwartz had gone ahead with the dispersal of his breeding stock at Saratoga in August, selling twenty fillies and mares and a batch of yearlings in a sale that drew lots of attention from buyers, one of whom was Robert Justus Kleberg Jr., who had taken over the management of his family's vast Texas-based King Ranch holdings a few years earlier.

Kleberg's father had experimented with crossing Thoroughbreds and ranch horses. The experiment did not go particularly well but left the junior Kleberg with an abiding interest in Thoroughbreds, and a visit to Kentucky in 1935 during which he looked at the Schwartz breeding stock cinched the matter. He spent almost $40,000 buying mares, foals, and yearlings at Saratoga and developed a relationship with Schwartz that would prove to be his and the King Ranch's own "rendezvous with destiny."

As was the habit of many major Eastern stables of that era, Hirsch shipped Bold Venture and his other horses to South Carolina for the winter in preparation for a spring campaign. Schwartz, his appetite for racing whetted again by Bold Venture's promising-yet-frustrating juvenile season, had told friends he thought he might have a chance to win the Kentucky Derby with this horse, and Hirsch had a lot of confidence in the colt, as well.

Bold Venture's work in the winter consisted of long gallops to "leg him up," followed by a steady progression of longer and longer workouts, all designed to build him for the endurance tests that lay ahead. However, while his contemporaries, among them hot Derby favorite Brevity, were being cranked up in actual race competition in Florida, California, and other warm-winter climes, Bold Venture was not sent to the starting gate for something other than a workout until April 16. Only sixteen days prior to the 1936 Derby he went postward in the South Shore Purse, an allowance race at Jamaica over a mile and seventy yards. He faced only three opponents, none of them daunting, and led almost the entire way to win by four lengths under a hard hold. This was nothing more than an afternoon workout in company, but the New York racing reporters liked what they saw and tabbed him a live candidate for the Wood Memorial, to be run a week prior to the Derby, and for the Derby itself.

Four days after the South Shore, Hirsch galloped the colt a full mile and a quarter in 2:08 3/5. The trainer then decided to bypass the Wood and sent Bold Venture another mile and a quarter the day before that race, this time in 2:10 3/5. Two mile-and-a-quarter works in five days would be unheard of today and caused some comment then, but Hirsch said he'd seen enough in those two lengthy trials to tell him his horse was ready to go to Kentucky.

Even at a time when lightly raced horses coming into the Derby was no oddity, Bold Venture's single start since August of his two-year-old season was enough to shuffle him to the rear of the pre-race hype surrounding contenders. Another factor was Hirsch's choice of jockeys. The trainer had approached Sonny Workman about riding his horse, but Workman was already committed to Grand Slam, and Hirsch decided to go with apprentice Ira Hanford.

Hanford, a native of Omaha, Nebraska, was the youngest of three brothers who had all decided to pursue race riding as a profession. The oldest, Bernard "Buddy" Hanford, got off to a good start but was killed in a spill at Pimlico in May 1933. The middle brother, Carl, persevered and was already riding with success when the youngest Hanford, nicknamed Babe by the family, apprenticed himself to Max Hirsch's daughter Mary, the first woman licensed as a trainer by The Jockey Club, in the winter of 1935. Ira "Babe" Hanford would record eighty-four winners during his first year at the races and was fifth among the nation's leading jockeys by winners on Derby Day but had never ridden a stakes winner or been involved in a race of this magnitude before. The writers and broadcasters who were blanketing the Derby assumed, logically, that an eighteen-year-old apprentice with no major race experience would find himself in very deep water under such pressure against the nation's top reinsmen.

Hanford, still spry and charming at eighty-eight years young, has remarkable recollection of the circumstances of the 1936 Derby.

"I mostly worked with Mary [Hirsch] on the horses that Mr. Hirsch would ship to tracks outside New York, places like Maryland or the New England tracks," said Hanford. "I had never ridden Bold Venture until that prep race for the Derby [the South Shore] but I knew Mr. Hirsch was pretty high on him. He was going down to win the Derby — I think he knew he had the best horse."

There was, of course, the matter of the other horses, thirteen of them, in the entries for the sixty-second running of the race that was already considered, everywhere outside of New York, the premier three-year-old event in American racing.

Foremost in the estimation of the writers and fans was Brevity, a neatly balanced son of the Phalaris horse Sickle, bred and owned by Joseph E. Widener, one of the American Turf's most notable patrons. Brevity was officially listed as being by Chance Shot or Sickle, both standing at Widener's Elmendorf Farm, but it was evident from both his foaling date and his physical make-up that Brevity was a son of Sickle, whom he resembled closely. Sickle had been a good two-year-old in England, and so was Brevity, who, despite occasional bad racing luck, concluded his juvenile campaign successfully with a win over a large and well-regarded field in the important Champagne Stakes at Belmont. Although he skipped the season's major juvenile race, the Futurity, Brevity was still regarded by many observers as the top two-year-old male in training and a serious candidate for the 1936 classics.

His pre-Derby efforts only added to that notion. He ran a 1:36 mile in his seasonal debut at Hialeah, then stormed home five lengths the best in the Florida Derby, running a mile and one-eighth in 1:48 1/5, equaling the world record for the distance.

Such was Brevity's reputation afterward that his Derby odds in the winter books fell to 2-1, and his subsequent workouts drew wide attention. His only other start was an allowance race at Churchill Downs a week before the Derby, when he skipped over seven furlongs easily, setting strong fractions along the way. He started as the hot favorite in the Run for the Roses, at eighty cents to a dollar.

Second choice, a bit surprisingly, was Indian Broom, a Brookmeade Stud-bred colt who was, after a solid but unpretentious juvenile campaign, taken to the West Coast to begin his three-year-old season in Brookmeade colors. After he ran moderately in his winter starts at Santa Anita, Isabel Dodge Sloane, proprietor of Brookmeade, told her trainer to cut their losses and sell some of the stable's lesser lights, including Indian Broom, who was purchased by Canadian owner Austin Taylor. Under new management, he blossomed, eventually landing the Marchbank Handicap at Tanforan on April 11 over top-notch older horses Top Row and Azucar, in sensational style, breaking the track record at virtually every pole en route to a nine-furlong clocking of 1:47 3/5, smashing Brevity's world-record time! Although Easterners were suspicious of the West Coast tracks, this was clearly a very fast horse, and his works after he shipped to Churchill continued to make that point.

Next in the wagering was the entry of Granville and Teufel, coupled because although separately owned, Sunny Jim Fitzsimmons trained both. On his own, Granville would probably have been third choice because the son of Gallant Fox had been well regarded as a two-year-old and even more so at three, where it was believed his pedigree would make him formidable over longer distances. He had been beaten narrowly in the Wood Memorial by Teufel, a maiden receiving five pounds from Granville, but many onlookers thought Granville's rider, Jimmy Stout, had not given his best performance that day and were confident Granville would be a force at Churchill. Belatedly, Fitzsimmons decided to add Belair second stringer Merry Pete to his Derby entry to provide pace for Granville.

Local favorites, Bien Joli, campaigned by Colonel E.R. Bradley's famed Idle Hour Farm and a good two-year-old, and Coldstream, bred and owned by Dale Shaffer's Coldstream Stud, had good support in pre-Derby betting, as did The Fighter, a son of Bull Dog who as a juvenile had shown good form for owner Ethel V. Mars and her Milky Way Stables but who was generally regarded as a speed horse. The Fighter changed some minds when he went on a five-race sweep culminating in the Texas Derby at Arlington Downs, Texas' short-lived pari-mutuel facility. Because he had won at nine furlongs, some thought his speed might be dangerous at Churchill, although he was not really a front-running type. However, when one is looking for a Derby horse at a price, rationality and logic are seldom entry mates.

In 1936 the first Saturday in May dawned threateningly, with early morning sprinkles and forecasts of more serious rain for later in the day. There was such rain elsewhere in the Louisville area and throughout Kentucky, but Churchill Downs stayed miraculously dry, and the race was contested on a fast track under hazy sunshine, to the benefit of the crowd estimated at 60,000 to 70,000.

As Derby post time approached, early favorite Brevity continued to attract more and more wagering interest, to the point that only Indian Broom, at 5-1, was less than 10-1, the approximate odds of the Granville–Teufel–Merry Pete entry. Bold Venture? Well, he wasn't entirely friendless at 20-1, but outside of his owner, trainer, and jockey, few were expecting to see him near the winner's circle after the mile and a quarter test.

After the race, and for a long time, discussions about the 1936 Derby focused on the start of the race and its ultimate impact on the outcome.

Starting gates in those days had no front or rear doors; they were simply made of attached stalls, with little to control the behavior of the horses led into them. Although a great improvement over the old walk-up or tape starts, they didn't prevent numerous delays as horses acted up before being loaded or continued to do so afterward, requiring starters to be eternally patient while always aware of the need to get the field underway with some alacrity.

The 1936 Derby had its share of pre-race problems, caused by the antics of several members of the field. However, those theatrics were a minor sideshow compared to what happened when starter William Hamilton sent them away.

Hanford remembers it this way: "Bien Joli hit Bold Venture on the right shoulder, which turned him in and caused us [Hanford and Bold Venture] to bump into Granville, and Jimmy Stout came right off his horse. Had we not been hit so hard, we would have been in better position going into the turn."

The chart of the race has two telling comments, one an absolute certainty, the other a matter of dispute: "Granville unseated his rider when in close quarters shortly after the start." Granville got smacked and dumped Jimmy Stout, a matter of fact. Regarding Brevity, the chart said: "The latter [Brevity], probably best and knocked to his knees within a few strides after the start, had to race wide thereafter, closed resolutely and was wearing down [Bold Venture]."

There was, undoubtedly, some skirmishing at the break when Indian Broom, in post-position No. 2, came over a bit on He Did in post-position No. 3, who, in turn, bumped Granville, causing him to stumble sideways and drop Stout, thus eliminating the Belair colt from the race entirely, although he would join the field, riderless, for the trip around the course. Brevity, meanwhile, was involved in another skirmish farther out when Coldstream, in the outside post, broke in and forced the two horses just inside him into Brevity.

The Blood-Horse account of the race was emphatic in stating that Brevity, while jostled, did not go to his knees or anything close to it. The writer noted that most of those claiming to witness Brevity's mugging were at least a quarter-mile away from the action and grossly overstated what had happened to the favorite. Starter Hamilton, in post-race questioning, likewise said the damage to Brevity's chances resulting from the start were much exaggerated, although he might have been biased.

Regardless, the race was underway, and all except Granville were left to make the best of their respective fortunes. The immediate leader was He Did, with Coldstream and The Fighter his closest company, followed by Bien Joli, Grand Slam, Indian Broom, and Merry Pete, who hadn't gotten a chance to run interference for Granville and couldn't get to the front, anyway. Hanford, meanwhile, had dropped Bold Venture back to the middle of the pack while keeping him to the outside, away from the close quarters inside. After completing the long run out of the chute and into the first turn, Bold Venture was eighth, about six lengths off the leaders, with Brevity, having recovered from his earlier misadventures, trailing him in ninth by a length and a half. The front-runners were cutting out decent fractions for a mile and a quarter race (first quarter in :23 3/5; half-mile in :47 4/5), when Hanford, having followed instructions and keeping his horse out of trouble, decided to send him to the front. Sweeping out of the first turn, Hanford propelled his eager mount around the leaders and then, once in front, moved over toward the rail.

Hanford says his horse was getting a lot of dirt thrown in his face going into the first turn, so "I moved him outside to get away from that, and when I did, he took off on his own. He made the lead by himself, and he did it so easily that I thought, 'Why restrain him when's he's going so easily?' I didn't ask him to run until the stretch, and then we had a real horse race."

That move almost certainly gave him the race, that and Bold Venture's talent and tenacity. Jockey Wayne Wright on Brevity saw Hanford make his move but sat still on his colt, perhaps thinking Bold Venture was moving too early. The latter was sailing along as he raced into the final turn with a comfortable lead over He Did, Indian Broom, Coldstream, and Grand Slam, his most immediate attendants, and looking to extend his margin as he turned into the stretch. He was ahead of Indian Broom by a length and a half at the quarter pole and widening his advantage, but now Brevity was on the move, resolutely overhauling the leader as they came down the stretch.

The huge crowd, seeing the favorite making up ground on the outside, raised the noise level even higher as jockeys Hanford and Wright went to the whip to urge their mounts to greater effort. Bold Venture was still striding out, but Brevity was gaining, foot by foot, inch by inch. At the eighth pole, the margin was a diminishing length; at the sixteenth pole, a neck; and with twenty yards to go the pair were a head apart, but at that point Brevity had stopped gaining and Bold Venture held on determinedly, winning officially by a head over the unlucky Brevity.

The result was made official, and Bold Venture was the 1936 Kentucky Derby winner, paying $43 on a straight $2 wager, the fourth-longest price in Derby history. His final time of 2:03 3/5 was the third fastest in race history, and Hanford became the first apprentice jockey in history to win a Derby. Morton Schwartz, in receiving the Derby trophy from Kentucky Governor A.B. "Happy" Chandler, pronounced that "the ruling ambition of my life" had been realized. It certainly had to be a pleasing moment for Schwartz to win the country's most prestigious race in his hometown, especially after he had contemplated leaving racing behind only a year before and had tried to sell his eventual Derby winner.

Hanford, for his part, would get a fifteen-day suspension from the stewards for his crossover move at the head of the backstretch, along with two other jockeys, including Nick Wall on third-place Indian Broom for initiating the skirmish at the start.

Hanford says he got back to New York on Monday after the Derby and was told by Hirsch and New York steward Marshall Cassidy that he had been suspended by the Kentucky stewards for what they thought had happened at the start. "I always thought it was for bumping into Granville; years later I read it was for crossing over on the backstretch when we went to the lead. No one at the time ever told me that. I was just told by Mr. Cassidy that I was suspended for fifteen days."

After giving Bold Venture credit for a gallant effort, the racing writers of the day were virtually unanimous in proclaiming that Brevity would reverse the result next time out, as would probably Granville.

Hirsch had not formally said he was going to the Preakness, but in the interim he worked the colt as if he were preparing to face Man o' War: May 4 — six furlongs in 1:13 4/5; May 9 — a half-mile in :48 3/5; May 11th — nine furlongs in 1:53 2/5; May 12 — a half-mile in :49; May 13 — six furlongs in 1:12 1/5 (a half in :46 1/5). Bold Venture galloped a mile in 1:45 2/5 after arriving at Pimlico on Thursday. Imagine three-year-olds today going through a training regimen of that sort the ten days prior to a classic race.

Did Hirsch know his stuff, and his horse? Well, with new rider George Woolf subbing for the suspended Hanford, Bold Venture ran an even better race than in the Derby. It was his turn to get interfered with near the start, and he was near the back of the field early before Woolf gradually worked him into contention on the outside going into the final turn. Woolf then asked him to run at the top of the stretch, and the colt accelerated alongside the leader, Granville (Brevity had skipped the Preakness), hooked him, then edged by him and withstood a final surge by the tough Belair youngster, winning by a long nose.

Now, it was on to the Belmont Stakes, where he would try to join Sir Barton, Gallant Fox, and Omaha (Gallant Fox and Omaha were both Belair bred and raced) as the only winners of what was now being termed the American Triple Crown, and his doubters were now muted. Hirsch worked him five furlongs in 1:02 on the Tuesday after the Preakness, then followed with a half-mile in :47 4/5 on Thursday. On Monday, May 25, he breezed six furlongs in 1:15 but came back to his stall lame in his right foreleg, with a bowed tendon being the diagnosis. He was done for the year and could not, in fact, be brought back to the races. He was retired with a record of six wins from eleven starts and earnings of just $68,300, a testimonial to the paltry purses in Depression-driven America.

Bold Venture was retired to stud in Kentucky briefly but didn't get much patronage and was purchased in 1939 by Bob Kleberg to go to the King Ranch in Texas. Kleberg liked his pedigree, his looks, and

Kentucky Derby
Purse: $40,000 Added

Churchill Downs - May 2, 1936. Sixty-second running Kentucky Derby.
Purse $40,000 added. Three-year-olds. 1 1-4 Miles. Main Track. Track: Fast.
Gross value $40,000. Net value to winner, $37,725 and $5,000 gold cup; second, $6,000; third, $3,000; fourth, $1,000.

Horse	A	Wgt	Eqp	Odds	PP	St	1/2	3/4	1	Str	Fin	Jockey
Bold Venture	3	126		20.50	5	13	8^1½	1^1	1^1½	1^1	1^hd	I Hanford
Brevity	3	126	b	.80	10	10	9^1½	6^1½	3^1	2^2	2^6	W Wright
Indian Broom	3	126	b	5.10	2	7	6^hd	3^2	2^1½	3^5	3^3	G Burns
Coldstream	3	126		15.20	13	6	2^hd	4^1	5^3	5^3	4^5	N Wall
Bien Joli	3	126	b	14.90	6	2	4^hd	7^1	6^3	6^2	5^hd	L Balaski
Holl Image	3	126	b	f-43.40	14	12	12^1	11^1	11^1½	7^3	6^4	H Fisher
He Did	3	126	sb	33.80	3	1	1^2	2^½	4^4	4^hd	7^hd	C Kurtsinger
Teufel	3	126	b	a-10.60	8	9	11^½	10^1	8^hd	8^1	8^hd	E Litzenberger
Gold Seeker	3	121	b	f-43.40	12	14	13	12^2	10^½	10^4	9^4	M Peters
Merry Pete	3	126	b	a-10.60	1	8	7^1½	8^3	7^1	9^hd	10^6	T Malley
The Fighter	3	126		b-16.50	7	3	5^hd	9^hd	12^6	11^4	11^5	A Robertson
Grand Slam	3	126		19.10	9	5	3^2	5^hd	9^2	12^8	12^10	R Workman
Sangreal	3	126		b-16.50	11	11	10^2	13	13	13	13	M Garner
Granville	3	126		a-10.60	4	4	Lost rider.					J Stout

Off Time: 4:46   **Time Of Race:** :23¾   :47½   1:12¾   1:37½   2:03¾
Start: Good For All   **Track:** Fast
Equipment: s for spurs; b for blinkers
Coupled: a-Teufel, Merry Pete, and Granville; b-The Fighter and Sangreal; f- Field.

Mutuel Payoffs

6	**Bold Venture**	$43.00	$11.80	$6.60
12	**Brevity**		5.00	4.00
3	**Indian Broom**			3.80

Winner: Bold Venture, ch. c. by *St. Germans—Possible, by Ultimus (Trained by Max Hirsch).
Bred by M. L. Schwartz in Kentucky.

Start good and slow. Won driving; second and third the same.
BOLD VENTURE, in close quarters immediately after the start, began to improve his position fast on the outside after about three-eighths, took an easy lead approaching the final half-mile and, holding on with fine courage under strong handling, withstood BREVITY's bid. The latter, probably best and knocked to his knees within a few strides after the start, had to race wide thereafter, improved his position gradually and closing resolutely, was wearing down the winner. INDIAN BROOM, badly blocked in the first quarter, raced to a contending position quickly when clear, made a bid entering the stretch and weakened in the last three-sixteenths. COLDSTREAM lost ground while showing speed and failed to keep up. BIEN JOLI was jostled about on the far turn and did not threaten thereafter. HOLL IMAGE began slowly. HE DID had speed for a mile. TEUFEL showed nothing. GOLD SEEKER was outrun. MERRY PETE was bumped when swerving soon after the start. THE FIGHTER began well, but failed to stay after about three-quarters. GRAND SLAM crossed to the inside approaching the first turn and showed speed for five-eighths. GRANVILLE unseated his rider when in close quarters shortly after the start.
Scratched—Banister, Dnieper, Seventh Heaven, Forest Play, Silas.

Owners: (1) M L Schwartz; (2) J E Widener; (3) A C T Stock Farm Stable; (4) Coldstream Stud Stable; (5) E R Bradley; (6) Superior Stable; (7) Mrs S B Mason; (8) Wheatley Stable; (9) Foxcatcher Farms Stable; (10) Belair Stud Stable; (11) Milky Way Farm; (12) Bonmar Stable; (13) Milky Way Farm; (14) Belair Stud Stable
©EQUIBASE

his willing spirit, and thought he had a chance to be a good stallion, which turned out to be a "rendezvous with destiny" for both horse and buyer.

Bold Venture was not particularly fertile, a problem that had plagued St. Germans and many of his line (Twenty Grand would be sterile), but Bold Venture became the only Derby winner to sire two other Derby winners, the first being 1946 Triple Crown winner Assault (who proved to be sterile at stud!) and 1950 Derby and Belmont Stakes winner Middleground (ridden by Bill Boland, the only other apprentice to win the Derby). The latter sired only 130 named foals in his stud career, continuing his sire line's tradition of modest or worse fertility. Both Assault and Middleground were raced by King Ranch and trained by Hirsch, whose monumental training career would span seventy-two years before he died in 1969 at age eighty-nine. Hirsch had been inducted into the Racing Hall of Fame in 1959, a mere four years after it was created.

Of Bold Venture's contemporaries, Granville would go on to become the first official American Horse of the Year in 1936, the first year in which year-end championship polls were conducted, after winning the Belmont Stakes, Travers, Classic Stakes (Arlington), and Saratoga Cup. Brevity, continuing his luckless run, would run second in the Withers, then fifth in the Belmont, after which he was lame and retired for the year.

In the end, where did Bold Venture rank among his contemporaries, or other stars of the era? His abbreviated career makes comparisons difficult, but there can be no doubt he was a high-class and competitive colt and certainly had a good argument for being the best of his year.

Hanford believes the horse never received the credit he deserved. "There's been many a horse who paid a big price to win the Derby and didn't turn out to be that much. But, Bold Venture was one of the better horses to win the Derby. If he had not broken down, he might have won the Triple Crown."

Hanford, as fortune would have it, never rode in another Derby and did not return to Churchill Downs until 2006, when he was a guest for the Derby renewal of that year, seventy years after his greatest day at the races.

Regardless of their place in Turf history, Bold Venture and Hanford will be immortalized in Kentucky Derby history as true "upset" winners of America's most glamorous race, and one of its gamest duos. Given his win in the 1936 Derby, and the subsequent successes of Assault and Middleground, Bold Venture could be said to be the ultimate "Derby horse," and one whose momentous win in Louisville brought a "rendezvous with destiny" for him, his owner, trainer, and jockey, and presaged the building of a horse racing empire at the King Ranch.

By Timothy T. Capps

The Spoiler

IN THE SPRING OF 1940, it seemed as if just one horse would contest the Kentucky Derby. Reporters and racing fans alike could write and talk of no other entrant but the dark bay colt named Bimelech. He belonged to Kentucky's own "Colonel" Edward Riley Bradley, an owner so successful in racing that he had four Derby winners to his name. Yet, Bimelech was the one Bradley called the greatest who had ever carried his colors.

Amid the wild furor over Bimelech, a lanky colt called Gallahadion went nearly unnoticed. For all his obscurity, he would topple the champion, shocking America by crossing the Kentucky Derby finish line first. When Gallahadion beat the "mighty" Bimelech, wrote Henry McLemore of the United Press, it was "to win $60,150 and break nearly 90,000 hearts."

Before the heartbreak, there was a love affair between the racing public and Bimelech that had begun soon after the colt made his racing debut. "It is a pleasure simply to walk around that horse," Joe Estes wrote in the pages of *The Blood-Horse*, "for he is a study in perfection, and one gets from him the same lifting of the spirit that comes from the contemplation of some masterpiece of the fine arts." More importantly, the colt's race record was outstanding. As a two-year-old, he swept to six victories, including the Saratoga Special Stakes and the Hopeful Stakes. He was named champion male for 1939.

Bradley's belief in his colt, who had an oddly endearing habit of running with his tongue stuck out, made him so confident that he challenged other owners to a mile race, a contest he hoped would attract attention similar to the 1938 Pimlico Special pitting Seabiscuit against War Admiral. Bradley encouraged challengers after Bimelech's two-year-old season, but then asked that the race be a brisk mile and one-sixteenth and that older horses carry more weight. No owners agreed to Bradley's terms, so his gauntlet lay untouched.

It seemed the Kentucky Derby would give Bradley the chance to show the world Bimelech was something extraordinary.

Bimelech was the last son of Bradley's stud Black Toney, who stood at his Idle Hour farm outside Lexington and sired successful racehorses such as Black Gold and Big Hurry. Bimelech's dam was La Troienne, the blue-hen mare by Teddy who founded a female family that has produced more than one thousand stakes winners.

The colt's unusual name came from a biblical figure named Abimelech, a nickname the Colonel's friend John Harris had gone by, and the contraction fit with Bradley's tradition of using names starting with "B" for his horses, such as Blue Larkspur and Brokers Tip. Fans mainly avoided the colt's hard-to-pronounce name and called him everything from Bimmie to the Bimbo to Big Bim.

No one had extravagant hopes — or even so much as a nickname — for Gallahadion, a son of Sir Gallahad III and Countess Time, by Reigh Count. Unlike racing veteran Bradley, Gallahadion's owner, Ethel V. Mars, was relatively new to the sport. Her Milky Way Farm was named after a candy bar produced by the Mars company, owned by her late husband, Frank C. Mars. He became involved in racing in 1933, when he bought twenty yearlings from Claiborne Farm's owner, Arthur B. Hancock, and sent them to Pulaski, Tennessee, between Nashville and

Birmingham, with his riding horses. Frank Mars died in 1934, never seeing his own colors in a winner's circle.

Ethel Mars enjoyed having the horses and found moderate success with the farm. Her horses included Sky Larking, who won three stakes races, including the 1937 Hopeful, before breaking a leg during the Champagne Stakes. Her filly Mars Shield won the 1937 Kentucky Oaks. Mars had entries in the Derby five times before Gallahadion and had taken third with Whiskolo in 1935 and Reaping Reward in 1937. In the 1938 and 1939 runnings, however, Mars' entrants Mountain Ridge and On Location had finished last and had been eased in the stretch and pulled up, respectively.

Instead of breeding her own Thoroughbreds, Mars enjoyed acquiring racers — about a dozen each year — at the yearling sales at Saratoga. She was notorious for spending more money to buy more horses than any other buyer, which often paid off. In 1936 she was the country's top-grossing money-winning owner.

Mars had enjoyed success with Sir Gallahad III colts in the past. Her 1934 purchases, Sangreal and Sir Gawaine, were both winners, so when she saw a gangly 15.3-hand son of Sir Gallahad at the Saratoga sale in 1938, she bought him for $5,000.

Gallahadion was a maiden at two. In their laconic way, race-chart writers that season told the story of a trier who just couldn't make it. Some examples: "Gallahadion was in close quarters in the early stages, then faltered when clear," and "Gallahadion raced greenly throughout." And finally, when he did place: "Gallahadion was a forward contender in the early racing and finished gamely in the final test."

Trainer Roy Waldron took Gallahadion to Santa Anita for winter racing, and the bay colt began his three-year-old campaign with four losses. On January 5, 1940, he finally won a race. He won again on January 10 but then lost his next two races. His stablemate, a solid racer named Tough Hombre, beat him in the latter race, but Gallahadion showed enough promise to catch his trainer's attention. He was entered in his first stakes race, the February 10 San Vicente Handicap. He won. He finished unplaced in two more stakes before heading to Churchill Downs.

Unlike Gallahadion, Bimelech was resting on his laurels that long, cold winter, loitering at Idle Hour. His trainer, William Hurley, went to Florida with some other Bradley horses and either left unclear orders for Bimelech's exercise or simply miscalculated the colt's conditioning needs, wrote Peter Chew in *The Kentucky Derby: The First 100 Years*.

In any case, the colt was out of shape and fat going into the spring. Rival trainer Ben Jones advocated keeping Bimelech out of prep races and saving his energy for the big one. He told Idle Hour's longtime manager Olin Gentry that Bimelech would win the Derby only if he did not run between the winter layoff and the race. But Hurley scoffed, believing his horse would win any race, no matter what. Jones' advice might ring true for a weaker animal, "but Bimelech is an iron horse," he claimed. On April 2, Bradley publicly dealt with rumors that Bimelech's training was lagging. He told reporters a letter from the trainer had reported the colt was in "excellent condition."

And Bimelech certainly seemed ready for the Blue Grass Stakes, a Derby prep race, at Keeneland on April 25. He trounced the competition, easing past a colt named Roman with no problem. He was a bit sweatier than usual in the paddock, but after his victory Bimelech's fans breathed a sigh of relief, believing that a lack of consistent conditioning could not quash the amazing ability they had all grown to admire during the colt's stellar two-year-old season.

Bimelech then won the April 30 Derby Trial, another Derby prep race, proving to his fans he could overcome yet one more obstacle: a less-than-fast track. The colt had enjoyed fast tracks for six of his seven previous starts, and the track for the Trial had barely dried out after a morning downpour. Its official condition was listed as good.

In what seemed like a sure harbinger of a victory to come, Bimelech thundered around the track at Churchill Downs with little competition. (This was the first meeting between Bimelech and Gallahadion, who was one of seven other entrants facing the heavy favorite.) Bimelech was in command at the beginning, easily outpacing an early challenger named Designer. Bimelech's jockey, F.A. "Freddie" Smith, went to the whip only once, a move the rider claimed was only to keep the colt focused. But Gallahadion had come on at the head of the stretch, and though Bimelech coasted home to win by two and a quarter lengths, people wondered later if it was the Mars colt drawing near that had encouraged Smith to give Bimelech that swat. In coverage of the race, however, Gallahadion went generally unmentioned except that he had run second to Bimelech.

Despite the victory, Turf writers clucked over how exhausted Bimelech seemed as he headed into the winner's circle. They wondered whether the late-staying winter that year, along with the lack of training, had pushed Bimelech back. The two races in five days, with the Derby only four days away, also seemed like a challenge for any horse. For all the criticism, Hurley was not talking. He declined to explain his training strategy for his champion or to decry his critics. As Estes wrote, compared to Hurley, " 'Silent Tom' Smith is something of a chatterbox."

Meanwhile, Seabiscuit's famously terse trainer, who was training Charles Howard's Mioland for the Derby, wondered aloud about Bimelech's chances after the Derby Trial. "I saw Bimmie flatten his ears so tight against his head at the barrier Tuesday that he looked like he might be going to bite something. Then jockey Freddie Smith even hit him with the bat once in the stretch," he told a reporter. "What's more important to me, he only beat Gallahadion by a couple of lengths, and unless Gallahadion has improved a powerful lot from what he was on the Coast last winter, Bimmie's race wasn't too hot."

Waldron had noted his colt's powerful performance and chose Gallahadion to wear the farm colors over the other Milky Way eligibles because he liked how the colt had made up ground in the Derby Trial.

Waldron had his horse and just needed a rider. He selected twenty-one-year-old Carroll Bierman to ride Gallahadion. Known as Cal, or sometimes "Bad Luck Bierman," because he had labored under a loser's curse for years on Western and Midwestern tracks, Bierman had won ninety-six of 622 races in 1939 and had ridden the fourth-place Derby finisher that year.

Some questioned the inexperience of Bimelech's jockey, twenty-six-year-old Freddie Smith, who seemed ripe to be pushed around by the veterans, such as George Woolf and Buddy Haas. Smith had won eight races aboard the colt and called Bimelech the greatest horse he had ever ridden. He petted him but made sure to tell reporters he never smuggled Bimelech the sugar he craved and that Hurley forbade.

Bradley had passed up the seasoned and scrappy Don Meade, who had won the 1933 Derby — with its scuffling "Fighting Finish" — for Bradley aboard Brokers Tip. He wanted Smith, who had ridden Bimelech in every one of the horse's starts. The duo seemed invincible to Bradley and to almost everyone else.

Keeping in the voluble journalistic style of the forties, reporters showed no fear of hyperbole in discussing hopes for the Bradley colt. "Kentuckians in this crowded swirling bluegrass metropolis," reported Turf writer Grantland Rice from Lexington, "believe that they have the horse which will pick up where Man o' War left off — a thoroughbred which will move on beyond Man o' War's glory and Seabiscuit's gold."

"America's most spectacular horse race will have Bimelech and eight others in it," the *Los Angeles Times* said of the Derby field. A headline ran: "Louisville is One-Horse Town." "If the date line on this reads 'Bimelechville, Bimlechy,' don't blame the operator," wrote the *Washington Post*'s Walter Haight. "He is a Kentuckian, and Kentuckians, by this time, believe every word starts with B-I-M."

Louisville *Courier-Journal* reporter Jimmy Jones wrote up a pretend celebrity magazine "interview" with Bimelech, in which he asked the horse questions such as who his family was. Answer: "Son of Black Toney and La Troienne … and they say I have my father's head and my mother's figure."

The only news in Kentucky besides Bimelech was the unseasonably chilly weather. "This is the first Derby week I've attended when you can carry a frosted mint julep in your hip pocket for hours," Haight quipped. Silent Tom Smith ended up training Mioland and his other runners in the afternoon, when it was not so cold on the grounds. The carefully tended flowers of the Churchill Downs' infield had been damaged by the cold. Bands rehearsing for the race trampled the rest of the flowers, so the traditional blooms were muted. Potted plants were installed on the Monday before the Derby.

But May 4, Derby Day itself, dawned bright, warm, and still. Pennants barely fluttered, and Churchill Downs was resplendent in the sunshine. General manager Matt Winn (another honorary colonel) had installed a new public address system along with new dining rooms and julep bars. Movie star Irene Dunne's version of "My Old Kentucky Home" was almost drowned out by the cheers for Bimelech, as the 2-5 favorite came onto the track. Bimelech had the shortest odds of a Derby favorite in thirty-five years.

The raucous crowd was vast. Winn estimated it at 95,000, which was later found to be too high. The number was probably closer to 87,000. In any case, the crowd was so big that people sat on nearby roofs and packed the Downs, looking for the chance to see Bimmie wear his roses. The press "coop," situated on top of the clubhouse, hummed with activity as about two hundred sportswriters waited for the race to unfold.

The only people not there, it seemed, were the owners of Bimelech and Gallahadion, both of whom were sick. The eighty-year-old Bradley was laid up at Idle Hour, with his doctor, nurse, and brother gathered around him. Ethel Mars, in the midst of a similar group, was nursing a severe cold back at her home in Chicago.

Because of his No. 1 post position, Gallahadion, who at 35-1 was the third longest shot in the race, was the first to parade onto the track. His 16.3-hand frame made him easy to spot, as well as his jockey's orange silks with a white star on the front and back, black sleeves, and a chocolate and white cap — the same colors found on a Milky Way wrapper. On Bimelech, Smith wore the classic crisp green and white of the Bradley stable.

The start, as the race chart said, was "good and slow," once Roman stopped bouncing through the doorless Bahr gate. Finally, the starting bell sent off all eight contenders.

Roman, whom Bimelech had beaten so soundly in the Blue Grass, was in the lead at first. Smith kept his colt back and took him wide to the outside. At the first pass of the judges' stand, Roman was three lengths in front with everyone else bunched behind him. In the Blue Grass, Bimelech had cruised past Roman easily, but in the Derby, Roman was still well clear down the backstretch. He stayed in the lead, with the other horses clustered behind.

Bierman kept Gallahadion near the rail, and as the horses came down the backstretch, viewers were surprised to see how close Gallahadion was to their champion. All down the backstretch, the crowd waited for Bimelech to overtake Roman. When he did so, near the end of the backstretch, Gallahadion was close by. Gallahadion's looming bay body almost blocked any view of Bimelech from the main stands, a harbinger of what was to come.

Bimelech was wide in the stretch and entered a duel with Dit, who went with him on the outside. No one noticed what was happening on the rail, where Gallahadion chugged mercilessly along without tiring.

Dit and Bimelech raced on, close enough to touch, and the crowd roared for "Big Bim." Near the sixteenth pole Gallahadion got close enough to Bimelech to look him in the eye. Never before had a horse come alongside Bimelech like that, and when Gallahadion challenged him, the dark bay faltered.

Bierman called on Gallahadion (reports were that he was still hitting him a few yards past the finish), and the horse responded. Gallahadion crossed the line a length and a half ahead of Bimelech, who won a photo finish for second by a scant nose over Dit.

Bierman had saved ground throughout the race, keeping his mount close on all turns and in both stretches. He stayed to the inside and never got farther back than fourth. The strategy paid off. In the slow 2:05 it had taken to run the race, the unthinkable happened: Bimelech was defeated.

As Gallahadion returned for his roses, people sat stunned in the stands. Even the press box was silent. "Most of them," wrote Estes, "had long since imagined the beautiful Bimelech beneath the traditional blanket of roses."

Gallahadion's team paid no heed to the disappointment in the air but focused on their winner. As he headed back to the grandstand after the race, Bierman reached down to shake Waldron's hand. Waldron told his jockey it was a "million dollar ride."

"We talked it over last night," Waldron said, "and I instructed him to stay on the rail and take his chances on getting through. He couldn't have ridden a better race."

Bierman himself was so excited that he forgot to unsaddle the horse after pictures were taken and had to be called back to pick up his tack. "Why, I didn't have any trouble," he told reporters. "We broke with the bunch. I laid third nearly all of the way. At the head of the stretch, I called on him. We caught Bimelech at the eighth pole and from the sixteenth pole on we were pulling away."

"We looked Bimelech in the eye as we reached the sixteenth pole and from there on it was just a ride," he said. "I don't think Bimelech could have caught us if we had raced all the way to Chicago."

All the jockeys gathered around to congratulate Bierman, except for Smith, who had gotten dressed and departed before Bierman came back. Out at Idle Hour, Bradley himself behaved with equanimity at the news of his favorite's loss. He walked into his bedroom and lay down. A butler refused reporters admission to the house but admitted that Bradley was "disappointed." Neighbors without radios strained to hear the Idle Hour bell that had rung so clearly after the Derby wins of 1921, 1926, 1932, and 1933. But the bell never tolled.

Gallahadion was the longest-odds horse to win the Derby since Donerail won in 1913 at odds of 91-1. The colt's victory paid $72.40 for winning tickets. Even so, there was little praise for him. Simply because Gallahadion had spoiled Bimelech's reign, Ed Danforth called him "presumptuous" and a "villain" in the *Atlanta Journal*.

Gallahadion's sire, Sir Gallahad III, not only had sired 1930 Kentucky Derby winner Gallant Fox, but also had sired the dams of Omaha and Johnstown, who both had won the Derby, as well as the dam of Challedon, who had won the 1939 Preakness. Gallahadion still came under fire as the "despised offspring of a royal family, a horse who had been whipped 14 times," as United Press International's Jack Guenther wrote. But even the doubters had to admit, however grudgingly, that it was more than luck that trounced Bimelech. "Rose Wreath, Cut For Bimelech, Fits Gallahadion Perfectly," ran one headline.

Gallahadion's backers claimed to have known his abilities all along. The Tennessee papers seemed delighted as the Mars farm was in Pulaski. Mars' daughter, Patricia Feeney, told reporters, "I'm sure mother would have fainted had she not already been in bed." Ethel Mars said Gallahadion's win made for the happiest day of her life. Milky Way's employees had backed their faith with bets and were rewarded with cash in their pockets, as well as bragging rights.

"This was her first Derby victory, and there never was a sweeter lollypop," wrote one reporter of the candy queen. Mars scoffed at the insinuation that Gallahadion's victory constituted an upset. She saw him as an example of her own skill in picking winners. "Certainly, I expected him to win," she said. "I have always been very confident of Gallahadion. I liked him when I bought him, and I liked him as a 2-year-old, and I liked him in the Derby."

It was the first time a woman had owned a Derby winner since 1934 when Isabel Dodge Sloane's Cavalcade took the roses.

The Blood-Horse used pedigree research to explain the victory. It was the old Teddy blood, which Gallahadion shared with champions such as his lookalike Johnstown, that gave him the ability to pull it out in the last sixteenth, the reasoning ran. (Of course, Teddy was Bimelech's grandsire on his bottom side. But it wasn't the time to mention that.)

So the question remained: What happened to Bimelech? Was it the track condition? Was he simply too exhausted after racing on Tuesday and after a winter of relaxing? Or was it all the jockey's fault? ("Bierman Gives Smith Riding Lesson," ran one subhead in the *Courier-Journal*.) Some blamed track superstition, such as the old saw that a two-year-old champion does not have a chance at the Derby. And the No. 1 post position did, in 1940, prove to be lucky, as it had for War Admiral in 1937 and Lawrin in 1938.

It was tough to find fault with Bimelech. His status as hero was too well entrenched, and he had as good a start as any other horse in the race. Many blamed Smith as Bimelech broke fast and was away well. It was Smith's keeping the colt out toward the middle of the track all the way around, they argued, that cost him the race. He was, in effect, running over a longer distance than the rail-hugging Gallahadion. Smith also heard plenty of criticism for allowing Bimelech to surge up early on.

For his part, Smith blamed the surface. "The track actually wasn't fast," he said. "It was about a second off. And that beat my horse. He wasn't used to the cuppy conditions. He has always run on going that he liked, and this time he tired in the stretch and let Gallahadion finish ahead of him. That is about all I can say."

Many pointed accusing fingers at Hurley. Bimelech had gone over five months without a race but then had two prep races in quick succession before the Derby. Racing three times in the space of nine days would have been tough for a seasoned campaigner, but Bimelech had a long winter of rest without conditioning. Also, both races took all his effort, and neither was a sprint. He had worked hard up until Derby Day, and he just wasn't there. He showed his lack of preparation, the argument went, in that last tough quarter, when three-year-olds are tested.

Bimelech seemed to prove this theory right when he won both the Preakness and Belmont in fine style, with a second in the Withers in between. At Pimlico, he won by three lengths, and Gallahadion took third. At Belmont, he fought hard to win, while Gallahadion finished next to last. With the proper balance of rest and preparation, the champion had returned.

After the Triple Crown races, Bimelech struggled and lost the Arlington Classic, finishing ten lengths off the pace. A little later the colt injured himself during a workout, and X-rays showed a snapped bar wall in his foot. News of the break caused speculation that he was hurting during the Classic. After watching one failed attempt at a comeback to stakes competition in the Widener the next year, Bradley retired Bimelech for good.

Bradley, whose name was synonymous with Derby winners for years, never saw the roses on his two best horses, Blue Larkspur and Bimelech. Bimelech was named champion three-year-old colt for 1940. But Bradley would not win a fifth Derby.

Bradley died in 1946. A syndicate made up of John Hay Whitney, Robert Kleberg, and Ogden Phipps bought Bimelech, and he was sent to stud at Whitney's Greentree, near Lexington. He sired thirty stakes

Kentucky Derby
Purse: $75,000 Added

Churchill Downs - May 4, 1940. Sixty-sixth running Kentucky Derby.
Purse $75,000 added. Three-year-olds. 1 1-4 Miles. Main Track. Track: Fast.
Net value to winner, $60,150 and gold trophy; second, $8,000; third, $3,500; fourth, $1,000.

Horse	A	Wgt	Eqp	Odds	PP	St	1/2	3/4	1	Str	Fin	Jockey
Gallahadion	3	126	b	35.20	1	4	3^{hd}	2^{hd}	4^1	3^2	1$^{1\frac{1}{2}}$	C Bierman
Bimelech	3	126		.40	2	1	2$^{\frac{1}{2}}$	3^{hd}	1^{hd}	1$^{\frac{1}{2}}$	2no	F Smith
Dit	3	126	b	6.70	6	5	4^1	4^1	3^3	2$^{\frac{1}{2}}$	3^1	L Haas
Mioland	3	126	b	6.40	3	3	5^2	5$^{\frac{1}{2}}$	5^2	4^1	4^2	L Balaski
Sirocco	3	126	b	42.70	5	6	6^1	6^3	6^5	6^6	5^2	J Longden
Roman	3	126	b	24.20	4	2	1$^{1\frac{1}{2}}$	1$^{1\frac{1}{2}}$	2^{hd}	5^{hd}	6^6	K McCombs
Royal Man	3	126	b	61.20	7	7	7^2	7^{hd}	7$^{\frac{1}{2}}$	7^3	7^3	J Gilbert
Pictor	3	126		18.00	8	8	8	8	8	8	8	G Woolf

Off Time: 4:50   **Time Of Race:** :23⅗   :48   1:12⅖   1:38⅖   2:05
Start: Good For All   **Track:** Fast
Equipment: b for blinkers

Mutuel Payoffs

1	Gallahadion	$72.40	$13.80	$4.80
2	Bimelech		3.20	2.40
7	Dit			2.80

Winner: Gallahadion, b. c. by Sir Gallahad III—Countess Time, by Reigh Count (Trained by Roy Waldron). Bred by R.A. Fairbairn in Kentucky.

Start good and slow. Won driving; second and third the same.
GALLAHADION, away well from his inside post position, held a contending postition while saving ground, moved forward with BIMELECH, responded to strong urging when wearing down BIMELECH then drew out impressively, but won with little left. BIMELECH was first in motion, went wide throughout, moved into command nearing the final quarter, bore out on the stretch turn, held the lead under strong handling approaching the final eighth and was unable to hold the winner. DIT, steadied along early, improved his position on the outside, was forced wide entering the stretch, but held on well under good pressure. MIOLAND, unable to improve his early position, responded well after reaching the stretch and finished resolutely. SIROCCO, unable to improve his early position, was put to strong handling in the drive and tired near the end. ROMAN established a good early lead, held command under light urging, then gave way when challenged and tired in the stretch. ROYAL MAN and PICTOR raced well back and were unable to improve their positions under severe pressure.
Scratched—True Star.

Owners: (1) Milky Way Farm; (2) E R Bradley; (3) W A Hanger; (4) C S Howard; (5) Dixiana; (6) J E Widener; (7) Tower Stable; (8) W L Brann

©EQUIBASE

winners, one of whom was Better Self, the broodmare sire of Dr. Fager. Bimelech was elected to the Racing Hall of Fame in 1990.

And Gallahadion? Many shared the view of Joe Estes, who wrote in *The Blood-Horse* that "Gallahadion went back to a surprised staff of Milky Way Farm grooms who thought they had rubbed far better horses than this one." Once Bimelech beat him in the Preakness, the public was satisfied. Gallahadion had gotten lucky once, but once was all Bimelech would allow.

By 1941 Jack Guenther in the *Los Angeles Times* called Gallahadion "America's forgotten horse." His article about the 1940 victor depicted a "lonely" Thoroughbred stabled at the "extreme fringe" of Churchill

Downs. "He came out of nowhere, unloved and unwanted by anyone except Mrs. Ethel Mars and Roy Waldron, and his only sin was that he beat Bimelech — the darling of the hard boots. The experts laughed at him, the public laughed at him and rival owners laughed at him. None of them forgave him when he proved them wrong."

After a mediocre career Gallahadion went to stud in 1942 to Henry Knight's Almahurst Farm near Nicholasville, Kentucky. All in all, he had started thirty-six times, won six, and finished second six times and third four times. He had earned $92,620. In 1951 Gallahadion was purchased by a bird-dog breeder named John Holliday and moved to Oklahoma. He sired four stakes winners total and died in 1958.

Mars retired the Milky Way colors in 1944. She had been cutting back on racing since the bombing of Pearl Harbor. The Tennessee farm was put on the market and purchased by a cattle breeder.

Gallahadion will always be considered a spoiler. His name is linked to the great Bimelech's as surely as the two were locked for one brief moment near the sixteenth pole at Churchill Downs before Gallahadion finally pulled away to win the Kentucky Derby. Beating a horse as accomplished and adored as Bimelech kept Gallahadion remembered as a fluke, instead of as a champion. But for one sunny day in May, he was the best horse. And he wore his roses proudly.

By Eliza R.L. McGraw

Defeating the Dancer

ON THE LAST SATURDAY of April 1953, Native Dancer certified his standing as America's favorite Thoroughbred by easily winning the Wood Memorial Stakes before 40,000 spectators at Aqueduct and millions of television viewers watching a coast-to-coast broadcast on CBS. A thunderous, fast-finishing gray owned by millionaire Alfred Vanderbilt, Native Dancer had never lost a race, winning eleven in a row and earning more than $340,000. He was an overwhelming favorite to win the Kentucky Derby a week later. No three-year-old had ever run for the roses with a better record, more career earnings, or — thanks to television, the fantastic new medium sweeping the country — more fans.

As Native Dancer was adding to his glowing credentials by winning the Wood, a brown colt named Dark Star was resting in his stall inside Barn 12 at Churchill Downs. He was Native Dancer's polar opposite in many ways, as obscure as the great horse was famous, a seemingly mediocre runner with less than $30,000 in career earnings. His owner, Harry Guggenheim, and his trainer, Eddie Hayward, were still trying to decide whether to run him in the Kentucky Derby. His jockey, Henry Moreno, was holed up at a Louisville-area tourist camp, a crude cabin hostelry, while he waited for his bosses to make up their minds.

The spring of 1953 was an epic time for myth making in America; in the aftermath of the Great Depression and World War II, people were communing over a new generation of celebrities hatched in their living rooms on flickering black-and-white TV sets. Comedians Milton Berle and Lucille Ball made them laugh. Boxer Rocky Marciano made them cheer. But at a time when American horse racing was more popular than pro football, Native Dancer loomed as large as any other figure. Many of his races had been televised across the country; he had become a Saturday afternoon programming staple, knocking out rivals and strutting to the winner's circle. His human connections — Vanderbilt, trainer Bill Winfrey, and jockey Eric Guerin — were household names because of their attachment to the majestic gray.

He received full-blown star treatment as he traveled by train from New York to Kentucky for his expected coronation in the Derby. Several top New York sportswriters took the overnight train with him so they could chronicle his every move. His brief layover in Cincinnati was covered by the local papers there. His presence would make the 1953 Derby easily the most-watched ever to that point; the race was being nationally televised for just the second time, and CBS' broadcast would draw an estimated 20 million viewers, equal to audiences for World Series games.

The Dancer's train trip was not without incident. His train unexpectedly screeched to a halt in the middle of the night to avoid hitting a car outside Columbus, Ohio, giving the standing colt a frightening jolt. Winfrey raced from his berth shouting, "My horse! My horse!" But the Dancer was sporting a leather headgear that prevented an injury.

As the horse disembarked in Louisville the next day, the Louisville *Courier-Journal*'s Jerry McNerney observed him and later wrote, "I've seen 20 Derby winners arrive in Louisville, including Count Fleet, Citation and Whirlaway, and none gave the impression of such sheer power and bubbling-over energy as this big gray." It was almost assumed he would soon join that roll call of legendary Derby winners.

The public paid little attention to the cadre of horses set to run against him in the Derby, although several had accomplished enough to be given a chance. A speedy front-runner named Correspondent had won the Blue Grass Stakes at Keeneland in Lexington, Kentucky, and would be ridden by Eddie Arcaro, the famous jockey who had won five Derbys and two Triple Crowns. Royal Bay Gem was a little black colt known for rallying from far back to finish in the money, a style suited to the Derby. But few others were thought to have any chance of even staying within sight of Native Dancer, much less beating him. Dark Star had finished a distant second to Correspondent in an allowance race at Keeneland. A colt named Money Broker also had finished well behind Correspondent in the Blue Grass Stakes.

Guggenheim, a wealthy and prominent sixty-two-year-old descended from Gilded Age high society, desperately wanted to run Dark Star. He had succeeded at everything else in life except racing. He had fought as a naval aviator in World War I, served as ambassador to Cuba, bankrolled rocketry pioneer Robert Goddard's early experiments, founded a Long Island newspaper, and established a foundation that funded aviation research and had helped the American airline industry get off the ground. But his Cain Hoy Racing Stable had produced only one champion in two decades of steady financial backing, and that champion, Crafty Admiral, 1952 older horse, had run for another stable. Another of its best-known horses was the 1951 Derby betting favorite, Battle Morn, who had finished a disappointing sixth in the big race. Guggenheim hoped for more from Dark Star. He had picked the colt out himself, paying $6,500 for him at a yearling sale instead of relying on the opinions of his trainers and agents, as he usually did.

Dark Star's Derby credentials were not entirely lacking. Sired by Royal Gem II, an Australian import who had won twenty-two races Down Under, he had started his career impressively, winning the three-furlong Hialeah Juvenile Stakes in Florida. But he faded as his two-year-old season progressed, finishing a distant third to Native Dancer in the Futurity Stakes and all but quitting in the Champagne Stakes. Guggenheim changed trainers after that, firing Moody Jolley, a taciturn Tennessean, and giving Dark Star to Hayward, a genial Canadian-born former jockey.

"Go train the horse and win the Derby," Guggenheim told Hayward.

It seemed an outlandish challenge. With Hayward now calling the shots, Dark Star opened his three-year-old season by winning an allowance race at Hialeah but then finished out of the money in the Florida Derby. With just four wins in nine starts and no major stakes successes, he was a dubious Derby entry, especially against the great Dancer.

Guggenheim and Hayward decided to give him one last chance to prove himself, in the Derby Trial, a mile-long race run at Churchill four days before the Derby itself. It would be Dark Star's second race under Moreno, a twenty-four-year-old California-based jockey whom Hayward had hired to guide Cain Hoy's horses.

Leaving the starting gate as the third betting choice before 23,000 fans on a cloudy afternoon, Dark Star zipped to an impressive victory in the Trial. He lay third after a half-mile, then accelerated when Moreno urged him and ran off to win by four lengths, missing the track record for a mile by less than a second. The performance convinced Guggenheim and Hayward to run him on Saturday. "I just wish we could have run the Derby today," Hayward told reporters. Money Broker, a sturdy if unspectacular colt from New Orleans, finished second behind Dark Star.

Sitting in traffic as he drove from the track to the annual Derby trainers' dinner that evening, Hayward was rammed from behind by a driver who hit the gas pedal instead of the brake. Hayward wasn't injured, but his car took a hit and he joked at the dinner that now he had to win Saturday to pay for the damages. It was hard not to view him and his horse as lighthearted bit players in the Dancer-dominated Derby drama.

Dark Star's victory in the Trial was overshadowed by what most fans saw as a more newsworthy event that took place at Churchill earlier that Tuesday — the Dancer's first visit to the racing strip where he was expected to dominate on Saturday. It happened during morning training hours, a time of great bustle. All activity abruptly stopped when the big gray took his first steps on Kentucky soil, jogging twice around the damp oval. "The most talked-about horse since Man o' War seemed to know he was the center of attention," the Associated Press reported.

The Dancer returned to the track for light training the next morning and then engaged in an unusual public workout with a stablemate in between the third and fourth races that afternoon. Winfrey had scheduled the colt's only serious pre-Derby exercise for Thursday morning, but with the weather forecast calling for storms, he asked Churchill officials if he could beat the rain and run the horse that afternoon instead. The officials happily said yes.

When the Dancer and another Vanderbilt-owned colt named Social Outcast stepped onto the track after the third race, the fans cheered wildly, thrilled to see the great horse in person. The horses warmed up and started to run. The exercise riders on both horses were under strict orders from Winfrey, who wanted Social Outcast to take a lead and have Native Dancer make a run through the stretch. The six-furlong exercise came off as planned. The Dancer dropped five lengths back and then made it all up with a mad dash, charging through the stretch with his powerful muscles straining against his hide. The fans buzzed as the horses reached the finish line together. What an animal the Dancer was!

Derby entries were due Friday morning. The connections of the Dancer and ten other horses paid their $250 fee before Hayward arrived with Guggenheim's money twenty-one minutes before the deadline. Dark Star was the last horse to enter.

After a stormy week the weather cleared for the Derby. More than

100,000 fans gathered at Churchill Downs under a brilliant blue sky. The temperature was seventy degrees by mid-afternoon. Spectators took off their jackets, enjoyed the sun, ogled celebrities such as Senator Lyndon B. Johnson and FBI Director J. Edgar Hoover, and bet on the races. The Dancer, paired as a wagering entity with Social Outcast, was 3-5 on the track-sponsored morning line and 7-10 on the pari-mutuel board as post time neared. Correspondent was the second choice at 3-1, and there was little respect for the rest of the field. Dark Star was the fifth choice, but he would leave the starting gate as a 25-1 shot.

Moreno was nervous. A Chicago barber's son, he was riding in the Derby for the first time. He wondered how he could beat more accomplished pros such as Arcaro, Guerin, and Ted Atkinson. Hayward gave him explicit instructions as the horses were being saddled in the paddock. The trainer told the young jockey to lay third or fourth early, watch Native Dancer up the backstretch, and then make a move in the stretch. After the trainer spoke and was out of earshot, Guggenheim grabbed Moreno's right foot — the jockey was already on the horse — and said, "Listen, son, you do what you think is best out there." Moreno took that as a mandate to be more aggressive than Hayward wanted if the situation warranted it.

Thanks to television, it was not an exaggeration to say America came to a halt when the starting gate opened at 4:42 p.m. The Dancer's big moment was at hand, and sports fans didn't want to miss it. Incredibly, almost three of every four TV sets that were on at the time across the country were tuned to the race.

Correspondent was expected to set the early pace, but he was squeezed back coming out of the gate. That enabled Moreno to swing down from the No. 10 post and take the lead coming through the stretch the first time. Arcaro recovered quickly and moved Correspondent into second, but with Moreno heeding Guggenheim's mandate, Dark Star was two lengths ahead after covering the first quarter-mile in a routine :23 4/5.

All eyes were on Native Dancer, of course. The gray broke cleanly from the No. 6 post and was settled in the middle of the pack coming through the stretch. He was famous for his finishing charges, and Guerin, the only jockey who had ever ridden him, wanted no part of the early lead. The colt was sixth, ahead of the stragglers, as he passed the finish line the first time.

One of those stragglers was Money Broker, the seemingly overmatched colt who had finished behind Dark Star in the Derby Trial. Al Popara, Money Broker's jockey, wasn't pleased to find himself so far back. A twenty-four-year-old Californian in his first Derby, Popara was under orders to press the lead in the early going. He worried he was disobeying. He planned to sit behind Native Dancer through the first turn and then make a move, but the pace was so slow that he decided to circle around the Dancer, cut in front of the favorite, and drop down toward the rail.

What happened next became instant Derby lore and ignited a controversy that will last for as long as the race is run.

Money Broker lugged in sharply just as Popara was completing his outside pass of the Dancer. It happened right in front of Bill Shoemaker, the future Hall of Fame jockey, who was riding a horse named Invigorator. "Money Broker bumped Native Dancer but good and knocked him back," Shoemaker recalled years later. Popara's intentions would be intensely debated, but there was no doubt the Dancer had been shaken and set back. The favorite now had ground to make up as he came out of the first turn. He was running eighth.

The commotion unfolded well behind Moreno and Dark Star. Still in the lead as he came out of the first turn and headed up the backstretch, Moreno had no idea where the Dancer was, or that the favorite had run into trouble. The jockey just figured — correctly, it turned out — that the big gray would eventually make a run. That expectation governed Moreno's tactics. He believed in his horse, but he knew Dark Star would be hard-pressed to hold off a full-steam Dancer in the stretch. His only hope, he figured, was to save as much of Dark Star's energy as possible for use in the final furlongs. He maintained a relatively deliberate pace while still in the lead, hoping no challenger would come forward and force him to push harder.

Ironically, Guerin, aboard Native Dancer, had employed the same strategy to win the 1947 Derby aboard Jet Pilot. He had taken the early lead and slowed the pace to a crawl, leaving Jet Pilot with just enough energy to hold off the heavy favorite, Phalanx, in the stretch. Now, six years later, Moreno was wielding the same strategy against Guerin.

Native Dancer's jockey didn't have time to think about that, of course. He had ground to make up, and he made it up in a hurry. Coming out of the first turn, he asked the Dancer to run, and the big gray responded with an astonishing burst up Churchill's back straightaway. The horse steamed past four rivals and closed in on the leaders approaching the second turn. He now stood fourth, trailing Dark Star by four lengths with a half-mile to go. Correspondent was in second, a half-length behind Dark Star, with a colt named Straight Face in third. Although the bump on the first turn had set him back, the Dancer was now in perfect position to make one of his patented stretch runs. Millions of TV viewers fully expected him to do so. Guerin found room inside and swung down to the rail to shorten his path to the lead.

When Correspondent and Straight Face faltered on the turn and swerved off the rail as they entered the stretch, the eleven-horse field was down to two contenders. Native Dancer, the popular TV star, was two lengths behind Dark Star, a colt few fans had ever seen before. It seemed a foregone conclusion that the Dancer would catch Guggenheim's obscure longshot.

Moreno, having brilliantly judged the pace of the first mile, just wanted to coax the horse to the finish line now. He moved Dark Star from the middle of the track to the rail. It was a move any jockey would make with the rail available, but it was critical now, as it moved Dark Star directly in front of the Dancer, cutting off his open lane to the finish.

Guerin waited to respond, thinking Native Dancer would begin to surge and sweep by Dark Star, but the Dancer gained no ground in the first hundred yards of the stretch. Dark Star still had something left, it seemed. The Dancer's fans gasped. Finally, the big gray began to gain ground. Urged by Guerin, he accelerated and pulled to within a length at the sixteenth pole.

Moreno had not seen the favorite since they loaded the starting gate. Curious, he glanced back and saw the Dancer bearing down on him. "I was pretty scared," he admitted later.

The lead was less than a length as the finish line approached. The Dancer, whose stride had been measured at a gargantuan twenty-nine yards, gained ground every time he hit the dirt. Dark Star had little left. The Dancer pulled within a half-length, then a neck, then a head as they neared the wire.

With their final bobs, both horses lunged for the finish … and Dark Star reached it first.

Although the judges ordered a photo to determine the winner, it was clear to many in the crowd that the 25-1 shot had beaten the unbeatable horse.

Standing in his box amid the pandemonium, Vanderbilt shouted to Winfrey, "Did he get there?"

Winfrey dolefully shook his head. "I don't think so," the trainer said.

Vanderbilt left the box and proceeded down to the apron, where he watched the jockeys dismount. He gave Popara a murderous stare. Much of the newspaper coverage of the race would focus on whether the first-turn collision between Money Broker and Native Dancer had been intentional.

Meanwhile, Guggenheim and Hayward all but danced their way from Guggenheim's box to the winner's circle, where they joined Moreno and the horse. The winners were jubilant and incredulous; although they had hoped Dark Star would give a decent account of himself, they hadn't expected this. Guggenheim was presented the Derby cup and a garland of roses on the victory stand, and movie actress Marilyn Maxwell kissed Moreno several times — photographers made them keep kissing until they got the shot they wanted.

As Guggenheim and Hayward headed back across the track for a reception in Churchill president Bill Corum's office, a fan reached out and clapped Hayward on the back.

"You did it, Eddie," the fan said.

Hayward smiled and said, "Yeah, I guess I did."

The trainer later admitted to reporters that Moreno had ignored his conservative instructions by going to the front. "But he went up so handily that [Moreno] just let him go. A [jockey] has to know when to do these things. He's on his own out there," Hayward said.

There was no doubt Moreno had given the winner a brilliant ride, controlling the pace from in front and then moving to the rail at the top of the stretch to block Native Dancer's path. The *Daily Racing Form* chart caller noted that Dark Star had been "alertly ridden" and "won with little left." The late move to the rail, which forced Guerin to swerve back off the rail before making a charge, probably made the difference at the finish line.

"I thought I had a wonderful chance all along," Moreno told reporters in the jockeys' room. "As I was going out onto the track, I got the feeling I was going to win."

Across the room, Popara vehemently defended himself against the charge that he had cost Native Dancer the race.

"I thought we were clear of him but Money Broker suddenly changed strides. I know it may have cost him the race, and I hated seeing a great horse get beat. But there was nothing intentional," he said.

He would stick to that story, but some doubted his intentions.

Kentucky Derby
Purse: $100,000 Added

Churchill Downs - May 2, 1953. Seventy-ninth running Kentucky Derby.
Purse $100,000 added. Three-year-olds. 1 1-4 Miles. Main Track. Track: Fast.
Gross value $118,100. Net value to winner, $90,050 and gold trophy; second, $10,000; third, $5,000; fourth, $2,500.

Horse	A	Wgt	Eqp	Odds	PP	St	1/2	3/4	1	Str	Fin	Jockey
Dark Star	3	126		24.90	10	3	1 ^{1½}	1 ^{½}	1 ^{1½}	1 ^{½}	1 ^{hd}	H Moreno
Native Dancer	3	126		a-.70	6	6	8 ^{3}	4 ^{½}	4 ^{2}	2 ^{1}	2 ^{5}	E Guerin
Invigorator	3	126		40.90	4	5	7 ^{½}	6 ^{½}	6 ^{1}	4 ^{1}	3 ^{2}	W Shoemaker
Royal Bay Gem	3	126		6.80	11	11	11	8 ^{2}	7 ^{½}	7 ^{1½}	4 ^{1½}	J Combest
Correspondent	3	126		3.00	2	2	2 ^{2}	2 ^{1}	2 ^{½}	3 ^{1}	5 ^{1½}	E Arcaro
Straight Face	3	126	b	10.40	9	7	4 ^{3}	3 ^{1}	3 ^{½}	5 ^{hd}	6 ^{nk}	T Atkinson
Social Outcast	3	126		a-.70	8	10	10 ^{½}	10 ^{1½}	8 ^{2}	8 ^{2}	7 ^{2}	J Adams
Money Broker	3	126	b	45.80	7	9	5 ^{½}	5 ^{½}	5 ^{hd}	6 ^{3}	8 ^{3½}	A Popara
Ram O' War	3	126	b	85.10	3	8	9 ^{½}	11	10 ^{1}	9 ^{1}	9 ^{nk}	D Dodson
Curragh King	3	126	b	99.10	5	4	6 ^{2}	9 ^{1}	11	11	10 ^{hd}	D Erb
Ace Destroyer	3	126	b	91.80	1	1	3 ^{½}	7 ^{2}	9 ^{3}	10 ^{1}	11	J Jessop

Off Time: 4:42	**Time Of Race:** :23½	:47½	1:12½	1:36½	2:02			
Start: Good For All	**Track:** Fast							
Equipment: b for blinkers								

Mutuel Payoffs

10	Dark Star	$51.80	$13.60	$7.00
1	Native Dancer		3.20	2.80
5	Invigorator			9.40

Winner: Dark Star, br. c. by *Royal Gem II—Isolde, by *Bull Dog (Trained by Eddie Hayward).
Bred by W. L. Jones Jr. in Kentucky.

Start good from stall gate. Won driving; second and third the same.
Coupled: a—Native Dancer and Social Outcast
DARK STAR, alertly ridden, took command soon after the start, set the pace to the stretch under steady rating, then responded readily when set down in the drive and lasted to withstand NATIVE DANCER, but won with little left. NATIVE DANCER, roughed at the first turn by MONEY BROKER, was eased back to secure racing room, raced wide during the run to the upper turn, then saved ground entering the stretch and finished strongly, but could not overtake the winner, although probably best. INVIGORATOR, in close quarters entering the backstretch, raced well when clear and closed willingly under urging, but could not threaten the top pair. ROYAL BAY GEM, away sluggishly, was forced to lose ground while working way forward and could not reach the leaders when set down through the stretch. CORRESPONDENT, bumped after the break by ACE DESTROYER, recovered under good handling and raced nearest DARK STAR to the stretch, but had nothing left for the drive. STRAIGHT FACE raced prominently to the mile, then weakened. SOCIAL OUTCAST lacked early speed and was never dangerous. MONEY BROKER swerved into NATIVE DANCER at the first turn, raced well to the stretch, then gave way. RAM O' WAR was far back all the way. CURRAGH KING was through early. ACE DESTROYER began fast, bumped CORRESPONDENT and showed early speed but failed to stay.
Scratched—Spy Defense, 126.

Owners: (1) Cain Hoy Stable; (2) A G Vanderbilt; (3) Saxon Stable; (4) E Constantin Jr.; (5) Mrs G Guiberson; (6) Greentree Stable; (7) A G Vanderbilt; (8) G & G Stable; (9) B S Campbell; (10) E M Goemans; (11) Mr & Mrs T M Daniel

©EQUIBASE

"Sure, Popara knew what he was doing, and he did just what I would have done," Arcaro, who finished fifth on Correspondent, told a Baltimore reporter several days after the race. "When you're going after a big one like the Derby, you don't let any horse through the middle, especially a favorite like the Dancer."

The consensus explanation for the upset would also eventually include the suggestion that Guerin, a future Racing Hall of Fame inductee, had contributed a less-than-sparkling ride. Although neither Vanderbilt nor Winfrey criticized him after the race, years later Vanderbilt told a reporter, "the bump probably shook up Guerin more than the horse." Indeed, Native Dancer swerved to the outside after the bump, charged up the backside, swerved back to the rail at the head of the stretch, then swerved back off the rail before making his final charge. Winfrey's son Carey said years later, "My father once said to me he felt Native Dancer probably raced thirty or forty yards farther than any horse in the race. He also said he felt Eric moved too late in the stretch. He didn't know why [Guerin] hung back."

Guerin would win 2,712 races over thirty-five years but, fairly or not, would always be best known for having lost the Derby on Native Dancer.

Upsets usually thrill sports fans, but this one elicited the opposite response. Although the people who had bet on Dark Star and earned $51.80 for a two-dollar wager were thrilled along with Guggenheim, Hayward, and Moreno, a larger share of the public was disappointed and even depressed. Native Dancer's immense legion of fans could scarcely believe what they had seen on TV. "Thousands turned from the screens in sorrow, a few in tears," *Time* magazine reported. Even a steely *New York Times* columnist wrote, "This reporter was never as emotionally affected by a race as this one. At the end, he felt heartbroken."

The improbability of the upset would soon become evident. Native Dancer rebounded to win the Preakness Stakes, the Belmont Stakes, and every other race he entered until he retired in August 1954. The potential he had shown before the Derby would flower into greatness. His career record was twenty-one wins in twenty-two starts, with his one setback by a nose in the Derby.

Dark Star, on the other hand, bowed a tendon in the Preakness and was immediately retired. He never won a race after the Derby and finished with a career record of six wins in thirteen starts. His human connections would become known as the quintessential one-hit Derby wonders. Hayward never brought another horse to the big race. Moreno finished fourth and eighth in his other two chances. Guggenheim invested enough money in his Cain Hoy Stable to turn it into a top outfit, but he never produced another Derby winner.

It also turned out that Vanderbilt, one of the lions of American racing, never brought another horse to the Derby. For that matter, he never saw the race in person again, even though he lived another forty-four years. It was as if the Dancer's defeat had sapped him of his enthusiasm for the race. His daughter Heidi said years later, "He never put on a big opera about it [but] not winning the Derby was very important to him. That loss in 1953 was a very big sadness and a very big sorrow."

The hurt lingered because no one doubted what happened that day. As Moreno told a reporter in 1978, "The best horse got beat. We all know that."

By John Eisenberg

The Second-Stringer

THE GREATEST DERBY UPSETS often don't begin in the starting gate at Churchill Downs. Instead most begin at an indefinite point in time, and their confluence beneath the Twin Spires sets the stage for the much-anticipated showdown the first Saturday in May.

The 1957 Kentucky Derby was going to be the convergence of several exceptional horses — Bold Ruler, Gallant Man, Round Table, Federal Hill, and Gen. Duke. These horses had blazed down the Derby trail, trading blows and setting records at almost every turn. Calumet's Iron Liege had competed ably in the fray but often ended up overlooked in the formidable shadow of stablemate Gen. Duke.

Gen. Duke, a small and aggressive brown colt named for an obscure Civil War officer, tightly held Calumet's hopes for grabbing an unprecedented sixth Derby title. Gen. Duke's sire, Bull Lea, already had produced two of the famed farm's Derby winners — Citation in 1948 and Hill Gail in 1952.

Gen. Duke's dam also had an impressive set of stripes.

"Wistful was a grand mare who ran far and beat everything in her division and gave those colts a fit," bragged Calumet general manager Ben Jones while touting Gen. Duke to reporters in February 1957. Jones had trained Wistful with the help of his son, Jimmy, who had now taken over the mantle and was training the Derby hopefuls for Calumet.

Since winning the Derby in 1952, Calumet had been in a bit of slump by its own lofty standards. In 1954, for the first time since 1929, the farm had dropped to fourth on the list of leading owners by winnings. In 1955 Calumet had descended further to eighth. The farm rebounded to the top of the list in 1956, but 1957 was looked upon as the year to regain Derby glory. Visions loomed of Gen. Duke draped in red roses.

Albeit, Calumet's strongly made Iron Liege was "no frail reed upon which to lean," as Len Tracy pointed out in his 1963 retrospective of the race. The striking, strong bay was by Bull Lea as well. And Iron Maiden, a tough-as-nails daughter of War Admiral, was Iron Liege's dam.

Iron Maiden lived up to her name by racing sixty-one times, taking a hiatus to give birth to Iron Reward in 1946. The foaling almost turned tragic when Iron Reward became breach and her hind feet tore through Iron Maiden's vaginal wall. The veterinarian was able to right the foal but the damage required thirty-eight stitches to repair.

Iron Maiden recovered, but it seemed doubtful she could bear any more foals. She was sold to Ellwood Johnston, who thought she looked sound enough to be put back in training. The next year she became the first of only two fillies or mares ever to win the Del Mar Handicap, and at 28-1 odds. She was retired again in 1948. Calumet quickly sent a representative to inquire about buying her, provided she was capable of bearing offspring. It turned out she was, having raced that year in foal to Old English.

Iron Liege and Gen. Duke were not the only Derby hopefuls holding strong pedigrees. Almost all the top contenders for 1957 were by high-class sires, and all were the sons of elite race mares. Many speculated, and still do, that this group represented the best foal crop in American racing history.

Wheatley Stable's well-poised Bold Ruler was by the fast-rising and ornery sire Nasrullah and out of the stakes-winning Miss Disco. Oil-man Ralph Lowe's Gallant Man was a versatile little English fellow, bred by the Aga Khan for the hilly courses of Ascot and Epsom. He was by Prix de l'Arc de Triomphe winner Migoli and out of Majideh, winner of the Irish Oaks and Irish One Thousand Guineas. Claiborne Farm's Round Table was a bay son of the good handicap horse and capable sire Princequillo and out of the proven producer and runner Knight's Daughter.

The other five horses that rounded out the field did not garner nearly as much attention in the months leading up to the Derby, with the exception of manufacturer Clifford Lussky's colt. Federal Hill, by Cosmic Bomb and out of Ariel Beauty, showed brilliance as a two-year-old. The brown-coated colt finished first in seven of thirteen starts, going unplaced in only one race. His star shone so brightly that he was ranked second, tied with Bold Ruler, on the 1956 Experimental Free Handicap for two-year-olds, a year-end assessment by respected handicappers of how the juvenile crop would fare at three.

Gen. Duke's limited showing as a juvenile — he won one of two starts — wasn't enough for him to make the list, which was led by another stablemate, Barbizon, who had taken sick with a respiratory disease late in the year.

The Derby hopefuls began crossing paths as early as January 3 in the 1957 season with Gen. Duke, ridden by William Hartack, finishing second to Gallant Man in a $2,800 six-furlong race at Tropical Park in Florida. Gallant Man, with John Choquette in the irons, zipped clear of the field to win the race by a decisive six lengths. Gallant Man followed the victory with a speedy win in his opening race at Hialeah, the six-furlong Hibiscus Stakes. The field included the favored Federal Hill, who finished fifth, giving the colt his second out-of-the-money finish in fourteen starts.

Glamorous Hialeah also spelled good fortune for Iron Liege and

Gen. Duke, both of whom won their opening races at the Florida track, with Iron Liege throwing in a second win in his second race there for good measure.

But what looked to be the first clash of the young titans took place January 30 in the $20,000 seven-furlong Bahamas Stakes at Hialeah. Gallant Man, coming off his two wins, was favored over Bold Ruler, who was going off at 3-1 odds, the highest odds the Sunny Jim Fitzsimmons-trained colt ever drew. As a juvenile, the colt had won three stakes races, but in his previous start, the Remsen Stakes on November 6, he had finished a bewildering last.

"There's absolutely nothing wrong with him that I can find, but I think I'll wait until next year with him rather than keep him in training," Fitzsimmons had told reporters after the colt's baffling performance.

The exceptional eleven-horse field in the Bahamas Stakes offered the opportunity for redemption. In addition to Gallant Man, runners included Gen. Duke, Federal Hill, and Bold Ruler's old rival King Hairan, who had won eight stakes at two.

Bold Ruler, ridden by Ted Atkinson under 126 pounds, rushed out of the gate to a three-length lead in the first two hundred yards. He ran unchallenged for the rest of the race and won with four and a half lengths to spare in 1:22, equaling the track record set by Crafty Admiral under 107 pounds. Gen. Duke rallied from among the tail-enders and wore down the others to take second place, two lengths in front of Federal Hill. Gallant Man finished fourth.

The race led *Daily Racing Form*'s Evan Shipman to characterize Bold Ruler's treatment of his opposition "as if it had been so many platers instead of a field for which its connections entertained the most serious aspirations."

"It fairly took your breath away to see Mr. Fitz' talented charge … snatch the lead in the first few strides out of the gate, run them ragged for every step … and return to the winner's circle as if all of this had been a routine chore," Shipman wrote.

"Bold Ruler, as if to justify his regal name, dealt harshly with these pretenders to his throne as if to serve notice on the generation of what awaits those with the temerity to challenge him," he continued.

The colt's outstanding performance led the eighty-two-year-old Fitzsimmons, revered for his kindness with horses and people, to compare Bold Ruler to Nashua. Under Fitzsimmons' tutelage Nashua had become racing's money-winning champion in 1956 with earnings of $1,288,565.

"Bold Ruler has done just as much as Nashua up to this point, and I think he is just as good of a prospect," the trainer said after the balm of the Bahamas Stakes had salved the sting of the Remsen.

The next match-up among Derby contenders took place February 9 over more Hialeah ground, in a mile and one-sixteenth allowance race. Iron Liege, Gen. Duke, and Round Table faced off in a seven-horse field, with Iron Liege taking the honors over Gen. Duke. Round Table could not keep the pace and finished an uninspiring sixth.

Stablemates Gen. Duke and Iron Liege were back a week later in the mile and one-sixteenth Everglades Stakes for three-year-olds. This time Bold Ruler had his hat in the ring, Eddie Arcaro on his back, and odds of 2-5. Bold Ruler's incredible mile workout of 1:35 — one and three-fifths seconds better than the track record — three days before the race had apparently persuaded the crowd of 26,276 that the colt could still be successful while carrying 126 pounds and giving twelve to Gen. Duke and nine to Iron Liege.

Just days before the race, Fitzsimmons had signed the famous and talented Arcaro to ride the Wheatley Stable ace in all of his 1957 races.

"Eddie fits any horse," Fitzsimmons explained to reporters after he had signed America's top reinsman. "He plans ahead in a race. He makes sure he can go up in a spot before he moves. If he can't make it, he just sits still, [he] isn't weaving and bobbing all over the place."

Under Arcaro's steady hands in the Everglades Stakes, Bold Ruler swung in toward the rail and led the pack at a rapid pace. Gen. Duke sat within easy striking distance under Hartack's heavy restraint. Midway through the backstretch, Iron Liege, ridden by Dave Erb, attempted an unsuccessful run at Bold Ruler. That left it to Gen. Duke. Unleashed by Hartack, he moved to second place within a length of the leader at the quarter pole.

A tremendous duel ensued in the stretch. Gen. Duke was a half-length off when Hartack whacked him once at the eighth pole. Arcaro answered with two whacks to his mount. The jockeys then settled down and hand rode with everything they had.

Bold Ruler remained a neck in front until the final seventy yards. Gen. Duke edged by him in the final jump to win by a head in 1:47 2/5 — a stakes record. Iron Liege, almost forgotten, finished third six lengths behind.

"The entry wasn't working as a team out there," an ebullient Hartack told *Blood-Horse* writer Art Grace after the race. "We were both out to win. I knew my horse would run late; I knew I had Bold Ruler at the finish. I wasn't so sure at the head of the stretch, though. All I knew was I had a horse who responded perfectly. No telling how good this colt is going to be."

Earlier that morning, trainer Jimmy Jones had touted Gen. Duke and the ailing Barbizon, omitting Iron Liege from his predilections.

"A little bit of luck could have a big bearing on what happens," he had told Grace. "Barbizon is probably the best three-year-old in the barn, but he's still not ready for a race after that coughing spell. Gen. Duke is coming along fine; he looks like he'll go a distance."

Hartack, though, had definitely favored Gen. Duke, the smallest of the "big three" Calumet horses.

"Gen. Duke is highly intelligent and does everything you ask of him. This is the horse I prefer over Barbizon and Iron Liege," the jockey said.

But it was Iron Liege who had garnered attention before he was even born. *Sports Illustrated* had approached Ben and Jimmy Jones about picking a foal the magazine could follow from birth through its career. A story appeared February 25, 1957, chronicling the colt's first three years.

Famous nature photographer Ylla had taken the first pictures of Iron Liege coming into the world at 12:50 a.m. on March 10, 1954. (Ylla never got to see her pictures of him in print. She died in 1955 while photographing a bullock race in India for *Sports Illustrated*.)

A mare named Iron Maiden "dropped a frisky colt into the aristocratic stillness of Calumet," the story read. Calumet Farm manager J. Paul Ebelhardt told *Sports Illustrated* he had thought well of Iron Liege before he had ever set hoof on a track.

"You know, you might see five girls walking down the street, and you might like the conformation of one of them. It's the same with horses," Ebelhardt said.

His name at first was Iron Lea, but Mrs. Lucille Markey, who owned Calumet, decided to change it to Iron Liege. Iron Liege contracted a cough, slowing his training and delaying his debut until August 21, 1956, at Washington Park. After breaking slowly, he finished sixth.

"He ran green," Jones told *Sports Illustrated*. "The clods of dirt kept coming back at him from the horses in front and he ducked them like a toad in a hailstorm."

The story and photos followed Iron Liege's racing career up to publication. The story concluded:

"The alert, sensitive and mature head on the facing page now belongs to an established race horse. Iron Liege wintered well as a 2-year-old and early in 1957 earned the title of one of the best of the 3-year-old crop ... Last week he finished a creditable third to the same Gen. Duke and Bold Ruler, the two leading Derby contenders at this time. In three months, since his last disappointing race on Oct. 27, 1956, Iron Liege has found within himself a flicker of flame that pumped new vitality into the 3-year-old galaxy."

****

Coming into the March 2 Flamingo Stakes, though, the spotlight remained focused on Gen. Duke and Bold Ruler, with Iron Liege, Federal Hill, and the other three entrants nothing more than afterthoughts. The sole question was whether Gen. Duke could take on Bold Ruler at equal weights.

"Naturally, we're concerned," trainer Jimmy Jones told *The Blood-Horse*. "It'll be a different thing entirely in the Flamingo. If weight is the difference in horse races, it stands to reason Bold Ruler will beat us. It remains to be seen if my horse can improve enough to overcome 12 pounds.

"Bold Ruler is one of the very good ones. As a prospect, he's the best I've seen since Citation. He scares me when I see him work ... He scares me when I see him run. He just plain scares me, that's all."

Bold Ruler's trainer looked forward to a more level playing field.

"That other horse [Gen. Duke] had to run as fast as he could to catch us in the Everglades," Fitzsimmons said, "and he just barely did it. Twelve pounds, that was too much to give away. It'll be all equal this time — all equal."

As predicted, the Flamingo turned into a two-horse showdown. Federal Hill, ridden by Willie Carstens, took command at the start, while Arcaro kept Bold Ruler under restraint at easy striking distance. Gen. Duke, with Hartack aboard, sat well out of contention behind Iron Liege. Arcaro went for the lead on the far turn, and Federal Hill offered no resistance. Hartack also used the turn to make his move and emerged third coming into the stretch. Aware that Gen. Duke was coming on, Arcaro opened up Bold Ruler. In turn, Hartack went to work on Gen. Duke, who began closing Bold Ruler's two-length lead. Gen. Duke continued gaining, but Bold Ruler would not quit. He won by a neck in track-record time of 1:47. Iron Liege finished third, two and three-quarters lengths behind his stablemate and twelve lengths ahead of Mister Jive.

Hartack ballyhooed the additional weight as a factor in Gen. Duke's loss.

"It had nothing to do with the finish," he told *The Blood-Horse*. "When I moved with my horse he went just the way he wanted to. He was just a little shy at the wire, that's all. He'll be number one again. Just watch him next time."

Meanwhile, Claiborne Farm had sold Round Table for an estimated $140,000 to Travis M. Kerr, who took the colt out west. The same day as the Flamingo, the favored Round Table finished third to Sir William and Swirling Abbey, respectively, in the Santa Anita Derby in California. Round Table had entered the Santa Anita Derby off a win two weeks earlier at Hialeah. Federal Hill had been the overwhelming favorite in that mile and one-eighth race but finished last after throwing his rider at the start. Federal Hill, with Carstens up, went on to snap his losing streak and win the Louisiana Derby over Shan Pac on March 9. The time of 1:49 3/5 was a stakes record and equaled the track record for the mile and one-eighth distance.

On March 20, Barbizon emerged from the Calumet barn to contest the mile and one-sixteenth Fountain of Youth Stakes against his stablemates Gen. Duke and Iron Liege. The crowd slashed the trio's collective odds to 1-5. Of the other seven entries, only one, Safe Message, was less than 10-1. Gen. Duke easily prevailed over Iron Liege to win the race by a length and a half. Barbizon never posed a challenge, and his lackluster performance raised doubts that he was up to the rigors of the upcoming Florida Derby. Federal Hill served notice that he was willing and ready for the race with a world record-busting performance, running a sizzling six and a half furlongs in 1:15 in a betless exhibition race against three other horses at Gulfstream.

"Anyone who beats him will win the Florida Derby," said jockey Carstens.

A day later Bold Ruler worked seven furlongs in an amazing 1:22 2/5 at Gulfstream in preparation for the Florida Derby. Jimmy Jones had watched the work but remained unperturbed though wary.

"Bold Ruler's an awful good horse. Long as he holds together I don't think any of us can beat him," he told *The Blood-Horse*. "Gen. Duke has a chance. So does Federal Hill. Anybody that disregards that horse is asking for trouble. He's just beginning to form. He's a lot better horse than anybody thinks.

"Bold Ruler don't have to win them all," Jones continued. "He might fly to pieces one of these days. He might go right out of gear ... Or maybe he'll just run us out of gear.

"There's an awful lot of stakes coming up and Bold Ruler can't win 'em all. As long as they hang up $100,000 I got to keep shooting at 'em."

The warm, clear weather on Florida Derby day, March 30, provided perfect visibility for Jones to take aim. Iron Liege and Gen. Duke were coupled in the barrel as a nearly 2-1 entry against the 3-5 favorite Bold Ruler, Federal Hill, and Shan Pac.

Carstens rushed Federal Hill into command, holding a lead over a tightly restrained Bold Ruler around the clubhouse turn and into the backstretch. Gen. Duke stayed close to the pace, with Iron Liege fourth and Shan Pac far back.

As the field approached the far turn, it became obvious that the Calumet pair had no intention of letting Bold Ruler get away from them. Hartack took his whip to Gen. Duke, and the colt moved within a head of his rival. Arcaro looked over and, seeing Gen. Duke and not Iron Liege, opened up on Bold Ruler.

Halfway through the stretch turn Bold Ruler was head and head with Federal Hill while Gen. Duke had dropped back two lengths off the

(above) Elwood after the Derby; (left) Boots Durnell
(on right) with John "Bet-a-Million" Gates; (below)
Donerail in the Derby winner's circle; (right) owner-
trainer-breeder T.P. Hayes

(above) "Work horse" Exterminator (outside) breezing with Sun Briar;
(below) Exterminator after his Derby triumph

(above) Bold Venture wearing the roses and receiving a pat from trainer Max Hirsch; (right) Mr. and Mrs. Morton L. Schwartz; (below) Brevity, the odds-on Kentucky Derby favorite, after his Florida Derby win

(above) Gallahadion gallops to Derby victory; (inset)
trainer Roy Waldron (third from right) receives the
Derby trophy; (right) Gallahadion after winning the
San Vicente Stakes at Santa Anita; (below)
E.R. Bradley's powerhouse Bimelech

(top) Native Dancer is stuck on the rail as Dark Star maintains the lead; (middle) Dark Star holds off Native Dancer's late charge; (above) Dark Star, with a jubilant Henry Moreno up, holds court in the Derby winner's circle; (right) Native Dancer, whose lone loss was the Derby

(Opposite, top) Gen. Duke takes the
Florida Derby over Bold Ruler and Iron
Liege; (middle) Bold Ruler (on inside)
edges Gallant Man in the Wood Memorial;
(left) Iron Liege noses out
Gallant Man at the Derby finish;
(above) Iron Liege with his Calumet
connections in the winner's circle;
(below) Iron Liege returns to the barn a
Kentucky Derby winner

Canonero II charges toward a stunning Derby win; (opposite, above) galloping out after the finish; (above) a South American celebration in the winner's circle

(left) Derby favorite Rockhill Native gallops under the Twin Spires; (right) top contender Plugged Nickle bests Genuine Risk in the Wood Memorial; (top, inset) Genuine Risk takes command entering the Derby stretch; (above) Genuine Risk becomes only the second filly to capture the roses, which she wears proudly in the winner's circle (top right, inset)

The popular Arazi (left) commands attention before the race, but at the wire it is the unknown Lil E. Tee (above, on left); (top, inset) Governor Brereton Jones presents the trophy to trainer Lynn Whiting, owner W. Cal Partee, and jockey Pat Day

(above) Champion Timber Country is part of the favored entry with Serena's Song, but their other stablemate, Thunder Gulch (right), takes the Derby glory

(top) The brilliant filly Serena's Song leads the way in the early going; (middle) Thunder Gulch wins by daylight; (left) trainer D. Wayne Lukas, owner Michael Tabor; and jockey Gary Stevens hoist the Derby trophy

(above) Post-time favorite Bellamy Road gallops at Churchill Downs; (right) fan favorite Afleet Alex would finish third

(above) Giacomo prevails in the final strides; (above, inset) Giacomo's payoff for a $2 win ticket is second to Donerail's record; (left) trainer John Shirreffs leads Giacomo into the winner's circle; (below) Giacomo receives a loving pat from Ann Moss as Jerry Moss looks on

pace. Coming into the stretch, Bold Ruler got a head in front of Federal Hill. Erb, meanwhile, snuck Iron Liege through on the rail to within a half-length of the leaders. Gen. Duke was fourth on the outside.

The crowd of 24,409 roared its approval as the field dashed toward the finish line. Iron Liege managed to get his head in front, appearing as if he might win it. Federal Hill was tiring. But Bold Ruler was holding on, and Gen. Duke, seemingly out of it, was moving up again on the outside. At the sixteenth pole, Calumet's favored son got in front and pulled away to a length and a half victory. Bold Ruler finished second by a head over Iron Liege. Shan Pac passed Federal Hill in the final yards.

Gen. Duke ran the mile and one-eighth in 1:46 4/5, equaling the world record held by Noor, Swaps, and Alidon and cutting one and four-fifths seconds from the former track record, set by Needles in winning the 1956 Florida Derby. In fact, all five starters in the 1957 edition broke Needles' record.

After the race, Jimmy Jones summed up his feelings succinctly: "I'm too happy to say much."

The next day the trainer was back at work at his barn at Hialeah and was a little more talkative as he looked at pictures from the race with his father, Hartack, and Hartack's agent.

"Look at that bow-legged son of a gun. Legs just like a bulldog," Jimmy Jones said as he looked affectionately at a close-up of Gen. Duke.

Out in California, Round Table was staying busy making a name for himself. On April 6 the colt won the mile and one-sixteenth Bay Meadows Derby in track-record time of 1:41 3/5. Trainer John Nerud also had taken his horse, Gallant Man, out of the fray in Florida. Gallant Man didn't fare as well as Round Table that day, finishing fourth in the Swift Stakes at Jamaica in New York. A week later Federal Hill also ventured out of the shadow of Gen. Duke and Bold Ruler, running in the Biscayne Bay Handicap and finishing second.

"I'd be silly to keep running against those other two," Federal Hill's trainer Lussky said in an interview with *The Blood-Horse* following the race. "After the Derby I'm going to start picking spots. There are so many big races around, Bold Ruler and Gen. Duke can't possibly run in them all. When you shove that pair out of the way, my colt's as good as any."

In preparation for the Derby, Jimmy Jones moved his string to Kentucky to race at Keeneland. The trainer planned to bypass the mile and one-eighth Blue Grass Stakes later in the month in favor of an earlier seven-furlong race to keep his charges sharp. Only Cain Hoy Stable's One-Eyed King joined the Calumet stablemates in the betless event on April 19. Iron Liege, given eight pounds by Gen. Duke as was One-Eyed King, won in track-record time of 1:22 2/5. Gen. Duke, with Hartack aboard, finished third, within three lengths of the winner.

"I told Hartack to remember this wasn't May 4 [Derby Day] and that all we wanted this afternoon was some exercise," Jimmy Jones told reporters after the race. "This run today is just what he needed. A nice but easy race. It should put him on edge. But Iron Liege ran good, too. They'll both be vanned over to Churchill Downs next Tuesday and both will run in the Derby Trial."

In the exodus from Florida, Bold Ruler had headed to the Northeast to join Gallant Man in the April 20 Wood Memorial in what turned out to be an amazing Derby prep race.

With seven entries in the race, Bold Ruler stood out as the only real contender. His trainer, Fitzsimmons, and his jockey, Arcaro, each had won seven previous Woods without ever having combined their skills in the victories. Bold Ruler was bet down to 1-2, while Gallant Man was fourth choice at 8-1. In between were Promised Land and Ambehaving, who got left at the gate after slamming into a sidewall. Jockey Willie Shoemaker tried to pull the colt up, and while he was looking down to check out the colt's legs, his saddle slipped forward.

"Shoemaker lost his purchase and Ambehaving took him on an un-guided tour of the mile track, the rider perched on the top like a kid with his feet held above the pedals as his bike coasts down a hill," wrote Pat O'Brien of *The Blood-Horse*.

The other six horses had gotten away from the gate well, with the fa-vorite a bit off the rail. With Mister Jive, winner of the Gotham Stakes a week earlier, filling the void along the rail and pushing Bold Ruler, the Wheatley colt ran the first two quarters in twenty-four seconds apiece.

Going into the big turn, Bold Ruler edged ahead. Arcaro glanced over his left shoulder to see Mister Jive give way. Had he looked over his right shoulder, the jockey would have seen Gallant Man and Choquette steaming toward him and then past him. All Arcaro could do to stem the damage was urge on Bold Ruler, who responded by spending the next furlong getting the distance back. Arcaro switched the whip to his left hand, successfully convincing Bold Ruler to catch Gallant Man. The final furlong was an inch-by-inch battle with Bold Ruler crossing the finish line first by a nose and lowering the track record by two-fifths of a second.

"It was Gallant Man who brought out the courage in Bold Ruler, the mastery of Arcaro, and the thrill of the race," wrote racing journalist O'Brien.

Round Table made his way east to be the lone top Derby contender to contest the Blue Grass Stakes at Keeneland. One-Eyed King, con-sidered a Derby possibility, also was part of the six-horse field. As the even-money favorite, Round Table took the lead at the start and held a two-length margin into the backstretch. In the stretch turn, One-Eyed King and Manteau almost pulled even, but with a reminder from jock-ey Ralph Neves' whip, Round Table surged away, was hand-ridden to a six-length victory in the last furlong, and soon was on his way to Churchill Downs to prepare for the Kentucky Derby.

Over at Churchill, the Derby Trial Stakes wasn't much of a race, despite the inclusion of Federal Hill, Gen. Duke, and Iron Liege. Federal Hill emerged an easy winner, but Gen. Duke, after a second-place finish, captured much of the attention the following morning when he came out of the race lame and Jimmy Jones said he was unsure whether the colt would be able to run in the Derby.

Jones told reporters Gen. Duke's injury to his left forefoot had first appeared after he finished third to Iron Liege and One-Eyed King in the betless race. After that race the foot appeared to be bruised, but the colt seemed better when he was shod again and the pressure removed from the sore spot.

The next morning, however, the hoof and leg were extremely sore, and Gen. Duke winced visibly each time the area was touched. Jones ordered X-rays immediately.

"It's just one of those things that happens in racing. If it's only a bruise, we will try to put a bar plate on him and see if he can go in the Derby. If it's a break, that's another matter, of course," he said.

The day before the Derby, Jimmy Jones had Gen. Duke on the track at a slow trot. "He's much, much better," Jones told reporters. "We've got a chance now."

Still, Jones said, he would not decide until Derby morning whether to start Gen. Duke.

"You make a million decisions that are not easy," he said. "But you do the best you can."

On that cold Saturday morning, the best Calumet could do was scratch Gen. Duke, who still had heat in his foot. Calumet had to hang its hopes for a sixth Derby title on a horse that had finished a lackluster fifth in the Derby Trial. Gen. Duke's rider, Hartack, would take the reins of Iron Liege.

"I never felt more miserable in my life," Jimmy Jones told Joe Hirsch and Gene Plowden for their book, *In the Winner's Circle — The Jones*

Boys of Calumet Farm (Mason & Lipscomb, 1974). "... My name was to go on the program as trainer for Calumet Farm, and here I was scratching the horse I had been sure would give me my first credited win of the Derby."

With the better half of Calumet's entry out of the race, Iron Liege's odds lengthened to 8-1. Bold Ruler, Arcaro aboard, took most of the action at 6-5, followed by Gallant Man at 3-1 with Shoemaker replacing the suspended Choquette in the irons. The winter-jacket weather had kept many race fans home, attendance and handle dropping more than 10 percent over the previous Derby's.

The crowd of 58,465 that showed up, though, saw a race to be remembered — not just for its photo finish but also for the drama that preceded it and the questions that followed it about what might have been.

The early running of the nine-horse race — which also included Shan Pac, Mister Jive, Indian Creek, and Better Bee — went as experts predicted it would. Front-runner Federal Hill, ridden by Carstens, took his place at the lead, with Bold Ruler and Iron Liege keeping the pacesetter in check and waiting for any sign of his faltering. Gallant Man sat eight lengths off the pace, Shoemaker keeping a tight hold.

A few nights before the race, owner Ralph Lowe had dreamed Shoemaker would misjudge the finish line, take his horse up too soon, and lose the race, as he had on Swaps in California several months earlier. Lowe had told trainer Nerud about the dream, Nerud told Shoemaker, and the story made its way around the backstretch. Whether it made its way into Shoemaker's subconscious as he made his move is still debated.

As Gallant Man began to pass horses on the outside at the far turn, Arcaro went to work on Bold Ruler, and Hartack put the pressure on Iron Liege. Down the long Churchill Downs stretch, Federal Hill began to drift in, and Hartack, who had been on the rail, reined out to go around him. Arcaro tried to keep up, but Bold Ruler pinned his ears in protest, vetoing the decision.

Iron Liege continued his big move, edging around Federal Hill, who tried gamely to match strides with the Calumet colt, giving way inch by inch down the stretch. Meanwhile, Gallant Man continued his surge on the outside. Shoemaker pumped his colt, and by mid-stretch it became obvious the deciding battle would take place between Iron Liege and Gallant Man.

At the sixteenth pole, Nerud's premonition became a reality as Shoemaker, misjudging the finish line, suddenly stood up in the saddle. Apparently realizing his error just as quickly, he sat back down and drove Gallant Man toward the finish line. But Iron Liege fought back, and the two horses finished the race neck and neck. A photo determined Iron Liege the winner, by a scant nose.

Round Table, who had run steadily in fourth most of the race, passed the fading Bold Ruler to finish third by three lengths. Bold Ruler took fourth, followed closely by Federal Hill. The remainder of the field was never in contention. The time for the race was 2:02 1/5, with Iron Liege paying $18.80 to win.

Following the race, Shoemaker readily admitted he had stood up but said Gallant Man never broke stride. He was set down for fifteen days for "gross carelessness." In later interviews with the press, however, the jockey said his mistake accounted for Gallant Man's defeat.

Jimmy Jones did not see it that way,

"There were all kinds of stories after that Derby," he told Hirsch and Plowden years later for his biography, "... I was standing at trackside, not thirty feet from where the horses were battling, and I also saw the film patrol movie many times. Gallant Man never changed stride at any time, and I am still certain Iron Liege won on his merits. At the moment that Iron Liege's number flashed on the board, however, I didn't think about merit.

Kentucky Derby
Purse: $125,000 Added

Churchill Downs - May 4, 1957. Eighty-third running Kentucky Derby.
Purse $125,000 added. Three-year-olds. 1 1-4 Miles. Main Track. Track: Fast.
Gross value $152,050. Net value to winner, $107,950 and gold trophy; second, $25,000; third, $12,500; fourth, $5,000.

Horse	A	Wgt	Eqp	Odds	PP	St	1/2	3/4	1	Str	Fin	Jockey
Iron Liege	3	126	w	8.40	6	4	3^3	$2^{1½}$	$2^{1½}$	$1^½$	1no	W Hartack
Gallant Man	3	126	w	3.70	4	6	7^2	7^1	$5^½$	$3^½$	$2^{2½}$	W Shoemaker
Round Table	3	126	wb	3.60	3	5	4^3	4^3	4^2	4^h	3^3	R Neves
Bold Ruler	3	126	w	1.20	7	3	2^h	$3^{1½}$	$3^½$	5^3	$4^{1½}$	E Arcaro
Federal Hill	3	126	wb	7.90	2	1	$1^{1½}$	$1^½$	1^h	2^h	$5^½$	W Carstens
Indian Creek	3	126	wb	73.10	5	7	$6^{2½}$	$6^½$	7^3	7^3	6^1	G Taniguchi
Mister Jive	3	126	wb	55.90	1	2	5^3	$5^{2½}$	$6^½$	$6^½$	$7^{3½}$	H Woodhouse
Better Bee	3	126	w	42.40	9	9	9	9	8^3	8^6	8^{10}	J Adams
Shan Pac	3	126	wb	46.50	8	8	$8^½$	$8^½$	9	9	9	J R Adams

Off Time: 4:32	Time Of Race: :23¾	:47	1:11½	1:36½	2:02½
Start: Good For All	Track: Fast				

Equipment: w for whip; b for blinkers

Mutuel Payoffs

1A	Iron Liege	$18.80	$9.40	$6.20
5	Gallant Man		5.00	4.00
4	Round Table			4.00

Winner: Iron Liege, b. c. by Bull Lea—Iron Maiden, by War Admiral (Trained by H. A. Jones). Bred by Calumet Farm in Kentucky.

Start good. Won driving; second and third the same.
IRON LIEGE, away alertly, saved ground while racing nearest FEDERAL HILL to the mile, took command during the drive and, responding to strong handling, held GALLANT MAN safe but won with little left. GALLANT MAN, in hand and saving ground to the last three-eighths mile, moved up determinedly in the early stretch, reached the lead between calls and was going stoutly when his rider misjudged the finish and he could not overtake IRON LIEGE when back on stride. ROUND TABLE, well placed and racing evenly to the stretch, closed willingly under punishment but could not reach the leaders. BOLD RULER, a sharp factor from the outset but racing well out in the track, failed to stay when set down through the stretch. FEDERAL HILL took command at once, set the pace until inside the stretch, then gave way when challenged by IRON LIEGE. INDIAN CREEK was never prominent and had no mishap. MISTER JIVE could not keep up. BETTER BEE was never dangerous. SHAN PAC was overmatched.
Scratched—Gen. Duke, 126.

Owners: (1) Calumet Farm; (2) R Lowe; (3) Kerr Stable; (4) Wheatley Stable; (5) C Lussky; (6) Mrs A L Rice; (6) J L Applebaum; (7) W S Miller; (8) T A Grissom
©EQUIBASE

"I was never so happy to win a race in my life. It was my first official Derby victory, and it was all so unexpected."

Though he finished second to Bold Ruler in the Preakness and by-passed the Belmont, Iron Liege proved his mettle by beating one of the most exceptional fields of horses in Derby history.

****

One measure of how outstanding the 1957 Kentucky Derby field was lies in the figures that show the first four finishers earned a grand total of $3,428,577 in their racing careers. The trailer among them was the winner, Iron Liege, whose lifetime earnings were $404,169.

Round Table, Bold Ruler, and Gallant Man all went on to be named in *The Blood-Horse*'s *Thoroughbred Champions: Top 100 Racehorses of the 20th Century*, with Round Table and Bold Ruler making the top twenty.

Gen. Duke, unfortunately, never raced again. He developed an incurable spine disease and was put down in 1958.

By Rena Baer

Viva Canonero!

THERE IS A CHAPTER in the annals of Thoroughbred racing and the Kentucky Derby that sadly has withered with the years. But beyond the faded words and photos, beyond the madness that swept through the sport in the spring of 1971, the legend of Canonero II cries out to be told after all these years.

No detailed introduction is needed, for nothing can prepare the reader for the incredible tale about to unfold. The opening chapter begins in the rolling hills of Kentucky, where most sagas of the Turf unfold, and ends in the barn of Venezuelan trainer Juan Arias. From this unlikely place emerged a skinny, crooked-legged colt who would arrive at Churchill Downs for the ninety-seventh Kentucky Derby a forlorn-looking creature, ridiculed by the entire racing community. By the time he departed, however, he no longer was a clown, but a hero known throughout the Western Hemisphere as "The Caracas Cannonball."

At the 1967 Keeneland fall breeding stock sale, horsemen gathered as they do every year in search of bargain-basement bloodstock. Among the numerous broodmares sold that year was the six-year-old Nantallah mare, Dixieland II, in foal to the young stallion Pretendre, runner-up in the previous year's English Derby at Epsom Downs. The pedigree held little interest to American breeders, and when the bidding stopped at

$2,700, Claiborne Farm manager William Taylor, acting as agent for Dixieland II's breeder, Edward B. Benjamin, took it upon himself to buy the mare back. Benjamin then gave the mare to Taylor, who told him he could have her back any time he wanted. Several months later, just before Dixieland II foaled, Benjamin told Taylor he had changed his mind and wanted her back.

Dixieland II gave birth to her Pretendre colt on April 24, 1968, at Claiborne Farm, where Benjamin boarded his horses. Benjamin tried to sell the colt the following year at the Keeneland July yearling sale, but the horse was rejected due to his crooked right foreleg. He was so awkward and ungainly someone commented that he "had a stride like a crab." Benjamin consigned him to the then less-prestigious September yearling sale, where one could sell just about anything. But even at this sale a deformed colt by an unfashionable European stallion, out of a mare that couldn't even bring more than $2,700, had little hope of selling, especially on the last day of the sale. That is unless someone was willing to pick him up for practically nothing.

Venezuelan bloodstock agent Luis Navas, who had a reputation as an equine junk dealer, was that someone. Navas would buy young horses at dirt-cheap prices, then put together package deals and sell them to Venezuelan owners who were willing to pay decent prices for American-bred youngsters. Navas, acting under the name Albert, agent, made one bid of $1,200 and the colt was his. He immediately packaged him up with a Ballymoss colt and a filly and sold them to Venezuelan businessman Pedro Baptista for $60,000.

Baptista was forty-four years old, but his bald head, scar on his nose, and missing teeth made him look older. This wasn't a particularly good time for Baptista to be buying horses. His plumbing and pipe manufacturing company was in dire financial straits, and he was on the verge of bankruptcy. To continue purchasing horses, he registered them under the name of his son-in-law, Edgar Caibett. After Navas sent him his three new yearlings, Baptista turned them over to a young, up-and-coming trainer named Juan Arias.

Arias was born in 1938 in the small town of Marin in Yaracuy State. His family moved to the slums of Caracas, where his father abandoned him. Raised by his mother and grandmother, he escaped into the world of horses, whose beauty provided a stark contrast to the poverty in which he lived. Whenever he could, he would sneak away to the racetrack, where he would clean out stalls for free. When he turned sixteen, he enrolled in trainer's school at the old El Paraiso Racetrack, after which he got his first full-time job at the track. With little pay and nowhere to live, he slept in the stalls. He eventually began to put a small string together and several years later was introduced to Baptista, who took a liking to him and gave him sixteen horses to train.

One of the horses arriving at Arias' barn in the spring of 1970 was that ungainly colt from the Keeneland sale, whom Baptista had named Canonero after a type of singing group. Baptista had been forced to sell twenty-four of his forty-eight horses to raise some cash, and his instructions to Arias were to get started quickly and have the colt ready to win first time out. When Arias first laid eyes on Canonero, the trainer knew he had his work cut out for him. Not only was the colt's crooked leg still noticeable, but Canonero had a split right hoof and a bad case of worms. Arias had to clean out the colt's stomach every thirty days and put him on a special diet, which included seaweed from Australia.

Although Canonero had numerous physical problems, he showed promise in the morning and didn't need much training to get in shape. He made his debut at La Rinconada (which opened after El Paraiso closed down) on August 8, 1970, and despite being sent off at 12-1 in the six-furlong race, he won by six and a half lengths. Baptista, who was considered an eccentric, then came up with a plan to send him to the United States to race at Del Mar in the hopes of getting him sold.

In his first start, an allowance event, the repatriated colt raced under the name Canonero II, because a horse with the name Canonero had already been racing in the United States. After finishing third at 21-1 in the allowance, Canonero finished fifth in the Del Mar Futurity, beaten seven and three-quarters lengths in 1:08 4/5. One trainer at Del Mar, Charlie Whittingham, thought the colt had promise, and when he heard Canonero could be purchased for about $70,000, he attempted to buy him for one of his main clients, Mary Jones. Unfortunately, no one with the horse could speak English. Unable to get a firm price, Whittingham gave up, and Canonero returned to Venezuela.

Having failed to sell the horse, Baptista told Arias, "Don't worry, we'll win the Kentucky Derby next year." Arias replied, "The Kentucky Derby? What's that?"

Canonero won his next two races; then, following two defeats, he stretched out to a mile and a quarter on March 7, 1971, and defeated older horses in 2:03 2/5, with new rider Gustavo Avila aboard. Here it was only March, and Canonero had already beaten older horses and won at the Derby distance, two feats unheard of in the United States. A week later he dropped back to a sprint and finished third before winning his next two starts. On April 10 he stretched back out to nine furlongs and finished third, carrying 112 pounds. It was his ninth start in four months and his fifth in the last thirty-five days.

Baptista then hurled a bombshell at Arias, telling him he seriously wanted to run Canonero in the Kentucky Derby, which was only three weeks away. Little did Baptista realize, however, how close the horse had come to not being nominated. That February, Baptista was in Florida and heard that Pimlico vice president Chick Lang was there taking nominations for the Preakness and might do him a favor and put in the nominations for the Derby and Belmont as well. Baptista found out that Lang was staying at the Miami Springs Villas near Hialeah and called him.

Also staying at the hotel were John Finney and Larry Ensor from the Fasig-Tipton Sales Company. "I get this call from a guy with a Spanish accent who says his name is Baptista," Lang recalled. "I immediately thought it was a joke because the guys from Fasig-Tipton and I were always playing practical jokes on each other. When he said his name was Baptista, I kept thinking of the guy that Castro had removed from power in Cuba and thought someone was pulling my leg.

"He said he had a horse he wanted to nominate for the Preakness named Canonero. I said, 'Who are you?' and he told me he was the owner. I told him to spell the horse's name because I had never heard of him. He said, 'You will.' "

Lang wrote the nomination down on the back of a cocktail napkin and told Baptista he'd contact the representatives for the Derby and Belmont and put in those nominations as well. After Lang hung up, he went in the other room where Finney and Ensor were having evening cocktails. Finney asked who was on the phone, and Lang said, "I don't know; I thought it was you playing a joke on me." Finney assured Lang it wasn't he. Lang then asked him if he'd ever heard of a horse named Canonero. Finney left the room and did some checking, then came back a few minutes later and said, "Someone's pulling your leg; I can't find any horse by that name."

Lang took the napkin out of his pocket and started to crumple it up and throw it in the trash, but he decided he'd better put in the nomination and if it turned out to phony, so be it. The following day he phoned in the nomination to the racing secretary's office but had them check first to see if the horse really existed. They processed the nomination and found that the horse was legitimate.

With the Derby getting close, Baptista, according to his close friend and adviser, Miguel Torrealba, had a dream in which his deceased mother told him Canonero was going to win the Kentucky Derby. That was good enough for him.

Meanwhile, in the United States the Derby picture was wide-open following injuries to early favorites Hoist the Flag and His Majesty and the defection of Flamingo winner Executioner, who would wait for the Preakness. The big horses remaining were the indefatigable Jim French, the Santa Anita Derby winner who had already run in nine stakes across the country that year; San Felipe Handicap and California Derby winner Unconscious; the Calumet Farm entry of Bold and Able and Florida Derby winner Eastern Fleet; and Blue Grass Stakes winner Impetuosity.

One week after his third-place finish at La Rinconada, Canonero boarded a plane for Miami with his groom, Juan Quintero, whose expenses came out Arias' pocket. The colt was sent without any papers or blood work. Shortly after taking off, the plane was forced to return due to mechanical failure. The second attempt wasn't any more successful as one of the engines caught on fire and the plane had to return once again. The only other plane they could find was a cargo plane filled with chickens and ducks, which became Canonero's travel companions.

Finally, a weary Canonero arrived in Miami. But airport officials quickly discovered the horse had no papers, so he was forced to remain on the plane for twelve hours in the sweltering heat, nearly becoming dehydrated. With the papers finally in order, Canonero was allowed off the plane. One report, from someone close to Baptista, said the colt actually was forced to fly to Panama and wait there until the papers were in order. In any event, Canonero was back in the United States, but with no blood test results, officials placed him in quarantine for four days while his blood work was sent to a U.S. Department of Agriculture lab in Beltsville, Maryland.

By the time he was released from quarantine, Canonero had lost about seventy pounds and was a physical mess. But his problems were far from over. Baptista had not sent enough money to pay for a flight from Miami to Louisville, so Canonero had to be vanned the 1,200 miles, a trip that took nearly twenty-four hours. Neither Arias nor Quintero could speak English, and when the van arrived at the Churchill Downs

stable gate, no one at the track had any idea who the horse or the trainer was. After a short while, the matter was resolved, and Canonero was
allowed entrance into Churchill Downs. The Kentucky Derby, set for
May 1, was one week away.

When Canonero's name popped unexpectedly into the Derby picture,
the Caliente Future Book quoted him at odds of 500-1.

Canonero's stay at Churchill became a freak show, as curiosity seek-
ers would come by just to take a look at this harlequin of a horse. Instead of a conventional forelock, he sported bangs, much like Moe of
the Three Stooges, and every one of his ribs could be counted. When
Arias inquired how much a sack of bran cost, he was told forty-five dollars. "Too much," he said. "Can we have half a sack?"

Arias became almost as much of a curiosity as his horse. Here was a
black man from Venezuela who spoke no English, who was rarely seen
without a cigarette in his mouth, and who usually wore a sport jacket
and tie to the barn in the morning.

All the while, Arias kept what little media that showed up at the barn
amused by telling them that Canonero was a horse of destiny and would
win the Kentucky Derby. He trained Canonero whenever the horse felt
like training, and the times he did, Arias put up a 165-pound exercise
rider and had him gallop the colt without a saddle. When reporters
asked Arias what Canonero was going to do on a particular day, the
trainer would go through a pantomime of a horse galloping. Louisville
horseman Jose Rodriguez, a native of Puerto Rico, was helping out
Arias, serving as his assistant and interpreter.

Canonero and Arias had almost a spiritual relationship. If the horse
didn't eat, Arias would go into his stall and talk to him and pet him,
and he would start eating. If he felt Canonero had something to say
to him, he'd press his ear against the horse and listen. Before sending
him out to the track, he'd ask Canonero how he was feeling and how
he slept the night before. If Canonero "told" him he didn't feel like

training that day, Arias would say, "Okay, if you don't feel like it, I won't force you. Just relax, go eat, and wait for tomorrow."

Quintero took almost the same kind of approach. "I speak to him with affection and love," he said. "In other words, I treat him like I was raising my own son."

The "Canonero Show" became a running joke, especially when the horse finally did work, crawling a half-mile in a lethargic :53 4/5. What was lost behind all the laughter was that Canonero was beginning to thrive physically and had put back fifty of the seventy pounds he had lost.

Through an interpreter Arias tried to explain to people that he knew his horse, but few listened. "I have my methods," he said. "Most of the American trainers train for speed. I train Canonero to be a star, a horse of depth who is versatile and can be ridden in front or from behind. They say I work my horse too slow. Let's see if he runs that slow on Saturday."

Three days before the Derby, jockey Gustavo Avila arrived at Churchill Downs. Known in Venezuela as "El Monstruo," or "The Monster," Avila was one of the country's leading jockeys and had ridden Canonero on three occasions earlier in the year, winning twice.

So little was known about Canonero and his record in Venezuela, the *Daily Racing Form* past performance lines for his last three starts did not provide the name or conditions of the race, the jockey, weight, first three finishers, and comments. All it said was, "Missing data unavailable at this time."

Arias was invited to a pre-Derby party and felt as if some people there were mocking Canonero. "They made us very mad," he recalled. "They made fun of our horse. They said his workout was no good. They said we're clowns and we're crazy. They came to see my horse and turned away and wrinkled up their noses. Someone wrote he crawls like a turtle."

Arias said one rival owner proposed a mock toast, holding up his glass of champagne to him and saying, "Mucha suerte" (good luck in Spanish).

On Derby morning Arias worked Canonero under the cover of darkness. This time he put a saddle on him to let the colt know it was time to get serious. Canonero was razor-sharp, breezing three furlongs in about :35, a workout that was not revealed until two years later.

Unconscious was made the 5-2 favorite, with the Calumet entry 7-2, and Jim French 9-2. Canonero was put in the six-horse mutuel field, which closed at a meager 8-1. Baptista decided not to attend the Derby, and instead stayed home to take care of business, while sending his son to represent him. Avila put on Baptista's brown silks and brown cap and headed out to get his instructions from Arias.

Arias accompanied Canonero to the paddock but was too nervous to saddle the colt and left that task to Jose Rodriguez. Instead of going up to the boxes, Arias watched the race from the rail, along with the grooms.

As the field of twenty broke from the gate, Canonero immediately dropped to the back of the pack. When they charged past Arias, the colt was sixteenth, already some twenty lengths off the lead. The pace was a strong one, with Bold and Able, the lesser of the Calumet Farm entry, battling with three mutuel field horses — Barbizon Streak, Jr's Arrowhead, and Knight Counter.

By the time the field hit the backstretch, after a quarter in :23 and a half in :46 4/5, Canonero had dropped back to eighteenth and was still about twenty lengths off the pace. Bold and Able shook off the three longshots and opened a two-length lead as the horses headed down the backstretch. His stablemate, Eastern Fleet, began to move closer along the inside as the field bunched up a bit. Avila steered Canonero to the outside to give him a clear run, but he was still back near the rear of the pack.

Bold and Able, still leading by a length and a half, hit the far turn in a solid 1:11 3/5 for the six furlongs. Eastern Fleet moved strongly into second, with the favorite, Unconscious, a couple of lengths back in fifth. Jim French, who had been in mid-pack throughout, maintained his position and was about to launch his bid. Canonero had inched closer but still was in fifteenth, with eighteen lengths to make up and only a half-mile in which to do it.

Around the far turn Eastern Fleet charged up inside Bold and Able, and the two Calumet colts battled head and head, while opening a clear lead on their closest pursuers. It looked like a flashback to the Calumet glory days when the famed devil's red-and-blue silks dominated Thoroughbred racing. Unconscious and Jim French were getting in gear, but then all eyes caught sight of a brown blur streaking past horses as if it were moving in a faster time frame than the others.

"Who is that?" everyone in attendance and watching on television asked. Even as the mysterious figure came hurtling out of the turn and engulfed the two Calumet colts, no one had a clue who it was except Arias and his Venezuelan entourage, who already were jumping up and down and screaming "Canonero! Canonero!"

Canonero charged by the Calumet duo as if they had run into a brick wall. With Avila just hand-riding him, he quickly drew clear, while still racing on his left lead. He opened a three-length lead at the eighth pole and continued to pour it on. Jim French finally found his best stride and clear sailing and came with a strong late run, but Canonero was long gone. He crossed the wire three and three-quarters lengths in front, still on his wrong lead. As soon as he crossed the finish line, most everyone simultaneously scrolled down the names of the horses in their program to see who had won the Kentucky Derby. Even after they had matched up the number fifteen horse with the name, many still had no idea who it was.

Up in the press box even the majority of reporters didn't know who had won. When Chick Lang heard who it was, the name didn't ring a bell. After the horses had pulled up and the winner came jogging back, it finally hit him "like a bolt of lightning."

The horse whose name he had scribbled down on the back of a cocktail napkin and almost tossed in the garbage had just won the Kentucky Derby. "Jesus Christ!" he shouted. "It's the mystery horse. I can't believe it. This is like a fairy tale."

Reporters in the press box could not believe it either. It was the horse they had been mocking for the past week. Quasimodo had turned into Prince Charming right before their eyes.

Arias burst into tears and dashed onto the track where he hugged Quintero and just about everyone else who spoke Spanish. But the indignities were not over. When he tried to go into the winner's circle, the security guards wouldn't let him in. It was a repeat of the scene that had played out at the stable gate entrance a week earlier. Fortunately, one of his fellow countrymen who spoke English explained who Arias was and the Derby-winning trainer was allowed in.

Meanwhile, back in Caracas, Pedro Baptista had no idea what had happened. When a friend called ten minutes after the race and shouted into the phone that Baptista had just won the Kentucky Derby, the owner thought it was a joke and hung up. But the friend called back and swore he was telling the truth. Then, when the phone began ringing non-stop, Baptista, like Arias, broke into tears. He told his father the news and the two of them had a good cry. They then drove to the cemetery, where they prayed over the grave of Baptista's mother, who had paid him that fateful visit in his dreams.

That night Baptista threw a party for some two hundred guests. After twenty hours of revelry and drinking vino punche — a mixture of lemon, bitters, and "mucho" whiskey — Baptista told his guests the party would continue until Tuesday when Avila returned.

By then Caracas was in full celebration, with people singing and dancing throughout the city. When Avila returned, he was carried through the streets of Caracas. He also received a telegram from the president of Venezuela, which read in part: "This great victory will stimulate Venezuela's progress in all its efforts ..."

For Arias there wasn't much time for celebration. He and Quintero had to pack up and head to Baltimore for the Preakness. They had won the Derby, and now it was time to start thinking about a sweep of the Triple Crown, a feat that hadn't been accomplished in twenty-three years.

Arias said the one thing that gave him satisfaction following the Derby was running into the owner who had given him the mock toast before the race. When Arias saw him, the trainer raised his hand as if proposing a toast, and said, "Mucha suerte."

Perhaps the headline that best described the Derby appeared in *Sports Illustrated*. It read: "Missing Data Unavailable," referring not only to the comment in the *Daily Racing Form* past performances, but also to the mystery and confusion surrounding this curious invader from South America.

When Arias and Canonero arrived at Pimlico, more problems awaited them. Shortly after arriving, Canonero refused to eat. All communication between Arias and veterinarian Ralph Yergey was conducted through an interpreter, and it was debatable whether he actually was interpreting anything Arias and Yergey were saying. Canonero was developing a case of thrush, a foot infection usually caused by a horse standing in his own urine, an ordeal that Canonero was subjected to while in quarantine. The morning after the Derby, Chick Lang went to visit the colt and observed the same conditions.

Not only did Canonero have foot problems, but he also was cutting his tongue on a loose baby tooth, and he had contracted a low-grade fever. Six days before the race his medication was switched from pen-strep, a standard antibiotic mixture, to ampicillin because the lidocaine in the pen-strep would have showed up in the urine.

Despite Canonero's victory in the Derby, very few people were convinced the race wasn't a fluke. The final time was a slow 2:03 1/5, and Canonero's running style of coming from twenty lengths back was not suitable to the Preakness, which was run at a shorter distance and over a speed-favoring track with tighter turns. Eastern Fleet looked to be the perfect Preakness-type horse, and many of the "experts" seemed to favor him over Canonero.

Disdain for the Derby winner grew after Canonero worked a snail-like five furlongs in 1:06. One trainer commented afterward, "That was about a fifth of a second faster than might have been expected of a plow horse." Another said, "If I had that horse and he worked that slow, I'd put him on the first slow boat to South America."

Arias, however, was thrilled with the work. "Perfecto!" he said. "He's ready for Saturday." He later told the *Baltimore Sun*, "They laughed at us in Louisville, and they are laughing at us in Baltimore. But it is we who will be laughing at the whole racing world!"

What people didn't realize was that there was more to Canonero than what appeared on the surface. When a Baltimore radiologist, Dr. George Burke, took an electrocardiogram of the horse, he discovered the animal's heartbeat was only thirty beats per minute, which was five fewer than the average horse. "Fantastic; that's about as low as a horse will go," Burke said. A low heartbeat signifies exceptional stamina.

Canonero and Jim French were made co-favorites at 3-1, with Eastern Fleet the main danger to steal the race, getting bet down to 6-1. This time Baptista came for the race. What happened next was in some ways even more remarkable than what was witnessed on the first Saturday in May. Eastern Fleet, as expected, shot to the lead, but to everyone's shock, here was Canonero bursting out of the gate from post position nine and taking up the chase.

Canonero collared the Calumet runner as they turned up the back-stretch, and the pair were at each other's throat every step of the way down the backstretch and around the far turn. After a half in :47, they sizzled the next quarter in :23 2/5, while opening up five lengths on the rest of the field. The farther they went, the more they opened up.

With three-quarters run in a demanding 1:10 2/5, and the mile in

1:35, someone had to crack, and it was Eastern Fleet. Canonero, despite having run six furlongs four and two-fifth seconds (or twenty-two lengths) faster than he had in the Derby, showed no signs of tiring. He drew clear of Eastern Fleet inside the eighth pole and, again on his wrong lead, crossed the wire a length and a half in front, with Eastern Fleet four and a half lengths ahead of Jim French. The horse that people laughed at as being as slow as a "plow horse" had just run the mile and three-sixteenths in 1:54, breaking Nashua's track record by three-fifths of a second.

Back in Venezuela five million people watched the race on television, and again the country erupted in celebration. Baptista headed to the winner's circle pumping his fist, then pointing it up to the sky, shouting, "Belmont! Belmont! Belmont!"

When asked how he felt, Baptista said, "We have come up here — two Indians (he and Avila) and a black man (Arias) with a horse that nobody believed in, and we're destroying two hundred years of American racing tradition, dominated by the cream of your society. This is a monumental event for international relations. You can't imagine the impact this has had in Venezuela. Canonero is truly a horse of the people."

Arias was asked how he got Canonero to run so fast off such a slow work. All he said in response was, "They could not hold back destiny."

Before vanning to Belmont for the final leg of his amazing journey, "The Caracas Cannonball," as Canonero was being hailed, was honored at Pimlico between the fourth and fifth races. He was led onto the track to the playing of the Venezuelan national anthem, with the applause building as he approached the finish line. In the winner's circle Maryland Governor Marvin Mandel signed a document proclaiming the six members of the Canonero team honorary citizens of Maryland.

When Canonero arrived at Belmont Park, a circus had replaced the freak show of Churchill Downs. Between veterinarians and advisers for Baptista all trying to run the show, Arias also had to deal with new physical problems that were plaguing Canonero, as well as some of the old ones. The colt still was suffering from thrush, and now his right hock was swollen. He had burned his heels while galloping at Belmont, and he came down with a severe skin disease that covered a good portion of his body.

Security was posted at his barn twenty-four hours a day. He even appeared on the *Today Show* when former Major League Baseball player and author Joe Garagiola came out to the barn to "interview" him. Canonero was brought out, and Garagiola stuck a microphone in his face and began asking him questions, such as "Where'd you get that haircut?"

Canonero's physical problems forced him to miss a couple of days of training. Like at Churchill and Pimlico, the jokes started up. There was no way a horse in this condition could win the Belmont. "They still think we're a bunch of crazy Indians," Arias said.

But deep down Arias knew Canonero would not be at his best. Veterinarian William O. Reed examined the Triple Crown hopeful and told Arias the colt was only 75 percent ready to go a mile and a half. Even *Sports Illustrated* tried to convince Arias and Baptista not to run. An editorial that appeared in the magazine a week before the Belmont read: "Perhaps sometime before the Belmont this Saturday, Canonero's handlers will forego false national pride and scratch the horse. We hope so. He is in bad shape and has been for a week."

Arias knew in his heart Canonero probably shouldn't run, but there was too much at stake, and the trainer still believed his horse could win the race. After all, this was a horse of destiny. All of Venezuela had gone mad over the colt, and throughout the country came the cries of "Viva Canonero!"

Plans were in the works to erect a statue of Canonero at La Rinconada. Songs about Canonero were being played on the radio. At one civil registry office in Venezuela, a couple submitted the name Canonero Segundo (Canonero the second) for their newborn son. At Belmont a film was being made called *The Ballad of Canonero*, featuring a song of the same name. It was later shown on television and was named best sports film of the year by the Fifteenth Annual International Film and TV Festival of New York. It was too late to turn back now.

A group of about two thousand Venezuelans made the trip for the Belmont, many wearing T-shirts reading, "Viva Canonero!" and "Viva Venezuela!" New York's Puerto Rican community adopted Canonero, and Puerto Ricans and other Hispanics poured into the track by the thousands. The official crowd was listed at 82,694, destroying the previous record of 67,961. The new mark would stand for twenty-eight years.

Hours before the race, radio broadcasters in Venezuela asked the people to honk their car horns and churches to peal their bells at the precise same moment. Right before the race the city of Caracas was like a ghost town, with its citizens glued to their televisions.

Canonero's many maladies proved much stronger than destiny. The colt went to the front and ran as far and as fast as his battle-weary legs and body could take him. He tried gallantly but could finish no better than fourth, beaten only four and a half lengths by longshot Pass Catcher. Even as the Derby/Preakness winner began to fade turning for home, cries of "Canonero" still resounded from the huge grandstand. Jim French and Bold Reason, two colts Canonero had already manhandled, finished second and third, respectively.

The morning after the race Dr. Reed examined Canonero and said the gallant warrior still was showing signs of extreme fatigue. Baptista looked at the defeat philosophically and told those close to the horse not to hold their heads down. "Be cheerful," he said. "We have become rich and famous, the horse is all right, and the future is ahead of us."

Baptista had turned down several lucrative offers for Canonero but felt the time was now right to sell. Shortly after the Belmont he sold Canonero to Robert Kleberg, owner of King Ranch, for $1.5 million.

Canonero did not run again until the following May, losing his first six races. It was obvious he no longer was the same horse. His best effort was a second in the Carter Handicap in his first race back.

His new trainer, William J. "Buddy" Hirsch, tried blinkers, but that didn't help. As a last resort he summoned Canonero's old jockey, Gustavo Avila, to come up from Venezuela to ride Canonero in a mile and one-sixteenth allowance race at Belmont. Canonero showed some of his old spark, dashing to the lead and setting sizzling fractions of :45 2/5 and 1:09 1/5 before tiring to finish fifth. With the sleeping giant now showing signs of awakening, Hirsch and Avila agreed that a return to blinkers would help his concentration.

Hirsch entered Canonero in the mile and one-eighth Stymie Handicap at Belmont on September 20, 1972, with Avila back aboard. His main opponent was that year's Kentucky Derby and Belmont winner Riva Ridge, who was being asked to concede thirteen pounds to Canonero. Around the far turn Canonero collared Riva Ridge and the two Kentucky Derby winners battled head and head all the way to eighth pole. It was the Preakness Stakes all over again. Canonero, as he had done to Eastern Fleet, ran Riva Ridge into the ground and drew off to a five-length victory. His time of 1:46 1/5 broke the track record by three-fifths of a second and equaled the American record.

There was still greatness in Canonero, and he proved in the Stymie that his spectacular victories in the Derby and Preakness were no fluke. But the Stymie was to be his final hurrah. Still plagued by physical problems, he finished second in an allowance race in the mud and was retired to Gainesway Farm in Lexington, Kentucky.

Baptista managed to straighten out his business but died in 1984 at age fifty-seven. Juan Arias, despite his success with Canonero, never was able to build up his stable, and his career plummeted to the point where he barely was able to eke out a living training one or two horses. Married with two children, he was forced to retire from training and take a government job, working as a technician for Consejo Nacional

Electoral. But the horses were still in his blood, and on weekends he'd go to La Rinconada to visit with friends and occasionally work with the horses just to be around them, as he had as a kid.

Gustavo Avila continued to ride successfully for several years, winning numerous stakes, including the first Clasico del Caribe in Puerto Rico aboard a Venezuelan horse named Victoreado. He also rode regularly for a while in the United States. After retiring, he became involved with real estate investment, then was hired as a steward at La Rinconada. Several years later, in 2002, Arias also became a steward at La Rinconada, and he and Avila are now back together again.

Arias, now sixty-seven, said his eyes still tear up whenever he thinks back on Canonero's magical journey. "Canonero should be remembered as a great racehorse," he said recently. "He was a giant in the United States, even though no one believed in him. When we arrived in Kentucky, there were nothing but jokes. But Canonero had such a big heart. He was a battler and he loved competition."

Canonero never made it as a stallion and was sent back to Venezuela in February 1981 to stand at Haras Tamanaco. The only stakes horse he sired there was El Tejano, who finished second in the group II Premio Burlesco, with none other than Gustavo Avila aboard.

"I'm saddened that Canonero was not a successful sire," Arias said. "He never really had the opportunity. Many of his foals were raised at King Ranch in Texas, and that wasn't the best place to raise a young horse. And the quality of mares he was bred to was not appropriate for a horse they expected so much from."

On November 11, 1981, Canonero was found dead in his stall, the victim of an apparent heart attack. By then the magnificent decade of the seventies was history, with Secretariat, Forego, Seattle Slew, Affirmed, Alydar, and Spectacular Bid all stamping their place in the record books. But few remembered that it was Canonero who paved the way for these media stars and the resurgence of the sport.

Kentucky Derby
Purse: $125,000 Added

9th Race Churchill Downs - May 1, 1971. Ninety-seventh running Kentucky Derby.
Purse $125,000 added. Three-year-olds. 1 1-4 Miles. Main Track. Track: Fast.
Value of race $188,000. Net value to winner, $145,500 and gold trophy; second, $25,000; third, $12,500; fourth, $5,000.

Horse	A	Wgt	Eqp	Odds	PP	1/4	1/2	3/4	1	Str	Fin	Jockey
Canonero II	3	126		f-8.70	12	16^1	18^5	15^3	4^x	1^3	$1^{3¾}$	G Avila
Jim French	3	126	b	4.80	10	10^h	11^2	10^2	7^2	5^x	2^2	A Cordero Jr
Bold Reason	3	126	b	18.30	14	18^6	16^x	12^2	9^2	6^2	3^{nk}	J Cruguet
Eastern Fleet	3	126	b	a-3.80	17	6^2	3^h	2^{1x}	2^{1x}	2^h	4^h	E Maple
Unconscious	3	126		2.80	8	7^2	6^2	5^1	5^h	4^x	5^{1x}	L Pincay Jr
Vegas Vic	3	126	b	19.30	7	13^3	13^3	13^1	13^x	7^1	6^{nk}	H Grant
Tribal Line	3	126	b	80.80	15	15^2	14^h	17^6	8^{1x}	8^2	7no	D E Whited
Bold and Able	3	126	b	a-3.80	1	1^h	1^2	1^{1x}	1^h	3^h	8^3	J Velasquez
List	3	126	b	8.60	18	17^h	17^x	14^2	14^{1x}	9^2	9^3	J Nichols
Twist the Axe	3	126		c-5.10	11	9^x	10^1	7^1	6^{1x}	10^2	10^{1x}	G Patterson
Going Straight	3	126		45.60	2	11^2	8^h	6^h	10^3	12^2	11^h	O Torres
Royal Leverage	3	126		b-41.60	5	19^8	15^2	16^1	18^5	11^h	12^2	M Fromin
Impetuosity	3	126		c-5.10	20	8^{1x}	9^2	8^2	15^1	13^h	13^{1x}	E Guerin
Helio Rise	3	126		58.20	16	12^x	12^1	9^h	11^1	14^1	14^3	K Knapp
On the Money	3	126		b-41.60	9	20	20	20	17^x	15^{1x}	15^1	M Solomon
Barbizon Streak	3	126		f-8.70	6	2^h	5^1	11^1	12^1	16^6	16^{18}	D Brumfield
Knight Counter	3	126	b	f-8.70	13	4^2	4^{1x}	3^1	3^1	17^6	17^{11}	M Manganello
Jr's Arrowhead	3	126	b	f-8.70	4	3^h	2^1	4^1	16^{1x}	18^2	18^6	A Rini
Fourulla	3	126		f-8.70	19	5^h	7^x	18^3	19^4	19^4	19^{14}	D MacBeth
Saigon Warrior	3	127		f-8.70	3	14^3	19^9	19^8	20	20	20	R Parrott

f- Mutuel field.
a-Coupled, Eastern Fleet and Bold and Able; b-Royal Leverage and On the Money; c-Twist the Axe and Impetuosity.

Off Time: 5:43   **Time Of Race:** :23   :46½   1:11¾   1:36½   2:03¼
Start: Good For All   **Track:** Fast
Equipment: b for blinkers

Mutuel Payoffs

15f	Canonero II	$19.40	$8.00	$4.20
7	Jim French		6.20	4.40
8	Bold Reason			12.60

Winner: Canonero II, b. c. by Pretendre—Dixieland II, by Nantallah (Trained by J. Arias).
    Bred by E. B. Benjamin in Kentucky.

Start good. Won ridden out.
CANONERO II, void of speed and unhurried for three-quarters, was forced to come to the extreme outside to launch his bid upon leaving the backstretch, continued to circle his field entering the stretch to take command with a bold rush in the upper stretch and was under intermittent urging to prevail. JIM FRENCH, allowed to settle in stride, moved up along the inside when launching his bid on the second turn, was forced to come out between horses entering the stretch, commenced lugging in to brush with BARBIZON STREAK, continued gamely to move through close quarters in midstretch, but could not reach the winner. JIM FRENCH came back with a cut on the coronet band of his right rear foot. BOLD REASON, badly outrun for six furlongs, moved between horses until forced to steady when blocked in the upper stretch, dropped to the inside when clear and finished with good courage. EASTERN FLEET, away to gain a forward position along the inside, moved through in slightly close quarters leaving the backstretch, moved to the fore between calls in the upper stretch, commenced drifting out in the closing drive and gave way willingly. UNCONSCIOUS, never far back while along the inner railing, continued to save ground while moving into serious contention on the final turn, came out for the drive and had little left when the real test came. BOLD AND ABLE was sent to the fore at once, bore out entering the first turn, came back to the inside when clear to make the pace to the top of the stretch, at which point he dropped back steadily. LIST failed to enter contention while closing some ground in the late stages. TWIST THE AXE, in hand early, moved up along the outside after three-quarters to loom boldly on the final turn but could not sustain his bid. IMPETUOSITY, breaking smartly from his outside positioon, continued slightly wide to midway down the backstretch where he was dropped in to move up between horses, was forced to check sharply when JR'S ARROWHEAD dropped over at the half-mile ground, losing his action, and failed to recover when clear. BARBIZON STREAK, away in good order, was caught in close quarters entering the first turn, continued slightly wide and commenced dropping back after five furlongs. KNIGHT COUNTER was bumped and forced out entering the first turn. JR'S ARROWHEAD came away alertly to gain a striking position along the outside, commenced lugging in at the half-mile ground and dropped back steadily. FOURULLA bore out badly entering the first turn.
Overweight—Saigon, 1 pound. Scratched—Sole Mio.

Owners: (1) E Caibett; (2) F J Caldwell; (3) W A Levin; (4) Calumet Farm; (5) A A Seeligson Jr; (6) Betty Sechrest-C Fritz; (7) J E-T A Grissom; (8) Calumet Farm; (9) Mrs J W Brown; (10) Pastorale Stable; (11) Donamire Farm; (12) P Teinowitz; (13) W P Rosso; (14) R W-R T Wilson Jr; (15) Teinowitz-Schmidt; (16) Mrs H J Udouj; (17) R Huffman; (18) Walnut Hill Farm; (19) A H Sullivan; (20) C M Day
©EQUIBASE

By the time of his death, the cries of "Viva Canonero" had faded to a mere whisper, and the horse who had electrified the racing world like no other before him had slipped quietly back into the obscurity from which he had come.

But those who were there to witness the frenzy of that unforgettable spring will never forget Canonero. *Washington Post* columnist and handicapper Andrew Beyer wrote: "Even in a decade that was to produce such horses as Secretariat, Affirmed, and Spectacular Bid, there was no Triple Crown series that evoked such passions as that of 1971."

Canonero's Derby and Preakness trophies were given to La Rinconada, but they are not even exhibited anywhere. As the years pass by and new generations of racing fans emerge, the name of Canonero drifts deeper into memory, as do his amazing feats. The legendary sportswriter Red Smith wrote that the ninety-seventh Kentucky Derby "was won by a colt in a plain brown wrapper." In many ways he was correct, but the truth is, there was never anything plain about Canonero II.

By Steve Haskin

(Reprinted from The 10 Best Kentucky Derbies, *© 2005 Eclipse Press)*

Risk and Reward

ONE OF THE MOST COMPELLING mysteries of life is how the truly exceptional can suddenly appear among the commonplace, inspiring and transforming the world.

The yearning of the human psyche to experience such uplifting examples, even if only momentary, is one of the reasons that the sport of horse racing — and the Kentucky Derby in particular — can so stir the soul. For two minutes the ordinary becomes extraordinary, sometimes enduring in the memory far beyond the fleeting shadows of the first Saturday of May.

Such was the case in 1980, when, at the peak of the women's liberation movement, a bright chestnut filly with a bold stripe splashed down her face defied history, colts, and the racing pundits who gave her little chance.

Genuine Risk accomplished what had not been done in sixty-five years, becoming after 1915 winner Regret only the second filly to be blanketed with the Derby roses. Only one since then, Winning Colors, has matched the feat, leaving three filly winners in 132 runnings of the Derby through 2006.

But even as remarkable as that statistic is, the story of Genuine Risk stands alone, unlike any other saga in the annals of racing.

Produced from a mare purchased as a birthday gift; selected at auction by a fourteen-year-old boy; trained by a wily Racing Hall of Famer, who initially didn't want the filly he fondly compared to a glamorous actress roughhousing with the Derby colts; and retired with fanfare to the broodmare ranks only to encounter great difficulty producing foals, eliciting a national outpouring of concerned affection, Genuine Risk's life is truly the stuff of legends.

Even in her advanced years, she remains a monarch, reigning as the oldest living American classic winner. At the end of 2006, she was still receiving visitors at Newstead Farm in Upperville, Virginia, where owners Bert and Diana Firestone watch over her in a paddock lying between their house and the farm office. She is more to them than their Derby winner; indeed, she has become a cherished member of the family and even served as a trustworthy mount from whose back a rider could easily open and shut gates while pleasurably strolling from field to field.

Still eager for peppermints as she awaited her thirtieth birthday, Genuine Risk is a long way from the yawning stretch of Churchill Downs, which echoed with the screams of women who cheered her victory at odds of 13-1 as a symbol of their own burgeoning aspirations in life.

Always known for her kind nature, she has shared her twilight years with young females returning home from the racetrack and, in the autumn, each year's crop of weanling fillies. They follow her like goslings in the wake of the mother goose, and in the green tranquility of the pasture, it is easy to imagine the vivid tales from her exceptional existence that she could impart if only she possessed words.

When Genuine Risk was born in 1977, she was one of 30,036 foals in the North American Thoroughbred crop. Counting all the foals born since Regret, it is no exaggeration to say that she was one in more than half a million, but numbers can't begin to describe the phenomenon that she became.

****

Like some fictional miracle, the story of Genuine Risk began with a wish.

Sally Schriber Humphrey was turning thirty in 1975 and wanted a special gift. She asked her husband, owner and breeder G. Watts Humphrey Jr., for her own broodmare to celebrate the occasion.

The grandson of breeder George M. Humphrey, who had operated Whileaway Farm in Lexington, Kentucky, and the great-nephew of Mrs. Parker Poe, from whom he inherited Shawnee Farm near Harrodsburg, Watts Humphrey agreed — as long as his wife picked out the mare herself.

Setting aside $30,000 for the present, Humphrey urged her to comb through the Keeneland November breeding stock sale catalog and inspect the prospects she pinpointed. Sally Humphrey managed to narrow her search to only one, a four-year-old chestnut daughter of Gallant Man named Virtuous, a multiple winner who had placed in a stakes in France.

Fortune smiled on Sally Humphrey, and with her husband doing the bidding and extending his generosity by another $1,500, they were able to acquire Virtuous, who was expecting her first foal on a cover by Belmont Stakes winner Stage Door Johnny. For her next breeding, they chose the young stallion Exclusive Native, who would become best known as the sire of 1978 Triple Crown winner Affirmed.

Virtuous gave lucky Sally Humphrey a special Valentine's present in 1977, foaling a big chestnut filly with a blaze on February 15. The filly grew and prospered and, as planned, was offered for sale as a yearling.

As there was nothing unequivocally smashing on the filly's catalog page at the 1978 Fasig-Tipton Kentucky July yearling sale, she had to sell herself. Out of all the horsemen inspecting the yearlings, she caught the eye of fourteen-year-old Matthew Firestone, one of seven children in the merged family of serious equestrians and owner-breeders Bert and Diana Firestone. Matthew already had been riding for years, knew how to decipher the *Daily Racing Form* as well as pedigrees, and enthusiastically participated in purchase decisions.

He urged his parents to consider the filly, even though she wasn't on their list. They took a look and decided to bid to $40,000. When the hammer fell at $32,000, they owned a new racing prospect.

The Firestones aimed high in the sport, and one of their targets was the Kentucky Derby. Their Honest Pleasure, a $45,000 yearling purchase, had finished second as the odds-on favorite to Bold Forbes in 1976 and homebred General Assembly would become the Derby runner-up to sensational Spectacular Bid and later win the Travers Stakes in 1979.

Years after the Fasig-Tipton sale Bert Firestone would recall that the unthinkable flickered through his head immediately after the purchase. What if this filly, whose second dam was a half sister to 1959 Kentucky Derby winner Tomy Lee, could be the horse for which they had been searching, the one that could garner the roses?

John "Buck" Moore, manager of the Firestones' farm, which at the time was Cactoctin Stud near Waterford, Virginia, had no such flights of fancy. "I had no clue," he said of the filly's potential when he and his assistants began to school her under bridle and saddle. But he did know that despite her generally gentle demeanor, she had a fire inside that matched her glowing coat.

"She had her own thoughts about doing things," recalled Moore. "She wasn't the type who would lay down and roll over. She always had to fight, but not to the point she was mean. If you treated her easily, she would go on and do what you wanted to do.

"She was opinionated, and I knew for fillies that was a good sign. But she didn't show anything special other than her attitude."

One of the farm workers recounted to *Centaur* magazine that the filly, whom the Firestones named Genuine Risk to match their outlook on the sport of racing, lulled riders because she usually was so quiet. Then, the first time she was ridden, she "let out a buck that sent me sailing, threw me against a wall, gave me a bloody nose."

When she was shipped to LeRoy Jolley, the son of trainer Moody Jolley and an astute, old-school horseman who had been working at racetracks since he began walking hots for his father at age seven, Genuine Risk again did not immediately telegraph her brilliance.

"She was a nice, big filly, but at the time we had a lot of nice two-year-olds and she was just one of the bunch," Jolley remembered. She did, however, gain a reputation for running off with exercise riders every now and then and throwing an occasional temper tantrum.

When Genuine Risk breezed five furlongs in company with another Firestone filly, Cybele, in less than 1:00, Jolley knew she could be above average. But because New York was beset with unusually wet weather during the summer of 1979, he trained her sparingly, letting her develop without too much pressure.

On September 30, she made her debut at Belmont Park a winning one, taking a six and a half-furlong maiden race on a sloppy track after rating fourth early under cagey veteran Jacinto Vasquez in the field of eleven.

Eighteen days later Genuine Risk was 3-5 to win again, and she did, running off by seven and a quarter lengths in a one-mile allowance event at Aqueduct. Another eighteen days passed and she was back again, this time cruising home at 4-5 after taking an early lead to record her first stakes victory in Aqueduct's one-mile Tempted Stakes.

By then, both Vasquez and Jolley had sensed the filly's exceptional promise. The outspoken jockey, best known as the regular rider of the sensational, ill-fated champion filly Ruffian, hopped off Genuine Risk after the Tempted and delivered a prophecy.

"I told LeRoy Jolley, 'If you don't screw her up, she can win the

Kentucky Derby next year,'" Vasquez said. "He thought I was crazy."

But at the time, Jolley spoke with his own deep admiration for his charge and revealed his own ability to gaze into the future. "She's a quick study," he told Joe Hirsch of the *Daily Racing Form* before Genuine Risk was to make her final start of the year, against division leader Smart Angle in the Demoiselle Stakes. "She picks things up very quickly, is a better filly with every race she runs. She's a bit leggy, but she's very rugged. Her disposition is perfect. She's quiet and refined and will rate off the pace. I think that the further they go, the better she will like it."

Displaying what would become her trademark iron tenacity, Genuine Risk battled Smart Angle down much of the Aqueduct stretch and prevailed by a nose in the Demoiselle's one and one-eighth miles. Although Smart Angle was given the championship, Genuine Risk was undefeated — and on her way to bigger things. First, however, she got to romp and play and grow some more during a winter vacation at Catoctin.

****

As the new year began to unfold, America was in transition. A weakened economy during the Jimmy Carter administration had set the stage for the election of Ronald Reagan, who would change the world by ending the Cold War. Women were widely demanding equal pay for equal work.

When Genuine Risk was sent back to Jolley in late January, he said he planned to take his time with her. The important goals were the Kentucky Oaks and the Filly Triple Crown Series in New York; there was no talk from him about the Kentucky Derby.

But quietly the Firestones began to stoke the fire of their Derby dreams again. Two seconds in the previous four years had only further whetted their appetite for roses, and they kept their eyes on how the young three-year-olds were developing to assess their chances.

Returning to the races in March at Gulfstream Park, Genuine Risk galloped home easily in a seven-furlong allowance as the 2-5 favorite, stopping the clock in a sprightly 1:22 3/5. Seventeen days later she took an early lead and won a one-mile handicap against fillies at 1-5.

Now was the time to see how good this filly could be, and such a test was not likely to come against her own gender. After two strong works at Belmont Park, six furlongs in 1:13 2/5 on April 12 and a half-mile in :47 3/5 on April 17, Genuine Risk was led to the starting gate in the Wood Memorial Stakes on April 19, a key prep for the Derby that also had drawn eleven males.

Despite her unbeaten record, she was dismissed by fans unaccustomed to seeing fillies race against classic-bound colts and went off at more than 8-1. Even other trainers scoffed. Tom Kelly, who had been kicked in the hip by odds-on favorite Plugged Nickle before the race, summed up the widespread sentiment: "She's a very nice filly, but the boys are stronger."

Plugged Nickle was viewed as a leader of his generation on the East Coast after winning four of seven starts as a juvenile, including the Laurel Futurity at Pimlico Race Course and the Remsen Stakes at Aqueduct. Following a runner-up effort in a Hialeah Park allowance race to begin his sophomore season, the son of Key to the Mint had notched the Hutcheson Stakes and Florida Derby in succession at Gulfstream Park prior to returning to New York for the Wood.

Kelly also saddled Colonel Moran in the Wood. The son of Sham was a promising contender with four stakes wins already under his girth in the young 1980 season, including the Bay Shore and Gotham, prep races leading to the Wood. Thus, this was no easy bunch for the filly to chase.

Breaking alertly under Vasquez, Genuine Risk pressed the pace from third behind Plugged Nickle and Colonel Moran, whom Jolley likened to "friendly enemies" as they, although campaigned by different owners, were from the same barn. But there ended up being little drama in this race — the trio went around the whole one and one-eighth miles in that order over a tiring surface.

Vasquez claimed foul after Plugged Nickle drifted in front of Genuine Risk in the stretch drive, but it was disallowed. And just like that, the dreams seemed to vanish in the one and three-quarters length margin of her defeat.

Seeing Genuine Risk heaving with weariness as she was being un-saddled despite the race being completed in the relatively slow time of 1:50 4/5, Jolley told a national television audience there would be no Kentucky Derby for the filly.

Two days later, however, Bert Firestone contradicted the trainer he had employed for a decade, confirming there was "a 90 percent chance" that he and Diana (in whose name Genuine Risk raced, along with the couple's other fillies) would send her out to make history on the first Saturday in May.

The media went wild with speculation. Was this the end of the Fires-tone–Jolley team? Why would they want to run her against colts in the biggest race of the year when she had not been successful in the Wood? Was it just a ruse before switching her to the Kentucky Oaks, where she "belonged"?

Headline writers had some fun with the trainer's last name and his reputation among the scribes of the Turf as a bit difficult to deal with; the Louisville *Courier-Journal*, for instance, blared: "A Genuine Risk—Decision to run filly in Derby may not be a Jolley good idea."

It was all blown out of proportion, however, Jolley said in 2006. Re-calling his concern for the special filly who had lost her unbeaten status in the Wood and seemed drained by the experience, he said he was voicing emotion more than anything else immediately after the race when indicating that the Derby would be nixed.

"We live with the horses every day," he noted of his attachment to Genuine Risk. "And it wasn't like she was your average everyday horse, or we wouldn't have run her in the Wood. She was beaten for the first time, and there was disappointment. She came back, and as she was being unsaddled, she looked pretty fatigued. My first thought was maybe [running against males] was too much to ask."

Jolley and the Firestones agreed to evaluate the possibilities further when Genuine Risk returned to the track after she had the chance to regain her strength.

"They flew up from Virginia [to Belmont] and Jacinto Vasquez got back on her. She had recovered so much that she had one of her tough days and ran off with him," Jolley recalled with a chuckle.

"She was a tough filly to gallop and to handle," Vasquez said. "If you fought her, she tried to get out — and she was very strong. You had to use finesse; you just had to know how to handle her."

With Vasquez, Jolley, and the Firestones all convinced the filly had bounced back well, the decision was made. They would go to the Kentucky Derby and try to rewrite the record books. An indication of the enormity of the challenge they were throwing at her was that no owner had even attempted the Derby with a filly since Silver Spoon had finished fifth in 1959.

****

Speculation, emotion, and opinions flow freely on the backstretch of Churchill Downs during any Derby week, and 1980 was no exception. Although peppered with questions about whether he really wanted to run Genuine Risk, Jolley patiently extolled her virtues.

"I don't think giving up is in her book," he declared.

Twenty-six years later the filly's attributes remain indelible in his mind. "If she had an outstanding characteristic, she was very determined. She gave everything she had," he recalled.

Derby week also is naturally shrouded with the unknown: Who will be able to stay the mile and a quarter? Who is coming up to the race in the best form? How will the strategies unfold?

That year a dense fog swooped in and blanketed Churchill Downs on the Wednesday before the race, disrupting workouts for several of the leading contenders and fomenting even more questions and mystery.

The breathless discussion even included a story in the *New York Times* reporting that Genuine Risk had been in season during the week, a sometimes ominous sign.

Rockhill Native, the little gelding who had been 1979 champion juvenile male and who was coming off a win in the Blue Grass Stakes at Keeneland, went out to drill five furlongs but went no faster than a pedestrian 1:04 2/5 over a muddy and choppy surface that had not been harrowed due to the dense fog. Before the iffy workout, trainer Herb Stevens had maintained that Rockhill Native "couldn't be coming up to this race any better" and was still a "fresh horse."

In contrast, Genuine Risk also went out in the fog and emerged with a time of 1:02 2/5 for the same distance, which, considering the circumstances, proved to be better than it otherwise might have initially appeared. When the past performances were published for the Derby, there was a bullet beside the time, indicating the fastest move of the day over the distance.

Vasquez was thrilled after jumping out of the saddle. With some backstretch gossip centering on Rumbo, the stretch-running California invader referred to in some press accounts as "Dumbo" due to his propensity to spook and otherwise act up, the jockey remembers saying, "If he is the horse to beat, then I'm a cinch in this race."

Plugged Nickle, who would go on to be champion sprinter of 1980, worked a mile in 1:41 3/5, and Kelly proclaimed the colt "dead fit."

Actor Jack Klugman, famous for his role as Oscar in *The Odd Couple* and star of the television drama *Quincy, M.E.* at the time, injected some extra excitement by appearing at the track with the California Derby winner he owned in partnership, Jaklin Klugman.

But as the Derby neared and the hoopla reached a crescendo, Jolley liked what he was seeing from his filly — and noticed that the prospective competition, which totaled only twelve, a small group for a Derby — didn't seem to be faring as well. He also took the time to escort Genuine Risk, whom he told the media was a "Candice Bergen type," referring to the stunning blonde actress, to the paddock several times to get her used to the scenery. The Churchill paddock on Derby day could be like "the Christians and the lions," he told the Louisville *Courier-Journal*, and he didn't want his filly getting swallowed up by the melee.

"It was one of those situations where when you go to the Derby and have only one horse, while the rest of your horses are back in New York, you stay very focused on your horse, and you have the time to see the other horses, too," Jolley said. "She didn't need much training. And some of the other horses had some difficulties and problems of one kind or another. I think everybody in our group was confident she was going to run her best. Everything was going her way."

The filly prepared herself mentally in her own eccentric manner.

"She had a strange temperament in that on the days that she raced, she would go to the back of her stall and get a miserable look on her face," Jolley said. "Seventy-five percent of the time we would take her temperature because of that miserable look. And if a bird would fly by or a car drove by outside, she would just tear up her stall. Then, she would go back to the back with the miserable look on her face. She was just very intent on her racing."

Yet most of the racing experts in the media apparently didn't see all the telltale signs that Jolley did. Although pedigree analyst Leon Rasmussen boldly wrote in his *Daily Racing Form* column that Genuine Risk's bloodlines "strongly indicate she has very much of a 'Derby pedigree,' " not many others took such a stand. Of the forty-four national and local media members polled by the Lexington *Herald* before the race, only five picked Genuine Risk to win. A whopping twenty-six indicated they thought the filly would not finish in the top three.

And the fans agreed, letting her go into the starting gate for the 106th running of the Derby on the sunny afternoon of May 3 as only the sixth choice in the wagering. Rockhill Native was bet down to 2-1 with Plugged Nickle at just fractionally higher odds. Rumbo, Jaklin Klugman, and Blue Grass runner-up Super Moment all were less than 9-1, with Genuine Risk at 13-1.

Among those hobnobbing on Millionaire's Row were former President Gerald Ford and a bevy of Hollywood entertainers, including Telly Savalas, Ann-Margret, Shelley Winters, and Sissy Spacek. Singer Willie Nelson and boxer Muhammed Ali also turned up at the Downs, although the latter boasted to a reporter, "I'm bigger than the Derby."

When the bell clanged at 5:39 and the starting gate stalls sprang open, the two favorites leapt out, with Plugged Nickle a head in front after going the first quarter-mile in :24 on the fast track. Rockhill Native then took over entering the backstretch.

Meanwhile, Vasquez settled the filly in seventh through the first half, gradually easing her to the outside to prepare for a closing rally. As Rockhill Native and Plugged Nickle both tired, longshot Bold 'n Rulling took over the lead.

But there on the outside was a red blur. Vasquez had asked Genuine Risk for her run, and she streaked past the leaders like a flame burning five-wide in the middle of the track. She took command entering the stretch, evoking astonished gasps from the crowd, and Vasquez kept her mind on running with one right-handed stroke of his whip followed by six lashes with his left hand.

From farther back in the field, the gray Jaklin Klugman and the dark bay Rumbo thundered toward her, with the latter seeming to slice threateningly into Genuine Risk's lead, which was reported at two lengths at the stretch call. But Vasquez never felt in doubt, and the filly danced home, clear by a length from Rumbo, with Jaklin Klugman another length back in third.

Rockhill Native faded to fifth, and Plugged Nickle dropped back to seventh.

Ecstatic, Diana Firestone raced to the winner's circle, followed by her husband and six of their children. "I knew she had it in her," the owner declared, jubilant over the landmark triumph.

Vasquez — who in a twist of fate also had teamed with Jolley for Foolish Pleasure's 1975 Derby victory prior to choosing Ruffian for what became her last run in the fateful match race against the colt — also was exultant. "Rumbo would have had to go around the world three times to catch her," he said in 2006.

Jolley, never one to seek the limelight, got caught in the crowd of 131,859 and was then held back by overzealous security guards. He didn't make it to the winner's circle until Genuine Risk was leaving, later telling reporters that he felt like "two ships passing in the night" as he caught a glimpse of his favorite redhead.

Even now, however, he doesn't remember this remarkable Derby in terms of his own role in the history-making event.

"It was more of a thing about the horse herself than anything else," Jolley said. "She herself tried so hard — all the time — that you kind of just felt very happy for her."

In making the trophy presentation, Kentucky Governor John Y. Brown proclaimed that 1980 was "a great year for women." Feminist Gloria Steinem was reported to have cashed a ticket on the winner and *Harper's Bazaar* later named Genuine Risk one of its seven top women achievers for the year.

Another one of her admirers that day was none other than jockey Angel Cordero Jr., who had only seen the flash of her heels as he finished next to last aboard Gold Stage.

"She ran a very good race and took the sport to another level — she became a hero. And on the racetrack, we're always looking for heroes, because we don't get very many," Cordero reflected in 2006.

Yet the rider, who was enshrined in the Racing Hall of Fame in 1988, ten years before Vasquez earned the honor, would wind up playing what was widely interpreted as a villainous role in the story of Genuine Risk just two weeks after the Derby.

****

As the enormity of the filly's Derby accomplishment sank in, her effort was compared to the first sub-four-minute mile run by Roger Bannister and to the perfect World Series game by pitcher Don Larsen.

Although her time of 2:02 was nowhere close to Secretariat's 1973 record of 1:59 2/5, her final quarter-mile in :24 2/5 bespoke outstanding quality, bettering the same figures recorded by Triple Crown winners Seattle Slew (:26 1/5) and Affirmed (:25 2/5). In fact, Triple Crown winner Secretariat is the only horse to finish the Derby faster, with a final quarter in :23 1/5, in all the years since 1941 Triple Crown winner Whirlaway raced home in :24.

Breeders and journalists were abuzz with ideas about Genuine Risk's future. A *Courier-Journal* columnist wrote, in what would become a terrible irony, that she could produce at least nine lifetime foals if bred for the first time at age four. Warner Jones of Hermitage Farm estimated she was worth $2 million, which was stallion range, and suggested she could be bred to Northern Dancer, Spectacular Bid, or Seattle Slew. Her first four yearlings could sell for an average of $1.5 million, he speculated.

But the more immediate issue was: Would Genuine Risk become the first filly in forty-one years to compete in the Preakness Stakes? Yes, the Firestones and Jolley answered after they concluded she had emerged from the Derby less tired than she did from the Wood.

This time Genuine Risk received the respect she was due and was made both the morning-line and wagering favorite over the seven males that were entered to stop her bid for the Triple Crown. Jolley correctly predicted that Santa Anita and Hollywood Derby winner Codex would be the toughest competition.

He could not have known how tough, however. A blocky son of Arts and Letters, Codex seized the lead under Cordero after six furlongs, moving three-wide. But then Cordero felt his mount beginning to pull himself up. Looking around, he saw the blaze-faced Derby winner flying at him from his outside.

"I knew she would be coming," he recalled, and he gathered Codex and steered him to his right so that he could see Genuine Risk. "We both had a lot of momentum, and we went out [toward the outside rail] a lot more than we should have."

Her rally snuffed out by the aggressive herding, Genuine Risk was second to Codex by four and three-quarters lengths as he stormed across the Pimlico Race Course finish line.

Vasquez, whose claim of foul was rejected by the stewards, remembers the incident differently.

"Cordero mugged me and got away with it," he said in 2006. "He impeded me and took me to the clubhouse and left me there."

The official chart of the race states: "Cordero looked back entering the stretch, angled extremely wide, intimidating and lightly brushing Genuine Risk."

To this day, Jolley maintains that Codex should have been disqualified but believes the stewards were not bold enough for such action because no horse had ever been taken down in a classic race for interference.

"Cordero was a great rider and a very daring rider," Jolley said, "and he took a shot and got away with it. It would have been a lot better had he stayed straight, and if he beat us, so be it." Vasquez agrees, suggesting that Cordero could have been on the best horse that day and should have just kept the colt straight to prove it.

Enchanted with Genuine Risk after her Derby performance, followers of racing around the country were enraged with what happened before a record Preakness crowd of 83,455. Word spread that not only had Cordero carried her wide, but he also hit her with his whip, leaving a welt above her eye, while Codex bumped her.

"We never had any contact, and I never hit her with the whip," Cordero said in 2006.

But the furor raged at the time, and complaints and even death threats to Cordero and his family were phoned in to the track, and the jockey vividly remembers being met after the race by two agents from the FBI. They told him they had received a tip that his New York home would be bombed.

Sentiment for Genuine Risk was so strong that a Knight-Ridder report on the race carried the headline "Stewards Ended Triple Crown Try by Genuine Risk," while the Lexington *Herald* editorialized that this was "no way to run a horse race" and that "Codex's Preakness win will always be sadly tainted."

The Firestones appealed to the Maryland Racing Commission, but to no avail. Meanwhile, hate mail poured in stacks to Cordero, who was so troubled by the boiling anger that, even following his retirement in 1992 and his subsequent work as agent for jockey John Velazquez, he has never again opened letters or packages sent to him at a racetrack. Codex's trainer, D. Wayne Lukas, also received numerous vitriolic missives.

"It was a big deal, and rightly so," recalled Jolley, who stayed out of the public fray for the most part, focusing on his horse.

Three weeks after the Preakness, Jolley had Genuine Risk ready to leave another enduring hoofprint in the record books as she became the first filly to compete in all three classic races. Emotions were still feverish, and those in the Belmont Stakes crowd of 58,090 who pressed around the Belmont Park paddock cheered so loudly for the filly that she jumped and nearly pulled away from her handler. Codex and Cordero were booed both in the paddock and on the track.

Sent off as the third choice behind Codex and Rumbo, who had skipped the Preakness, Genuine Risk beat them both but could not withstand the closing kick of huge Arkansas Derby winner Temperence Hill, trailing him across the finish line in second although she had the lead by a head at the stretch call. Codex could do no better than seventh on the muddy track and never raced again, while Rumbo was fifth.

Temperence Hill, who earned male championship laurels for the generation after also winning the Travers Stakes, Jockey Club Gold Cup, and Super Derby, had not raced in either the Kentucky Derby or the Preakness. Thus, as Hirsch wrote in his *Daily Racing Form* column after the Belmont, "by any consensus you care to invoke, [Genuine Risk] is the champion three-year-old of the United States."

****

Genuine Risk enjoyed a much-deserved rest in the summer of 1980 before resuming racing against fillies, finishing second by a nose to Bold 'n Determined in the Maskette Stakes before winning the Ruffian Handicap by a nose over older Misty Gallore. Her unprecedented year was recognized with the Eclipse Award as champion three-year-old filly while the Firestones were honored with the Eclipse as outstanding owners.

At four Genuine Risk won two allowance races, but there really was nothing she could do on the track to enhance her singular record, and as she had some niggling physical problems, the Firestones elected to retire her.

Such an exceptional mare was expected to found a dynasty in the next stage of her life. But after being bred to Secretariat in a history-making event of its own that drew a bevy of onlookers, she produced a stillborn chestnut colt, and the difficult delivery apparently compromised her ability to carry a foal to term.

After a series of spontaneous abortions and years of barrenness that were dutifully reported under headlines such as "The saddest story in racing," Genuine Risk finally produced two blaze-faced chestnut colts: Genuine Reward, by Rahy, in 1993, and Count Our Blessing, by Chief Honcho, in 1996. Neither made it to the races, however. By 2006 Genuine Reward was standing at stud in Wyoming while Count Our Blessing, who had been gelded, was being shown as a conformation hunter.

The national love affair with Genuine Risk was perhaps never more vibrant than when at age sixteen she foaled Genuine Reward. Congratulatory notes and letters from women who also had suffered problems producing children flooded Three Chimneys Farm near Midway, Kentucky, where she was boarded, even though often only addressed with simple lines such as "Momma Genuine Risk, Lexington, Kentucky." Photographs and stories about the remarkable mare and her son were carried around the nation, even in magazines such as *Newsweek*.

Although the world seems to have a shorter and shorter attention span, Genuine Risk has continued to be the subject of great interest all the days of her life.

"She's doing fine, eating good, and loving her mints," Buck Moore said in December 2006, noting that the arthritis in her left knee was less of a problem in colder weather. "She gets a lot of visitors — even many young people who never saw her race. People fly in from California to see her. At this time in her life, it's amazing.

"And she's smart as a whip. She knows when people come to visit and she will stand for pictures. But after so long, she says, 'No more pictures. I'm either going to eat grass or eat candy, one or the other.'"

Because they have spent much of nearly three decades in each other's company, Moore and Genuine Risk have a special bond. He regards her, he said, as a parent would a child and cherishes even her quirks, such as when she mildly threatens him with a kick when she's had enough grooming. But while she's still strong-willed, her kindness remains paramount, and he said he had never seen her kick any of the boisterous youngsters with whom she shares her pasture.

"I know she's getting old and the time is coming, and I don't want to

Kentucky Derby
Purse: $250,000 Added

Churchill Downs - May 3, 1980. One hundred sixth running Kentucky Derby.
Purse $250,000 added. Three-year-olds. 1 1-4 Miles. Main Track. Track: Fast.
Gross value $339,300. Net value to winner, $250,550; second, $50,000; third, $25,000; fourth, $13,750.

Horse	A	Wgt	Eqp	Odds	PP	1/4	1/2	3/4	1	Str	Fin	Jockey
Genuine Risk	3	121		13.30	10	7 $^{1\%}$	7 ^{3}	4 ^{hd}	1 $^{1\%}$	1 ^{2}	1 ^{1}	J Vasquez
Rumbo	3	126		4.00	9	13	12 $^{1\%}$	11 ^{3}	5 $^{\%}$	3 ^{3}	2 ^{1}	L Pincay Jr
Jaklin Klugman	3	126		7.10	2	8 $^{\%}$	8 ^{hd}	8 $^{\%}$	4 $^{2\%}$	2 $^{1\%}$	3 ^{4}	D McHargue
Super Moment	3	126		8.60	3	10 $^{1\%}$	9 $^{1\%}$	9 $^{1\%}$	9 ^{3}	5 $^{\%}$	4 ^{no}	D Pierce
Rockhill Native	3	126		2.10	6	2 ^{hd}	1 $^{1\%}$	2 ^{hd}	2 $^{\%}$	4 $^{1\%}$	5 ^{nk}	J Oldham
Bold 'n Rulling	3	126	b	68.70	1	6 $^{1\%}$	2 ^{3}	1 ^{1}	6 $^{\%}$	7 ^{3}	6 ^{nk}	P Valenzuela
Plugged Nickle	3	126		2.60	11	1 ^{hd}	3 $^{1\%}$	3 $^{1\%}$	3 $^{1\%}$	6 ^{hd}	7 $^{3\%}$	B Thornburg
Degenerate Jon	3	126	b	61.70	4	9 $^{2\%}$	6 ^{hd}	5 ^{hd}	8 ^{3}	8 $^{1\%}$	8 $^{1\%}$	R Hernandez
Withholding	3	126		64.10	12	4 $^{\%}$	10 ^{1}	10 ^{1}	11 ^{2}	9 ^{2}	9 ^{2}	M Morgan
Tonka Wakhan	3	126	b	f-58.90	5	12 ^{hd}	13	12 $^{\%}$	12 ^{3}	10 ^{2}	10 $^{2\%}$	M Holland
Execution's Reason	3	126		111.80	13	3 $^{1\%}$	5 $^{\%}$	7 $^{2\%}$	10 ^{1}	11 ^{3}	11 ^{3}	R Romero
Gold Stage	3	126		41.50	7	5 ^{hd}	4 $^{\%}$	6 ^{hd}	7 $^{\%}$	12 $^{1\%}$	12 ^{no}	A Cordero Jr
Hazard Duke	3	126	b	f-58.90	8	11 ^{3}	11 $^{\%}$	13	13	13	13	D Brumfield

Off Time: 5:39 **Time Of Race:** :24 :48 1:12½ 1:37¾ 2:02
Start: Good For All **Track:** Fast
f-Field
Equipment: b for blinkers

Mutuel Payoffs

8	Genuine Risk	$28.60	$10.60	$4.80
7	Rumbo		5.20	3.40
3	Jaklin Klugman			4.40

Winner: Genuine Risk, ch. f. by Exclusive Native—Virtuous, by Gallant Man (Trained by LeRoy Jolley). Bred by Mrs. G. Watts Humphrey in Kentucky.

Start good. Won driving.
GENUINE RISK, settled nicely as the field came away in good order and was reserved behind PLUGGED NICKLE and inside WITHHOLDING around the first turn and early backstretch. She was eased back slightly and moved to the outside smoothly approaching the half-mile pole, gradually raced to the leaders outside four rivals, and took command entering the stretch; was hit once with the whip right-handed, increased her advantage under six well-spaced strokes as Vasquez switched to the left, and continued resolutely to the end. RUMBO dropped back last soon after the start and was kept outside rivals, gradually improving position, swerved under right-handed urging after racing wide into the stretch, and gained steadily under heavy left-handed urging in the final furlong. JAKLIN KLUGMAN saved ground behind the first flight, worked between rivals around the final turn, and moved boldly in pursuit of the winner settling into the homestretch, but could not sustain his bid. SUPER MOMENT stayed close to the rail and closed well from the head of the stretch to outfinish the others. ROCKHILL NATIVE had no difficulty taking a clear lead from between rivals entering the backstretch, but swerved out and was lightly checked for a stride approaching the six-furlong pole, stayed with the pace to the top of the homestretch, and then weakened. BOLD 'N RULLING raced with the pace along the rail for six furlongs, gave way approaching the stretch and drifted out, then held on fairly well in the straightway, but pulled up lame. PLUGGED NICKLE rated near the lead outside ROCKHILL NATIVE and BOLD 'N RULLING, bore out slightly on the final turn, then raced true while tiring in the homestretch run. DEGENERATE JON was a factor for six furlongs and tired. WITHHOLDING was very wide outside the first flight and tired. TONKA WAKHAN was outrun. EXECUTION'S REASON was used up early. GOLD STAGE also tired early. HAZARD DUKE was not a factor.

Owners: (1) Mrs B R Firestone; (2) Gayno Stable and Bell Bloodstock Co.; (3) Klugman-Dominguez; (4) Elmendorf; (5) Harry A Oak; (6) Hughes Brothers; (7) John M Schiff; (8) Barry K Schwartz; (9) Russell Michael Jr. (10) Glenn Bromagen; (11) Howard B Noonan; (12) Mrs Philip B Hofmann; (13) Andrew Adams
©EQUIBASE

be around when it happens," Moore said in a hushed voice. "She's been an inspiration to be around. And she's done me big favors — no one ever knew me before, but now a few do.

"Being around her is just not like being around another horse. She's always been special."

By Michele MacDonald

Lil E. Who?

SEVEN MONTHS BEFORE the 1992 Kentucky Derby, the Thoroughbred racing world celebrated what it thought was the birth of a superstar. On a sunny November afternoon at Churchill Downs, Arazi, a two-year-old chestnut colt, won the 1991 Breeders' Cup Juvenile with a burst of acceleration so electric that he merited comparisons to the greatest runners ever seen.

Lying next to last in a fourteen-horse field after a half-mile, he took off under jockey Patrick Valenzuela, zipped around and between horses, and ran away in the stretch to win by five lengths. "I've never seen a horse do that," Valenzuela said. "It was like playing a video game where you're driving a little car. All I had to do was drive through the pack. That's your next Kentucky Derby winner right there."

Based in France, Arazi was overseen by François Boutin, a respected French trainer, and co-owned by Allen Paulson, the famous American industrialist, and Sheikh Mohammed bin Rashid al Maktoum of the ruling family of the Persian Gulf emirate of Dubai. Their exotic, exciting colt was nimble and devastatingly quick. Arazi had won six straight major races in France before the Juvenile. This latest victory stirred the imaginations of America's horse community. Eclipse Award voters named him North America's top two-year-old of 1991 even though the

Juvenile had been his only race on the continent. He was assigned the highest weight in twenty-seven years on the Experimental Free Handicap, an evaluation of North American two-year-olds made by a panel of racing secretaries at the end of the year.

Arazi fever became so hot in early 1992 that the horse's Kentucky Derby future book odds dipped to 2-1 at a major Las Vegas casino, an unheard-of show of confidence in any horse, especially months before a race. So many bettors wanted a piece of Arazi that the casino, needing to lay off some of the action, invented a gimmick wager in which the bettor took Arazi and the casino took every other horse. Even in those absurd conditions, some bettors still took the French superstar. The bright lights of his celebrity obscured all other Derby contenders, rendering them irrelevant in the public's eyes. It was as if no other horses would be running at Churchill Downs on the first Saturday of May 1992.

Amid the frenzy the American-based contenders slowly sorted themselves out in the prep season that precedes the Derby. A longshot named Technology won the Florida Derby. Devil His Due, trained by Hall of Famer Allen Jerkens, won the Wood Memorial. An impressive colt named Pine Bluff won the Arkansas Derby. Most experts agreed the best American-based challengers were running in California. A regally bred colt named A.P. Indy won the Santa Anita Derby. Sired by Triple Crown winner Seattle Slew, A.P. Indy had sold for $2.9 million as a yearling and hadn't lost a race in nine months. A colossal upstart named Casual Lies ran with him for most of the Santa Anita Derby.

Those horses gathered at Churchill Downs in the weeks before the Derby and continued their preparations for the big race. Arazi was not yet on the grounds; he had raced just once since the Juvenile and mostly had been in seclusion at Chantilly, a bucolic training center in the French countryside, where Boutin's stable was based. Boutin planned to bring the favorite from France to Kentucky just six days before the Derby.

A few lesser American-based horses were also at Churchill, preparing for the Derby. One was a seemingly pedestrian colt with a strange name: Lil E. Tee. He was certain to be among the longer shots on the board. He had been foaled three years earlier in Pennsylvania, a state that had never produced a Derby winner. His sire, At the Threshold, had no record of producing horses that competed on such a grand stage. His breeder, a Philadelphia businessman named Larry Littman, was strictly a small-time operator.

Trained by Lynn Whiting, a veteran based at Churchill, Lil E. Tee was a big, muscular horse who ran with his head high, but he was on the fringe of the Derby scene, stabled across the backside from the other entrants. Few reporters made the trek over to speak to Whiting as the race approached, and Lil E. Tee received almost no attention. But who could blame reporters for focusing on Arazi and A.P. Indy and ignoring Lil E. Tee? Whiting's horse seemingly had no chance.

Upon closer inspection, the obscure colt was not entirely without legitimate Derby credentials. He had recently won the Jim Beam Stakes, a $500,000 prep race at Turfway Park in Florence, Kentucky, and had finished second in the Arkansas Derby behind Pine Bluff. He had made eight career starts, won four, and never finished out of the money. The fact that Whiting was running him at all was interesting to fans of the Midwestern racing circuit, where Whiting operated. A judicious, old-school trainer, Whiting never ran a horse in any race unless he thought it had an excellent chance. His winning percentage was considerably higher than the national average for trainers. In his only other attempt to win the Derby, he had finished third in 1983 with At the Threshold, Lil E. Tee's sire.

Also going for Lil E. Tee was the fact that Pat Day was his jockey. An immensely popular rider who lived in Louisville, Day was at the crest of a career that had included more than five thousand victories and $100 million in earnings. Still in his prime at age thirty-nine, he had already been elected to the Racing Hall of Fame and had won every major race with one exception — the Kentucky Derby. Even though top trainers always sought his services and he had several leading Derby contenders to choose from every year, he had made nine starts in the race and come home a loser every time. Whenever he was asked about his "Derby hex," the modest Day just smiled and calmly said, "I know there's a Derby out there with my name on it." If Day had faith in Whiting's horse, the horse was legitimate.

Still, Lil E. Tee wasn't given much of a chance of capturing the roses. His cheap pedigree was a major strike against him. He had picked a bad year — Arazi's year — to be a three-year-old. If the unflattering details of his humble background had been known (they weren't at the time), he wouldn't have received a dime of wagering support, even with Day on his back. He had overcome a lot to become a Derby horse, but he was hardly the stuff of legend.

Arazi — now there was the kind of horse that won America's greatest race. He was treated as a visiting potentate, his winning move in the Juvenile still vividly recalled, when he arrived at Churchill six days before the Derby. After a brief stay in quarantine, he was released to his barn at dawn Tuesday and soon headed to the track to stretch his legs. With an exercise rider guiding him and a clattering phalanx of reporters and cameramen charting his every move, he walked up the chute, turned around, and cantered a mile before returning to the barn. The next morning he returned to the track for more light exercise. The hype machine was blaring full blast. The *New York Times* called him a "mythical and almost mystical" horse. *Time* magazine said he was "fast winning a reputation as the second coming of Secretariat." In the *Daily Racing Form*, columnist Joe Hirsch wrote that Arazi was "such an extraordinary animal he makes other great horses look like hacks."

Boutin scheduled a five-furlong workout for Thursday morning with Valenzuela riding. When Arazi reached the track, all activity stopped.

Spectators stood three-deep for several hundred yards along the backside fence. Julian "Buck" Wheat, Churchill's director of horseman's relations, called it "the biggest crowd I ever saw on the backside." Arazi warmed up, cantered a mile, and broke into a gallop. He followed a stablemate for three furlongs and then accelerated as he came through the stretch and hit the finish line. The spectators applauded, impressed by the horse's obvious quickness.

Valenzuela had predicted a Derby victory seven months earlier and did not back down when he spoke to reporters at the barn after the workout. "We could win running around the outside fence," the jockey claimed. "The other horses are running for second. We can go around them, go through them. I just have to pick the right route and point him. I'm on a horse with an afterburner. A push-button horse. The best I've ever ridden." Considering that he had ridden the 1989 Derby winner, Sunday Silence, that was quite a statement. "Arazi can do more," Valenzuela shrugged. "This race is over."

But was it? Beneath the hype, there were signs all wasn't well with Arazi. American horsemen had been shocked to see he was among the smaller horses on the track every morning; unlike many of the other Derby horses, he hadn't grown much since the Juvenile. He also seemed jumpy. Every morning when he went for exercise, he whirled and balked before he stepped onto the track, even dumping Valenzuela once. It seemed he was afraid of the commotion generated by other horses working out. That wasn't so surprising, considering he trained in serenity at Chantilly, but one had to wonder how he would react to the noise of 125,000 fans on Saturday. If his five-furlong workout was any indication of his state of mind, the news was bad. He had covered the distance in 1:03, a slow measurement.

As well, he had undergone surgery seven months earlier, days after the Juvenile, to remove bone chips from each of his front ankles, and while it was a relatively minor procedure and he had fully recovered, he had been forced to convalesce for several months, setting back Boutin's Derby prep schedule. Although Arazi had easily won his only race since the Juvenile, an eight-furlong grass event in France in April, his lack of prep races contrasted starkly with the preparations of the more hardened American-based horses. Some of them had raced a half-dozen times in 1992. They were ready to go.

Although many reporters and fans continued to believe Arazi would win the Derby with ease, skepticism swelled beneath the surface as the race neared. "Even though the hordes were following him, I thought they were following him to a hanging," trainer D. Wayne Lukas said. "He didn't look good, wasn't working well. Every day he was more reluctant, less eager to get into his morning. His legions grew day by day but he was going in the wrong direction."

Lukas, a keen observer, said he believed the Derby horses showing the most in training were his colt, Dance Floor, and the top finishers in the Arkansas Derby, Pine Bluff and Lil E. Tee. Whiting agreed with that assessment. The low-key trainer never boasted before a race, but as the Derby neared, he touted Lil E. Tee to anyone who asked. Day, hanging around the barn in the mornings, was surprised by Whiting's behavior. "It was almost like a change of person," Day said. "A normally reserved individual was bursting with optimism. It was something to see."

Many American trainers privately shared Lukas' increasing doubts about Arazi, the horse who had rendered their animals all but irrelevant in the pre-race discussion. By Friday, they could no longer contain their suspicions. "How are they going to fit the saddle over his wings?" Jerkens asked sarcastically.

When Arazi went for a gallop Friday morning, he again appeared fractious. Boutin admitted the atmosphere was getting to the horse. "He is used to a very calm life, not being around all these horses," the Frenchman said. "It is a change from his usual atmosphere, and it makes him nervous. He doesn't like it."

The likely second betting choice, A.P. Indy, also was having a hard time. His training was dull, and he was limping around the barn. "It was obvious something was not right," said Shelley Riley, trainer of Casual Lies, the longshot from California who shared a barn with A.P. Indy. Riley's concerns proved to be well founded. A.P. Indy turned up lame on Saturday and had to be scratched.

Many Derby bettors saw this development as yet another reason to bet on Arazi; the absence of his most serious challenger only increased his chances of winning. On Derby Day, as the crowd at Churchill swelled to more than 130,000, the French colt dominated all speculation and attracted 43 percent of the win pool.

Hours before the race Allen Paulson taped an interview with an ESPN analyst who asked, "Have you ever owned a horse like this?" Paulson, a longtime owner of top horses, responded, "No one has ever owned a horse like this."

In the frenzied paddock before the Derby, all eyes were on the French colt and Valenzuela. Few noticed Whiting and Day having their final conversation about tactics. Day wore the distinctive silks of W. Cal Partee, the wealthy Arkansas lumberman who owned Lil E. Tee. The silks were Dreamsicle orange with large white polka dots. Whiting advised Day to stay away from the early pacesetters and save the horse's energy for the stretch, but not to fall so far behind that he couldn't make up the ground at the end. "But you're just going to have to see what happens and use your instincts," Whiting said. Day nodded.

The crowd roared when eighteen horses broke from the starting gate a few minutes later. Arazi was an odds-on favorite at 9-10, the first individual Derby entry to run at less than even money since Spectacular Bid in 1979. (Easy Goer had been coupled at 4-5 in 1989.) With A.P. Indy sidelined, the French horse so dominated the wagering that only one other horse had single-digit odds (Technology at 4-1). Lil E. Tee left the gate at nearly 17-1, deemed a longer shot than the seven horses that made up the mutuel field.

Arazi immediately wanted to run, but Valenzuela pulled him back to save energy for later. The favorite was dead last as the field came through the stretch the first time, passed the finish line, and angled into the first turn. A longshot named Snappy Landing took the early lead, closely followed by Devil His Due, Casual Lies, Pine Bluff, and Lukas' horse, Dance Floor.

Lil E. Tee was pinched back when a colt named Thyer veered into his path in the first quarter-mile, forcing Day to pull up and angle to the outside. Watching with binoculars from Partee's box in the grandstand, Whiting feared that might do in Lil E. Tee. Instead of running fourth or fifth, the colt was near the back of the pack. "That's probably enough to get us beat right there," Whiting groaned.

But it didn't prove to be the disaster Whiting feared. Day found running room wide of the rail, and Lil E. Tee settled nicely rounding the first turn and heading up the backstretch. Ahead of him, Dance Floor had assumed the lead from Snappy Landing. The pace was unusually slow. The first quarter-mile (:23 2/5) was the Derby's slowest in eight years. The first half-mile (:47 2/5) was the slowest since 1980.

Then the show that everyone had anticipated began to unfold.

Running next-to-last and well off the rail after a half-mile, Arazi switched leads and accelerated when Valenzuela encouraged him to run. With one of his famous bursts, he quickly passed six horses on the backstretch.

"Arazi is moving up in the middle of the track. Arazi is flying!" ABC announcer Dave Johnson exclaimed on the national TV broadcast.

Approaching the second turn, Arazi encountered Lil E. Tee. Day had slowly gained on the leaders through the backstretch, making up the ground he had lost in the first furlong. He was running eighth and seemed to be in good shape, but Arazi easily passed him, just as he had passed the others. "He went by me like a shot," Day recalled. "I went,

'Wow, there he goes again. I guess I'm running for second money.' "

Up front, Dance Floor was still a length ahead of Pine Bluff, with Casual Lies, a 30-1 shot, in third. But the crowd erupted as Arazi moved into fourth and took aim on the leaders. By the middle of the second turn, he had passed thirteen horses in a half-mile. It was one of the most devastating moves in Derby annals, a near-exact replay of his performance in the Juvenile.

"Arazi is gaining ground with every stride!" Dave Johnson called.

In the middle of the race, Valenzuela, whose boasts had put him in a win-or-else predicament, experienced pangs of relief. "I didn't think there was any way we'd get beat," he said.

But in the rush to anoint Arazi, one key factor had been overlooked: The Derby is three-sixteenths of a mile longer than the Juvenile. The same move might not take Arazi all the way to the finish.

Day began to suspect the French horse was tiring as the leaders moved through the second turn. Arazi had quickly moved five lengths ahead of Lil E. Tee after passing him, but Day noticed the margin didn't continue to grow. In fact, when Day finally asked Lil E. Tee to start charging on the second turn, Lil E. Tee began to close the gap between them.

Several lengths ahead, Arazi challenged Casual Lies as the horses neared the end of the second turn. It was no contest. Casual Lies was a 1,300-pound behemoth. Arazi weighed less than a thousand pounds. Arazi pulled even and went head to head with the bigger horse for several strides, but then Casual Lies pulled in front as they came out of the turn and headed for home. Arazi began to weave.

"I had said before the race that there was no way that little horse was going to pass my big horse at the top of the stretch, if it came to that," said Shelley Riley, Casual Lies' trainer. "Arazi was going so fast, but my horse said, 'Not today, little guy.' "

Arazi's brilliant half-mile sprint had exhausted him. The favorite had nothing left for the stretch run.

As Arazi fell back, Lil E. Tee approached. This second meeting between the famous, silver-spoon favorite and the obscure longshot was
no more than a brief encounter. Charging for the finish line at full
speed, Lil E. Tee swept around Arazi and left the French horse behind.
The coronation that millions of fans had anticipated was not going to
happen.

Racing seven wide, Lil E. Tee only had two horses in front of him —
Dance Floor and Casual Lies. Chris Antley, riding Dance Floor, veered
off the rail to try to hold off Casual Lies, but his horse, like Arazi, was
spent. Casual Lies went by Dance Floor and took the lead with a furlong to go. Riley, who had purchased Casual Lies for $7,500, was about
to faint in the grandstand. "When he made the lead, I screamed," she
said. "But then I went, 'Oh, no, too soon.' I started looking for the come-
from-behind horse. And sure enough, I saw him coming like a rocket."

That was Lil E. Tee. With the normally passive Day whipping him
furiously, Lil E. Tee bore down on Casual Lies, whose ears had gone
up when he took the lead, indicating he was easing up. Gary Stevens,
aboard Casual Lies, tried to get the big horse to run again, but it was
too late. Day's horse had more momentum.

Lil E. Tee edged past Casual Lies just before the sixteenth pole and
pulled ahead by a half-length. Pandemonium reigned in Partee's box.
"Do you believe this? Do you believe this S-O-B is going to win?" Whiting shouted. Lil E. Tee hit the finish line a length in front of Casual Lies
and nine in front of Arazi, who staggered home in eighth place.

Churchill Downs fell strangely quiet in the moments after the race;
many fans had no idea who had won. Lil E. Tee was that obscure.

In the days after the race, as reporters dug into the background of
the surprising Derby winner, it became apparent he was an even longer shot than it seemed. Yes, he had paid $35.60 on a $2 win bet, and,
yes, he was the first Pennsylvania-bred to win the Derby, but his life

Kentucky Derby
Purse: $750,000 Added

Churchill Downs - May 2, 1992. One hundred eighteenth running Kentucky Derby.
Purse $750,000 added. Three-year-olds. 1 1-4 Miles. Main Track. Track: Fast.
Value of race $974,800. Net value to winner, $724,800 and gold trophy; second, $145,000; third, $70,000; fourth, $35,000.

Horse	A	Wgt	Eqp	Odds	PP	1/4	1/2	3/4	1	Str	Fin	Jockey
Lil E. Tee	3	126		16.80	10	12^{hd}	10^{2}	$7^{½}$	5^{3}	2^{1}	1^{1}	P Day
Casual Lies	3	126		29.90	4	3^{hd}	$6^{½}$	3^{1}	2^{hd}	1^{hd}	$2^{3¾}$	G Stevens
Dance Floor	3	126		a-33.30	16	$5^{½}$	$1^{½}$	1^{1}	$1^{1½}$	3^{2}	3^{2}	C Antley
Conte Di Savoya	3	126	b	21.30	8	$11^{½}$	$9^{½}$	$10^{1½}$	6^{2}	6^{2}	4^{1}	S Sellers
Pine Bluff	3	126		10.50	12	4^{hd}	$3^{½}$	$2^{½}$	4^{hd}	5^{hd}	$5^{¾}$	C Perret
Al Sabin	3	126		a-33.30	1	$6^{1½}$	5^{1}	5^{hd}	7^{3}	$7^{1½}$	6^{hd}	C Nakatani
Dr Devious (Ire)	3	126		20.80	15	15^{hd}	16^{hd}	17^{7}	$10^{½}$	$8^{1½}$	7^{hd}	C McCarron
Arazi	3	126		.90	17	$17^{2½}$	17^{hd}	$8^{½}$	3^{2}	4^{hd}	8^{2}	P Valenzuela
My Luck Runs North	3	126		f-12.80	14	18	15^{3}	18	17^{1}	9^{3}	$9^{2¾}$	R Lopez
Technology	3	126		4.20	2	$9^{1½}$	$8^{1½}$	$6^{½}$	$9^{1½}$	10^{2}	10^{2}	J Bailey
West by West	3	126	b	f-12.80	11	$14^{2½}$	$12^{½}$	$12^{1½}$	8^{hd}	$11^{½}$	11no	J Samyn
Devil His Due	3	126		21.60	6	$2^{½}$	4^{1}	11^{hd}	12^{1}	12^{5}	12^{6}	M Smith
Thyer	3	126	b	f-12.80	5	$10^{½}$	13^{hd}	13^{hd}	$15^{½}$	15^{4}	$13^{¾}$	C Roche
Ecstatic Ride	3	126	b	f-12.80	13	13^{1}	$14^{½}$	$15^{1½}$	$13^{½}$	$14^{½}$	14^{nk}	J Krone
Sir Pinder	3	126	b	f-12.80	9	16^{1}	18	14^{hd}	$14^{1½}$	13^{hd}	$15^{3½}$	R Romero
Pistols and Roses	3	126		13.40	7	8^{hd}	7^{hd}	$9^{½}$	11^{hd}	16^{2}	$16^{1½}$	J Vasquez
Snappy Landing	3	126	b	f-12.80	3	1^{1}	$2^{1½}$	$4^{½}$	$16^{½}$	$17^{1½}$	$17^{2½}$	J Velasquez
Disposal	3	126		f-12.80	18	7^{hd}	$11^{½}$	$16^{½}$	18	18	18	A Solis

f- Mutuel field.
a-Coupled, Dance Floor and Al Sabin.

Off Time: 5:34 **Time Of Race:** :23⅖ :47⅘ 1:12⅕ 1:37⅗ 2:03
Start: Good For All **Track:** Fast
Equipment: b for blinkers

Mutuel Payoffs

7	**Lil E. Tee**	**$35.60**	**$12.20**	**$7.60**
3	**Casual Lies**		**22.20**	**11.60**
1a	**Dance Floor**			**12.60**

Winner: Lil E. Tee, b. c. by At the Threshold—Eileen's Moment, by For the Moment (Trained by Lynn S. Whiting). Bred by Larry Littman in Pennsylvania.

LIL E. TEE relaxed nicely after coming away in good order, was unhurried into the backstretch, raced seven wide while advancing approaching the stretch, caught CASUAL LIES between horses while close up early, was sent after DANCE FLOOR nearing the stretch, brushed lightly with that rival inside the final three-sixteenths and continued on with good courage. DANCE FLOOR moved around three horses to take over entering the backstretch, quickly opened a clear advantage while remaining well out from the rail, brushed with CASUAL LIES while still vying for the lead approaching the final furlong and weakened. CONTE DI SAVOYA unhurried while saving ground to the backstretch, moved up along the inside to reach a striking position after entering the stretch but failed to sustain his bid. PINE BLUFF, prominent from the outset, moved closest to DANCE FLOOR approaching the end of the backstretch, remained a factor until near the stretch and lacked a late response. AL SABIN came out in front of TECHNOLOGY following the start, raced forwardly into the backstretch, while saving ground, came out between horses nearing the far turn, but was finished after angling ouside for the drive. DR DEVIOUS passed tired horses. ARAZI, unhurried while outrun into the backstretch, swung out eight wide to launch a run with five furlongs remaining, moved menacingly around horses on the final turn, then came up empty during the drive. MY LUCK RUNS NORTH leaned in after the start bumping ECSTATIC RIDE, fell back through the run down the backstretch and failed to seriously threaten. TECHNOLOGY steadied when AL SABIN came out after the start, gained striking position along the inside racing to the first turn but was finished soon after going six furlongs. WEST BY WEST failed to be a serious factor. DEVIL HIS DUE raced forwardly into the backstretch and gave way. THYER, between horses much of the way, was carefully handled nearing the end of the backstretch. ECSTATIC RIDE, bumped by MY LUCK RUNS NORTH after the start, raced seven wide into the backstretch and failed to reach contention. SIR PINDER, off slowly, was always outrun. PISTOLS AND ROSES raced within easy striking distance to the far turn and tired badly. SNAPPY LANDING showed good early foot, held on well until near the far turn and faltered badly. DISPOSAL, seven wide into the backstretch, wasn't able to keep pace thereafter.
Scratched—A.P Indy.

Owners: (1) W Cal Partee; (2) Shelley L Riley; (3) Oaktown Stable; (4) Jaime S Carrion; (5) Loblolly Stable; (6) Calumet Farm; (7) Sidney H Craig; (8) A Paulson & Sheikh Mohammed; (9) Melvin A Benitez; (10) Scott Savin; (11) John Peace; (12) Lion Crest Stable; (13) Maktoum al Maktoum; (14) DanDar Farm & Joan Rich; (15) James Lewis Jr; (16) Willis Family Stables; (17) Frederick McNeary; (18) Bramble Farm

was a rags-to-riches story so unlikely a Hollywood director would have turned it down as impossible.

As a yearling, he underwent major surgery at a New Jersey clinic because the end of his small intestine was being sucked into his large intestine, causing food to back up. It was a serious procedure, and Lil E. Tee lost 150 pounds. Three months later his breeder, Larry Littman, tried to enter him in a minor sale in Ocala, Florida, but the colt looked so haggard that the Ocala Breeders' Sales Company turned him down. "He looked like the wrath of God," the sales agent said.

Littman eventually found a pair of buyers to take the horse off his hands for $3,000. The buyers were an Ocala blacksmith, Mike Paramore, and a small farm owner, Chuck Wieneke. They bought and sold horses together. Wieneke was a pinhooker, a trainer who bought horses as cheaply as possible, turned them around, and sold them for a profit. Wieneke fed Lil E. Tee well, put him on a vitamin program, and gave him a single dose of a steroid. Lil E. Tee filled out and began to shine. Wieneke's wife exercised him in the mornings and was staggered by his sheer power. Lil E. Tee was a big, strong horse.

In April 1991 the Ocala Breeders' Sales Company accepted him when Wieneke and Paramore put him back up for auction as a two-year-old. Al Jevremovic, a Yugoslavian-born Florida businessman who owned motels and cheap horses, bought him for $25,000. Lil E. Tee seemed to fit right in. He raced twice in Jevremovic's colors at Calder Race Course in the fall of 1991, finishing second in his first race and then winning by nearly a dozen lengths. Lynn Whiting, who was always on the lookout for top two-year-olds with Derby potential, spotted him in the second race and bought him on Partee's behalf for $200,000.

Whiting, Partee, and Day knew nothing of the horse's hardscrabble background. Reporters dug up the details after the Derby and came to the owner and trainer for comment. Whiting was stunned. Colic surgery? How had he missed the scars? Sold for $3,000? Turned down by an auction company? Whiting just laughed. "It shows you what an amazing game this is," he said. "I guess the horse took a Charles Atlas [muscle building] course somewhere along the way," he said.

Arazi was never the same after his Derby loss. Skipping the rest of the American Triple Crown, he returned to Europe and raced three times on the grass, winning once, then came back to America for the Breeders' Cup Mile in the fall. Bettors again made him the favorite at 3-2 odds, but he finished out of the money in what proved to be his final race. He was retired to stud at Sheikh Mohammed's farm in England. His winning performance in the 1991 Breeders' Cup Juvenile is still recalled as one of racing's greatest efforts.

Lil E. Tee didn't fare much better than his famous rival after the Derby. He bled internally while finishing fifth in the Preakness, skipped the Belmont Stakes, and then missed the rest of his three-year-old season when bone chips were discovered in both of his front ankles. Returning for what many thought would be a stirring four-year-old campaign in 1993, he won two of three races (and finished second in the other) before a lung infection and a fractured ankle ended his career.

In a somewhat lackluster career at stud, Lil E. Tee has sired sixteen stakes winners, three of them graded.

"Was he a bolt of lightning horse? In a way," D. Wayne Lukas said. "He wasn't exactly what I would call a roulette horse, where you spin the wheel and it stops on black and you win strictly by luck. He had a good rider, a good trainer; he was running on a track where he was comfortable. But there are thousands of horses like him. Every year there are hundreds of Lil E. Tees. On a given day, in the right spot, with a Pat Day and a Lynn Whiting in their favor, and with the gods smiling on them, they can get there. That's what makes the Derby so great."

By John Eisenberg

Small But Mighty

SMALL AND SLOW by anything but carousel standards, Thunder Gulch didn't show much eagerness to be a racehorse when he began training. In fact, his early inclination of leaning on other horses would have been more appropriate for the rugby field than the racetrack.

And so buyers and bettors alike shunned him.

But in 1995, with an array of victories that stretched from California to New York and from Florida to Kentucky, Thunder Gulch put together one of the decade's more impressive campaigns. And after missing a sweep of the Triple Crown by less than a length, he became the season's champion three-year-old.

Nevertheless, he began the year as a champion's sidekick.

In the company of more celebrated horses, Thunder Gulch was often overlooked, his talents frequently underestimated. He was so lightly regarded that his victory as a 24-1 longshot in the Kentucky Derby elicited not only surprise but also complaint. Inveighing against the circumstances of the Derby itself, some critics cited the large field of nineteen horses and the troubled trips some encountered as the only possible explanation for so shocking an outcome, so unprepossessing a winner.

Most observers hesitated to accept the true explanation, which

175

Thunder Gulch would eventually force upon them: He was simply and deceptively that good.

Bred by Peter Brant in Kentucky, Thunder Gulch was a son of the 1988 Sprint champion Gulch, who, of course, was much more than a sprinter. The winner of the 1987 Wood Memorial, in which he defeated Gone West and Capote at nine furlongs, Gulch was sent after major sprint prizes as a four-year-old largely to avoid the dangerous forest of a handicap division inhabited by such standouts as Cryptoclearance, Lost Code, Bet Twice, and Alysheba.

Thunder Gulch's dam, Line of Thunder, had some success in England as a two-year-old, but she did little the following season and was said to be small and physically unimpressive. In size, Line of Thunder apparently was much like her dam, Shoot a Line, and in his modest appearance, Thunder Gulch, it would seem, favored the distaff side of his family. Nevertheless, from this side he also received a heady dose of stamina. Despite her lack of size and unprepossessing appearance, Shoot a Line was a champion in both England and Ireland, winning the Irish Oaks at a mile and a half and the Park Hill Stakes at a mile and three-quarters.

Ken Ellenberg purchased Thunder Gulch for $40,000 at the 1993 Keeneland July yearling sale. The plan was to "pinhook" the colt. In other words, Thunder Gulch was originally purchased for resale, not for racing.

But the following April, when Ellenberg put the colt in Keeneland's auction of two-year-olds in training, with the Jerry Bailey Sales Company as agent, buyers showed little interest. Ellenberg still owned the colt when the gavel fell.

Trainer John Kimmel, whose stable was based in New York, liked the diminutive colt well enough, however, to contact at least one of his clients about him. That night, as Howard Rozins of Bedford, New York, recalls it, Kimmel faxed him the catalog pages of seven horses from the sale. Rozins, who with his brother owned and operated five bagel shops, was an avid horse racing fan. With the Mutual Shar Stable as his *nom de course*, he had owned only one horse, a filly named Swift and Classy. And she had won all three of her races, including a stakes in Florida, before an injury ended her career.

Eager to replace the injured filly and find another racing prospect, Rozins had put together a tentative partnership with a couple of friends. And from the faxed catalog pages, with Kimmel's encouragement, Rozins selected Thunder Gulch as the group's new horse.

But by the time Thunder Gulch arrived in New York, the partnership Rozins had cobbled together had fallen apart. His friends had retreated. And he didn't have the resources, he explained, to buy 100 percent of the horse by himself for $120,000. Instead, he could buy only 60 percent of the colt.

And so when Thunder Gulch began training as a two-year-old at Belmont Park in the summer of 1994, he was still for sale. Or at least 40 percent of him was on the market, for Ellenberg, whose goal from the start had been resale, remained eager to complete a deal.

But Thunder Gulch did little in the mornings to entice potential buyers. If anything, he scared them away. Anybody willing to overlook his size and physical immaturity long enough to watch him run soon realized he was also slow.

"He was working so slow we couldn't sell him to anybody," Kimmel recalled, finding his notes from those early workouts.

On June 12, Thunder Gulch worked three furlongs in :39 2/5. Two weeks later, he worked a half-mile in :53 and two weeks later another half in :52. And the railbirds yawned.

But then one morning at Saratoga, specifically on August 17, Thunder Gulch went to the starting gate for a five-furlong move, and it was, as Kimmel remembers it, as if somebody flipped a switch. Maybe it was just the right time or, more likely, the presence of another horse in the gate and the encouragement of competition, but whatever the reason, that morning and that workout produced an awakening. A light came on, and Thunder Gulch, Kimmel said, suddenly woke up. He stopped the official stopwatch at 1:01 3/5.

As a general rule, that isn't the sort of clocking that's going to turn heads or drop jaws or cause lips to pucker in whistles expressive of pure astonishment. No, it wasn't like that. But for a lackadaisical colt who so far had displayed more indifference than ability, the move was a hint, a suggestion that wasn't quite a promise, of significant potential. And from that moment on, Thunder Gulch progressed steadily.

A month later, at Belmont Park, the diminutive chestnut made his debut with John Velazquez riding. They left the gate from post position No. 2, and the young jockey soon had to check in traffic. Then, in mid-stretch, Thunder Gulch found himself in such a tight spot that he slammed into the rail, but despite everything he finished third, beaten by just a neck and beaten more by his own inexperience and bad racing luck than by any talent deficiency. He could run and that was clear. How far and how fast and how well, those questions remained, but he dispelled any suspicion lingering from his first workouts that he might prefer to be a pad nag rather than a racehorse.

And after he won his next outing by a nose as the even-money favorite, potential buyers suddenly became keenly interested in that 40 percent that still remained available. Of course, that 40 percent interest in the colt had suddenly become more expensive, the asking price $75,000.

On October 23, in the mud at Aqueduct, Thunder Gulch made his stakes debut in the Cowdin at seven furlongs. He didn't leave the gate sharply and raced in sixth for the opening half-mile, but then he rallied to finish second, two and a half lengths behind Old Tascosa. Having already proven he could run, Thunder Gulch quickly took the next step and proved he could compete in stakes company. And the horse that once interested nobody immediately interested everybody in the market for a Triple Crown prospect. After the Cowdin, Rozins and Ellenberg turned down $250,000 for the colt.

Theirs must have been an uneasy, even if congenial, partnership because Rozins and Ellenberg approached the situation with very different motives. Bagels were Rozins' business, and horse racing his sport. He didn't come to the racetrack looking for a way to support his family; he came looking for a sporting adventure. He came so that he might give life the opportunity to astound him, the opportunity to lift itself above the quotidian. Ellenberg's business, on the other hand, was selling horses, and he came to the track looking for business opportunities. As their trainer, Kimmel had to try to serve both interests. Yes, it must have been an uneasy situation, but the partnership would soon dissolve.

Michael Tabor of Monaco, who owned the Arthur Prince chain of bookmaking shops in his native England, was eager to jump into the American horse racing game. Once suspended, or "warned off," for three years by the British Jockey Club for allegedly making illicit payments to jockeys, Tabor had returned to the sport, and to good standing, by campaigning several stakes horses in England, such as Royal Derbi, who won the 1993 Irish Champion Hurdle.

Tabor wouldn't become a prominent force at North American sales until 1995, when he bought thirteen yearlings for $5.755 million, and he wouldn't win his first European classic until 1997. But back in 1994, still relatively unknown in American racing circles, he began to expand his racing interests by first searching for a Triple Crown prospect.

Representing Tabor, an Irish veterinarian cum bloodstock agent named Demi O'Byrne examined Thunder Gulch. O'Byrne, of course, would soon ascend to prominence as the agent for both Tabor and John Magnier, the managing partner of famed Coolmore Stud in Ireland.

"He was small," O'Byrne said, recalling his first impression of Thunder

Gulch. "But he was sound and very good looking. And he had an excellent walk."

He also had an efficient stride and a measurably large heart. And so on behalf of Tabor, who didn't want just 40 percent, O'Byrne offered $475,000 for the horse.

"I loved that colt, and I loved the game. I never looked at this like a business," said Rozins, explaining that those who did indeed look with a businessman's eye persuaded him to accept the offer. "I was reluctant to sell. But in retrospect, it's clear to me that owning a horse like Thunder Gulch is one in a million, and I was very lucky to be involved with him."

On November 11, immediately after Thunder Gulch finished fourth as the 6-5 favorite in the Nashua Stakes, the money changed hands and the horse changed barns, moving to the stable of trainer D. Wayne Lukas, who had topped the national trainers' standings in eleven of the previous twelve years and who had won two-thirds of the 1994 Triple Crown with Tabasco Cat.

Two weeks later, in his initial race around two turns, Thunder Gulch won his first stakes, the Remsen.

Gary Stevens, who actually went to New York to ride Bertrando in the NYRA Mile at Aqueduct, got the mount on Thunder Gulch in the Remsen Stakes. Having teamed with Lukas to win the 1988 Kentucky Derby on Winning Colors, Stevens was an obvious choice. And the trip to New York paid off for him. Although Bertrando finished tenth that day, Thunder Gulch won the Remsen by a neck.

Nevertheless, Thunder Gulch didn't impress his jockey; then again, the colt never had a gift for making a good first impression.

"When I walked into the paddock and saw him, I thought to myself, 'What do we have here?'" Stevens remembered. "I could look right over his withers, and I'm only five-three. They told me this was a horse they had for a new client and just try to get the best out of him."

Stevens followed instructions perfectly. Seventh early, Thunder Gulch advanced steadily, to fourth, then second, and then into the winner's circle. At a mile and one-eighth, the Remsen was especially auspicious because it confirmed Thunder Gulch's stamina. Still, he was far from being the professional he would become.

"He was very difficult to handle," Stevens said. "He wanted to lean on horses. He was a playboy. He just didn't seem to have the right attitude for racing."

Thunder Gulch completed his juvenile campaign by traveling to California and finishing second to a rising star named Afternoon Deelites in the Hollywood Futurity. But his was a poor second, more than six lengths back, and the outcome would contribute to the growing impression that the most talented group of prospects for the next season's Triple Crown would come out of California.

At the start of the new year, Timber Country was everybody's early Triple Crown favorite. Some even thought this might be the one, the twelfth horse in the sport's history to sweep the Triple Crown series. A large, powerful chestnut, Timber Country had won four of his seven races in his championship campaign of 1994, and he was unbeaten beyond a mile. He overcame a stumbling start to win the Champagne, and then, in what was widely viewed as a foreshadowing, he overcame a troubled journey to win the Breeders' Cup Juvenile at Churchill Downs by two lengths.

Charismatic and enormously talented, Timber Country seemed to be everything the sport needed. Lukas trained him; Pat Day rode him; and surely, many thought, the stars would align themselves in favor of the handsome colt.

Lukas also trained the best three-year-old filly in the country, Serena's Song. And so with both Timber Country and Serena's Song in California, Lukas sent Thunder Gulch to Gulfstream Park in Florida.

With Stevens riding regularly in Hong Kong, Mike Smith became

Thunder Gulch's new jockey. They teamed up for the first time in the Fountain of Youth, where Thunder Gulch gave the best performance of his young career.

He was growing, getting stronger. Lukas and his assistant, Todd Pletcher, were becoming more familiar with the colt, who now raced in blinkers and who, they knew, preferred to race outside rather than inside horses. The result: Thunder Gulch rallied seven-wide and won the Fountain of Youth by a neck over Suave Prospect, with Jambalaya Jazz, the 9-5 favorite, third.

Despite the victory, Thunder Gulch still inspired more skepticism than conviction, and three weeks later he wasn't favored in the Florida Derby. As part of a three-horse entry, Suave Prospect caught the bettors' attention and became the 9-5 choice, but the outcome was the same.

Thunder Gulch stalked the pace, made his move on the turn, was forced down inside, and got up in the final stride to win by a nose over Suave Prospect, who drifted out in the stretch. Mecke, who raced wide, rallied to finish third. It was the fourth victory in Thunder Gulch's career, all of them in photo finishes.

On April 15, just three weeks prior to the Derby, Thunder Gulch seemed to regress in the Blue Grass Stakes at Keeneland in Lexington, Kentucky. Smith chose to ride Concern in the Oaklawn Handicap in Hot Springs, Arkansas, that same afternoon. And so Day rode Thunder Gulch for the first time. They finished fourth, beating only two horses.

Bumped around at the start, Thunder Gulch reverted to his old habit of leaning on rivals, as though he forgot this was a race and thought it was a scrum. Lukas, however, attributed the poor effort to the Keeneland surface, which, before Polytrack, generally favored early speed and frequently treated late runners with disdain. In fact, Wild Syn, who would go on to finish last at Churchill Downs, won the Blue Grass in front-running style.

And so Thunder Gulch went to Churchill Downs with a slightly tarnished image. Maybe he had been lucky in Florida, or maybe he just loved Gulfstream. After all, he never had drawn off and won with authority, and if Suave Prospect hadn't drifted and Mecke hadn't raced wide … well, maybe Thunder Gulch wasn't that good; after all, he didn't even have a jockey for the Derby — such was the thinking after the Blue Grass.

Smith was committed to Talkin Man, who won the Wood Memorial by nearly eight lengths; and Day to Timber Country. And so Lukas asked Stevens to ride Thunder Gulch.

Stevens had returned from Hong Kong a few times for special mounts in special races. He won the Santa Anita Handicap, for example, on Urgent Request and the Santa Anita Derby on Larry the Legend. He expected, he explained, to come home again to ride one of the favorites in the Kentucky Derby. But an injury to Larry the Legend dispelled that idea and left Stevens without a Derby mount.

Still, recalling the Remsen and his impressions from watching the Blue Grass, Stevens "wasn't interested," he said, in riding Thunder Gulch, the playboy who didn't have a racing attitude. But then Smith intervened. The jockeys had been friends for years, and Smith convinced Stevens that Thunder Gulch would have a legitimate chance in the Derby if the colt returned to his Florida form.

As Stevens remembers their conversation, Smith had no explanation for the poor Blue Grass performance but told him that Thunder Gulch had developed far beyond the "playboy" of the Remsen. And so Stevens took the mount. Despite having two major victories in Florida on his resume and one of the world's best jockeys on his back, Thunder Gulch entered the Derby as an outsider. He was, after all, the third stringer in his own barn, for in addition to Timber Country, Lukas entered Serena's Song, who had won five straight, including the Jim Beam Stakes by three and a half lengths against males.

"He was caught between a champion and a ballerina," Lukas said about Thunder Gulch. "But he was sound and very durable. And he got to where he loved to train."

Thunder Gulch had been a few months younger than most of his rivals, a little bit smaller, and generally a little behind, except in talent and determination. But everything flowed together for him in the weeks leading up to the Derby, and he began training especially well, with more purpose and energy.

Donna Barton, who would become Donna Brothers, was a successful jockey at the time. She frequently rode for Lukas and worked for him in the mornings, getting on many of his better horses. One morning, she recalled, just before he was to begin a routine gallop, Thunder Gulch dropped her, tossing aside like dirty laundry, and then momentarily ran free, giving his overflowing energy and exuberance expression. It wasn't orneriness, Brothers said, that made him do it, just energy.

"Thunder Gulch was a little bit of a plodder, but he really came to life before the Derby," she said.

Brothers got on all three of the Lukas horses in the mornings. And one morning, after she had given all three their final Derby workouts, she and Thunder Gulch were returning to the barn, with Lukas accompanying them on a pony.

"Well, you have the best seat in the house," Lukas told her. "Which one do you think has the best chance to win it?"

"The one I'm on," she said.

"It was kind of surprising," Lukas said, recalling that morning years later. "But she was dead right."

The entry of Timber Country and Serena's Song was favored at 3-1 in the Derby. Timber Country had lost three races at Santa Anita and was third in the San Rafael, second in the San Felipe, and fourth in the Santa Anita Derby. But he closed strongly in all three, and this was Churchill, after all, where he had won the Breeders' Cup Juvenile.

Kentucky Derby

Purse: $750,000 Added

Churchill Downs - May 6, 1995. One hundred twenty-first running Kentucky Derby.

Purse $750,000 added. Three-year-olds. 1 1-4 Miles. Main Track. Track: Fast.

Value of race $957,400. Net value to winner, $707,400 and gold trophy; second, $145,000; third, $70,000; fourth, $35,000.

Horse	A	Wgt	Eqp	Odds	PP	1/4	1/2	3/4	1	Str	Fin	Jockey
Thunder Gulch	3	126	b	24.50	16	$6^{1\frac{1}{2}}$	$5^{\frac{1}{2}}$	$5^{\frac{1}{2}}$	$3^{1\frac{1}{2}}$	$1^{1\frac{1}{2}}$	$1^{2\frac{1}{4}}$	G Stevens
Tejano Run	3	126		8.60	14	13^{hd}	12^{1}	10^{hd}	6^{hd}	3^{hd}	2^{hd}	J Bailey
Timber Country	3	126		b-3.40	15	$14^{\frac{1}{2}}$	13^{hd}	12^{hd}	11^{hd}	10^{hd}	$3^{\frac{3}{4}}$	P Day
Jumron (GB)	3	126		5.60	10	8^{hd}	$9^{1\frac{1}{2}}$	$9^{1\frac{1}{2}}$	$4^{\frac{1}{2}}$	$5^{\frac{1}{2}}$	4^{hd}	G Almeida
Mecke	3	126	b	f-11.60	18	$16^{\frac{1}{2}}$	$16^{1\frac{1}{2}}$	19	$13^{1\frac{1}{2}}$	$8^{\frac{1}{2}}$	$5^{\frac{1}{2}}$	R Davis
Eltish	3	126		10.90	7	10^{1}	10^{hd}	11^{hd}	9^{2}	$6^{\frac{1}{2}}$	6^{3}	E Delahoussaye
Knockadoon	3	126		f-11.60	2	19	19	18^{hd}	$14^{\frac{1}{2}}$	$12^{\frac{1}{2}}$	7^{nk}	C McCarron
Afternoon Deelites	3	126		8.70	12	7^{hd}	6^{hd}	$6^{\frac{1}{2}}$	5^{hd}	7^{hd}	8^{nk}	K Desormeaux
Citadeed	3	126		f-11.60	19	$3^{\frac{1}{2}}$	$7^{\frac{1}{2}}$	2^{hd}	$7^{\frac{1}{2}}$	$9^{\frac{1}{2}}$	$9^{\frac{1}{2}}$	E Maple
In Character -GB	3	126		f-11.60	9	17^{1}	15^{hd}	17^{hd}	$12^{1\frac{1}{2}}$	13^{2}	$10^{\frac{1}{2}}$	C Antley
Suave Prospect	3	126		13.10	6	$9^{1\frac{1}{2}}$	11^{4}	14^{1}	$8^{\frac{1}{2}}$	$11^{\frac{1}{2}}$	$11^{\frac{1}{2}}$	J Krone
Talkin Man	3	126		4.00	11	$4^{1\frac{1}{2}}$	3^{hd}	4^{hd}	2^{hd}	2^{1}	$12^{\frac{1}{2}}$	M Smith
Dazzling Falls	3	126	b	27.60	1	12^{hd}	$14^{\frac{1}{2}}$	$13^{1\frac{1}{2}}$	19	15^{1}	13^{nk}	G Gomez
Ski Captain	3	126	f	f-11.60	17	$18^{\frac{1}{2}}$	17^{hd}	16^{1}	$15^{1\frac{1}{2}}$	14^{1}	$14^{1\frac{1}{2}}$	Y Take
Jambalaya Jazz	3	126	f	a-18.00	5	$15^{\frac{1}{2}}$	$18^{1\frac{1}{2}}$	15^{hd}	16^{hd}	16^{2}	15^{nk}	C Perret
Serena's Song	3	121		b-3.40	13	1^{hd}	$1^{1\frac{1}{2}}$	$1^{\frac{1}{2}}$	1^{hd}	4^{1}	$16^{1\frac{1}{2}}$	C Nakatani
Pyramid Peak	3	126		a-18.00	3	5^{1}	8^{hd}	8^{hd}	17^{1}	17^{6}	17^{6}	W McCauley
Lake George	3	126		f-11.60	8	11^{1}	4^{1}	7^{1}	10^{hd}	18^{12}	18^{21}	S Sellers
Wild Syn	3	126	f	18.80	4	$2^{\frac{1}{2}}$	$2^{1\frac{1}{2}}$	$3^{\frac{1}{2}}$	$18^{\frac{1}{2}}$	19	19	R Romero

f- Mutuel field.

Coupled, a-Jambalaya Jazz and Pyramid Peak; b-Timber Country and Serena's Song.

Off Time: 5:33 **Time Of Race:** :22⅘ :45⅕ 1:10⅕ 1:35⅗ 2:01⅕

Start: Good For All **Track:** Fast

Equipment: b for blinkers; f for front bandages

Mutuel Payoffs

11	**Thunder Gulch**	**$51.00**	**$24.20**	**$12.20**
10	**Tejano Run**		**10.20**	**6.80**
2b	**Timber Country**			**3.80**

Winner: Thunder Gulch, ch. c. by Gulch—Line of Thunder, by Storm Bird (Trained by D. Wayne Lukas). Bred by Peter M. Brant in Kentucky.

THUNDER GULCH, away in good order, was reserved while within easy striking distance until near the end of the backstretch, made a run four wide approaching the stretch and, after putting TALKIN MAN away with a furlong remaining, was kept to pressure to increase his advantage. TEJANO RUN, unhurried while outrun early, rallied between horses racing into the far turn, came out to continue his bid approaching the stretch and continued on with good energy to gain the place. TIMBER COUNTRY, outrun into the backstretch, dropped back after moving up along the inside at the far turn, came out looking for room through the upper stretch and finished gamely while angling in between horses. JUMRON brushed with AFTERNOON DEELITES early, raced five wide while advancing nearing the stretch but failed to sustain his bid in a long drive. MECKE, outrun to the far turn, moved up inside horses around the far turn and into the stretch and continued on with good energy. ELTISH, in close after the start, rallied from between horses nearing the stretch, came out for the drive but hung under pressure. KNOCKADOON, bumped after breaking slowly, raced between horses to the stretch and failed to seriously menace after angling inside for the drive. AFTERNOON DEELITES appeared to try and savage JUMRON after brushing with that rival near the eighth-pole position the first time, reached an easy striking position outside horses at the first turn, continued five wide while between horses to the stretch and weakened during the drive. CITADEED, close up early, made a run between horses approaching the far turn but tired throughout the drive. IN CHARACTER, in close after the start, angled out approaching the stretch but failed to reach serious contention. SUAVE PROSPECT saved ground to the backstretch, angled out seven wide after going a half, continued very wide while remaining within striking distance for a mile and gave way. TALKIN MAN, close up early while saving ground, caught SERENA'S SONG from the inside leaving the far turn, held on well to midstretch and tired. DAZZLING FALLS bumped KNOCKADOON after the start, saved ground into the backstretch, then passed tired horses after angling out very wide for the drive. SKI CAPTAIN, off slowly, was never close. JAMBALAYA JAZZ, always outrun, was checked between horses on the far turn. SERENA'S SONG, away alertly, was pressed while showing speed in the three path to the backstretch, held on well for a mile while continuing out from the rail and tired badly. PYRAMID PEAK saved ground for six furlongs and had nothing left. LAKE GEORGE, in close after the start, moved up six wide down the backstretch but was finished before reaching the stretch. WILD SYN showed good early foot along the inside, came out between horses when uable to stay with SERENA'S SONG around the first turn, raced forwardly to the turn, stopped suddenly and was eased.

Owners: (1) Michael Tabor; (2) Roy K Monroe; (3) Gainesway Farm, R & B Lewis & Overbrook Farm; (4) Charles W Dunn; (5) James Lewis Jr; (6) Juddmonte Farms; (7) William K Warren Jr; (8) Burt Bacharach; (9) Ivan Allan; (10) Baker & Farr & Jackson; (11) William Condren & M H Sherman; (12) Kinghaven Farm & H Stollery & P Wall; (13) Chateau Ridge Farm, Inc; (14) Shadai Racehorse Co. Ltd.; (15) John C Oxley; (16) Robert & Beverly Lewis; (17) John C Oxley; (18) William Boswell & David Lavin; (19) Jurgen K Arnemann

Talkin Man, who had won his last two outings by a total of nearly fifteen lengths, was the second choice at 4-1. And at 24-1, Thunder Gulch had the second longest odds in the nineteen-horse field. He also had the No. 16 post position, which never had produced a Derby winner.

Serena's Song shot to the lead, followed by Wild Syn and Talkin Man. Although he would give the horse all the credit for putting them in perfect position, Stevens was able to move Thunder Gulch toward the inside just behind the leading group during the run to the first turn. Serena's Song led the group through a rapid half-mile (:45 4/5). After three-quarters in 1:10 1/5, Wild Syn surrendered and retreated, and the sensational filly took them through the second turn.

After a mile in 1:35 3/5, Serena's Song tired. But Talkin Man was still there, and from the back, Timber Country and Tejano Run were rallying.

"When we turned into the stretch, I knew we had a chance," Stevens said, "and I was preparing for the battle of a lifetime. I put my stick in my left hand and hit him [Thunder Gulch], and he just exploded. He picked the perfect day to grow up, and from then on he was the ultimate professional."

Thunder Gulch dismissed Talkin Man in mid-stretch and won by more than two lengths, completing the mile and a quarter in 2:01 1/5, with Tejano Run second, a head in front of Timber Country.

Fans might have been stunned, but Thunder Gulch's connections had retained their confidence, especially Tabor, who had been surprised his colt went off at such a long price. Nevertheless, he was moved by the victory. "I never thought I could shake so much," he said after the trophy presentation. "It's a dream."

Timber Country, though, had his moment at Pimlico, winning the Preakness by a half-length, with Oliver's Twist second, a neck in front of Thunder Gulch.

Thunder Gulch followed with an easy two-length win in the Belmont Stakes. Six weeks later he won the Swaps by two at Hollywood Park, then the Travers by four and a half. Then he defeated older horses in the Kentucky Cup Classic. Injured in the Jockey Club Gold Cup, he finished fifth and was retired, with sixteen starts, nine wins, two seconds, two thirds, and $2,915,086 in earnings.

"People like to talk about how modern horses can't take stress and can't endure a long campaign," Lukas said, reflecting on the career of Thunder Gulch. "But he could. He was so sound and so durable and so tough. He did it all."

And he has passed much of it along. As a stallion, he has sired such standouts as Spain, winner of the 2000 Breeders' Cup Distaff, and Point Given, the 2001 Horse of the Year.

By Gary West

Decreed By the Derby Gods

TURN THE CLOCKS BACK to a damp, miserable late afternoon in May 1994. The setting is Churchill Downs, just moments after the running of the Kentucky Derby. Jockey Mike Smith, his cheeks caked with mud, has just dismounted the vanquished 2-1 favorite Holy Bull, the greatest horse he has ever ridden and likely will ever ride. Dejected and perplexed by the colt's dismal showing, Smith has his head down and eyes nearly closed as he walks off the track, carrying his tack and saddle towel. Having already finished a fast-closing second in the 1993 Derby aboard the favorite, Prairie Bayou, the loss is even harder to swallow.

This low point in Smith's career is merely the prologue for what would become one of the great stories in the annals of the Kentucky Derby. Holy Bull, of course, would go on to become Horse of the Year, his Derby failure long forgotten.

For Smith, however, there would be more disappointments to come on the first Saturday in May. A fifth-place finish aboard the sore-footed favorite, Unbridled's Song, in 1996, followed by a third on Cat Thief in 1999, a second aboard Proud Citizen in 2002, and another second on Lion Heart in 2004.

Surely, no one deserved to get lucky in the Run for the Roses more than Smith, whose career had been rudely interrupted by a broken back in 2001. The chances of luck finally coming his way in 2005 seemed re-mote at best as he prepared to ride 50-1 shot Giacomo, who had only a maiden victory to his credit in seven career starts. But the Derby gods, as we all know by now, work in mysterious ways, and it was almost as if they were waiting for this moment to smile down on Smith. The reason for the wait was simple. Giacomo's sire was none other than Holy Bull. If there would ever be a year for redemption — for both Smith and Holy Bull — this was it. The storyline seemed too good to go to waste, and no one writes scripts like the Derby gods.

As history shows, the script did indeed become reality, as Giacomo and Smith stormed down the Churchill stretch to win the 131st Kentucky Derby, paying a whopping $102.60 and triggering a record $9,814.80 exacta; $133,134.80 trifecta; and a $1 superfecta of $864,253.50.

Giacomo was owned and bred by Jerry and Ann Moss, who had cam-paigned a number of top-class horses over the years, including Sardula, Ruhlmann, and Delicate Vine. Moss, born in New York City, co-found-ed A&M Records with Herb Alpert, of Tijuana Brass fame. It took him "only" thirty-five years to come up with his first major Kentucky Derby hopeful.

In early 2004, the Mosses sent their Holy Bull colt, out of the Stop the Music mare Set Them Free, to trainer John Shirreffs, with whom they had about thirty of their seventy-five horses.

Shirreffs, a shy, unassuming person, has been one of the most popu-lar and well-liked trainers in Southern California for years. He is known for the meticulous care he gives his horses. On many nights he and his wife, Dottie Ingordo, who is the racing manager for the Mosses, would grab a pizza and bring it back to eat at the barn just to be close to the horses and see how they acted.

"John is so dedicated and passionate and devoted," Dottie said. "It's really amazing to be around him. He always looks for the greater good, always looks for the positive. We both realize that in this job, things can change moment to moment, so why not have a happy home life? Our position is we're very fortunate to be blessed with what we have. John loves the time between noon and three when it's quiet and he can spend some time with the horses and watch them in their house, as he puts it. He goes out and grazes them twice a day and stands there and plays with them. We have a great rapport with the horses, and we have a ball being around them. We try to make it fun for them."

When Giacomo turned three and was about to embark on the Triple Crown trail, Shirreffs wanted to get more protein in him and concocted his own version of a smoothie, consisting of carrot juice, apple juice, and at times a little whey protein powder. "I gave it as an appetite stimulant and to give him a little more energy," Shirreffs said.

A veteran of the Vietnam war, Shirreffs had been an assistant to Brian Mayberry and Bill Spawr before going out on his own in 1994 as private trainer for Ed Nahem and Marshall Naify, who operated 505 Farms near Lexington, Kentucky. His most notable runners were Bertrando, Manistique, Borodislew, and Cliquot.

Following the death of Naify and the subsequent dispersal of the 505 Farms horses, Shirreffs trained for the Thoroughbred Corp., owned by Prince Ahmed Salman. That stable was dissolved following Salman's death in 2002. Over the years Shirreffs also won stakes with Radu Cool, Starrer, Swept Overboard, Tarlow, Hollywood Story, and many other top-class horses.

One horse Shirreffs remembers fondly is a daughter of Holy Bull named Styler, who had a good deal of ability but was hampered by a breathing problem. When he visited Robbie Harris' farm in Ocala, Florida, in 2003, where the Mosses' sent horses to be broken, he became enamored with Styler's full brother and knew right away that was one horse he wanted to train.

The colt was named Giacomo, after the son of rock star Sting, who had named his son for the great Italian composer Giacomo Puccini, famous for such operas as *La Boheme* and *Madame Butterfly*.

Giacomo didn't appear to be anything special in the beginning. "He was just a young two-year-old coming into the barn," Shirreffs recalled. But after a series of gallops and works, Shirreffs started to feel as if he just might have something special on his hands.

"Every exercise rider who got on him came back and said, 'Boy, he's got a real nice way of going,' " Shirreffs said. "They were all very impressed with the way he moved."

One morning at Hollywood Park, Shirreffs was about to breeze Giacomo three-eighths of a mile when he saw Smith standing by the gap. He went up to him and said, "Come by the barn. My two-year-olds are in, and we got a Holy Bull I want you to look at."

All Smith said was "great." In the world of jockeys, it's never too early to start lining up Derby mounts, and Smith wasn't about to pass up getting on a son of Holy Bull.

Smith stopped by the barn, took one look at Giacomo, and said to Shirreffs, "I'm tellin' you what, John, can I get on this colt?"

"Yeah, get on him and let me know what you think," Shirreffs replied.

After working Giacomo — like Holy Bull, a handsome, well-balanced battleship gray, Smith couldn't wait to get back to the barn. "Man, this is the first horse I've ever been on that reminds me so much of his dad," Smith told Shirreffs. "He isn't as big as Holy Bull, but he is very similar in looks and the way he moves."

That's when Smith dropped his bombshell: "This might be the horse who'll redeem his father's name in the Kentucky Derby." The conservative Shirreffs, however, had more immediate and realistic plans for the colt. "Well, let's break his maiden first," he told Smith.

Giacomo made his career debut at Hollywood Park on July 15, 2004. Shirreffs hadn't geared the colt down and was just looking to give him a race. He was up to five-eighths in his works, and there was nothing left to do but run him. Sent off at 8-1, Giacomo ran fifth, with the winner, Things Happen, running the five and a half furlongs in a scorching 1:02 4/5.

"He didn't have a lot of early speed, and we weren't pushing him to show any," Shirreffs said. "In all his training, we never emphasized getting out of the gate fast and getting right into the race. What I liked about him was that his stride was long and smooth and repeated itself."

Then came his second start at Santa Anita, at a mile and one-sixteenth. After the race, Smith, the Mosses, and, yes, even Shirreffs, began having visions of roses and mint juleps. Giacomo rallied from fifth in the seven-horse field to blow his field away, winning under a hand ride by ten lengths.

Shirreffs needed a prep for the Hollywood Futurity and found a mile and one-sixteenth allowance race, in which Giacomo finished third behind the speedy Texcess. In the Hollywood Futurity, at the same distance, he was sent off at odds of 15-1 and closed strongly to finish second, beaten one length by the eventual two-year-old champion Declan's Moon, while finishing ahead of Breeders' Cup Juvenile winner Wilko. Although Giacomo had been beaten, Shirreffs and Smith gained satisfaction in knowing that the colt belonged with the best young horses in the nation. It was now on to the Kentucky Derby trail.

But the winter and spring were not kind to Giacomo and his reputation as a legitimate Derby contender, as he suffered three consecutive defeats — in the Sham Stakes, San Felipe Stakes, and Santa Anita Derby — at odds of 7-5, 7-2, and 7-2, respectively. The experts thought the three-year-olds in Southern California were vastly inferior to the brilliant colts back east and that Giacomo was too slow to compete with the likes of Bellamy Road, Afleet Alex, and Bandini, who had all destroyed their opposition in their final Derby preps — Bellamy Road by seventeen and a half lengths in the Wood Memorial, Afleet Alex by eight lengths in the Arkansas Derby, and Bandini by six lengths in the Blue Grass Stakes.

But Shirreffs had a master plan, and that was to get Giacomo to peak on Derby Day. "We always felt there was one more thing we could do with the horse, but we never wanted to do it too soon as far as his training was concerned," Shirreffs said. "We never pushed him in the morning. We knew we hadn't seen the best of Giacomo. He threw a shoe in the Sham Stakes and still finished a good third. In the San Felipe, Consolidator ran an amazing race in very fast time, and I thought Giacomo ran well to be second after making a big move on the far turn. In the Santa Anita Derby, they went very slow early and then sprinted home, just like a grass race. Although he finished fourth, he was only beaten two lengths, and Mike said he galloped out like he wanted to go a mile and a quarter."

Smith had several opportunities to get off Giacomo and ride a horse with more brilliance, such as the D. Wayne Lukas-trained Going Wild, who had beaten Giacomo in the Sham, but he had faith in the colt and in Shirreffs. He opted to stick with the horse with whom he had bonded.

Smith said he thought a lot of Giacomo from the first time he got on him. He and Shirreffs felt the colt had the natural speed to compete with the quick California two-year-olds, but their plan was always long-range, with the following year's classics in mind. To assure that Giacomo had every chance to make it to the Kentucky Derby, Shirreffs took it slow with him, teaching him to relax early and save his speed for the end of the race.

After the Santa Anita Derby, Shirreffs thought it was time to get serious and start cranking Giacomo up in the morning. "At first, we were just looking to see how far he'd go running twelve-second eighths," Shirreffs said. "As he got stronger and fitter, we asked him to do more."

Giacomo responded by turning in two bullet works: seven furlongs in 1:23 4/5 on April 25 and six furlongs in 1:11 4/5 six days before the Derby. No one back east seemed to notice. But Shirreffs and Smith were gaining confidence, despite the likelihood that Giacomo was going to be one of the longest prices in the Derby field.

Ten days before the Derby, Smith drove to Churchill Downs from Keeneland, where he had been riding regularly, to watch the morning gallops. As he stood in front of the old racing office, he looked out at the track where he had seen so many dreams evaporate on the first Saturday in May and had to wonder if his day would ever come to grab that elusive Derby victory.

"As you start getting older, you do have to wonder if [a Derby win] is ever going to come," said Smith, who would be celebrating his fortieth birthday that August. "But this colt is a lot better than people think. He's been working great, and I really believe he's going to run a big race. He's consistent, he's athletic, and he acts like he'll handle the mile and a quarter. It's just a question how he'll handle this track."

On the Wednesday before the Derby, Giacomo boarded a Tex Sutton plane, along with Santa Anita Derby winner Buzzards Bay, for the trip to Louisville. Shirreffs, Dottie, and the Mosses had flown in the previous evening on the Mosses' private jet, and the following morning they headed back to the airport to greet their star.

"We couldn't believe it," Shirreffs said. "We were getting goosebumps standing there. After the plane landed, Mrs. Moss walked up into the cargo bay and got to see Giacomo. He was in the first row, so she was able to see him right away. To watch him walk off the plane was really special. But to drive into Churchill Downs, knowing we had a horse in the Kentucky Derby, that just put us over the top."

The next morning Shirreffs sent Giacomo out for his first gallop around the Churchill Downs oval. As the trainer stood at the gap watching the handsome gray colt, he was conspicuous by his solitude. Not a single member of the media was around, which is something one ordinarily doesn't see when it comes to a Derby trainer, especially on his and his horse's first day at the Downs. The media were busy either at

"Fort Zito," the name given the fortress-like fence outside trainer Nick Zito's barn, or at the barns of Afleet Alex and Bandini. Zito would be saddling a record-equaling five horses in the Derby, and for five different owners, which necessitated the construction of this odd barricade.

Shirreffs and Smith watched Giacomo gallop and were elated with what they saw. "When he went by us, I said to John, 'Oh, man, he likes it,'" Smith recalled. "You could see the way he moved over it."

Despite the lack of attention paid to Giacomo, and all the hoopla surrounding the top choices, Shirreffs remained focused on his own horse.

"Dottie and I and the Mosses came to Kentucky just happy to be there with a horse in the Kentucky Derby and to enjoy the whole Derby experience," Shirreffs said. "I wasn't paying much attention to what was going on around me, as far as Bellamy Road, Afleet Alex, and Bandini were concerned. There were a lot of good horses in the race, but we just focused on our horse and tried to have the best experience possible."

That year's Derby picture was dominated by some of the titans of the Turf, with Zito, Todd Pletcher, D. Wayne Lukas, and Bobby Frankel having eleven of the twenty Derby hopefuls. Lukas, however, was forced to withdraw Consolidator several days before the race due to a fractured sesamoid. In addition to Bellamy Road, Zito had the Florida Derby one-two finishers, High Fly and Noble Causeway; the Tampa Bay Derby winner Sun King; and the Arkansas Derby third Andromeda's Hero. Pletcher had a pretty potent arsenal himself, saddling Bandini, Lane's End Stakes winner Flower Alley, and the Lexington winner Coin Silver.

An interesting starter was a speedball named Spanish Chestnut. Although trained by Patrick Biancone, he was owned by Michael Tabor and Derrick Smith, who also owned Bandini. Pletcher thought he could serve as a "rabbit" for Bandini while helping to kill off Bellamy Road, who would go off as the 5-2 favorite, and he convinced Tabor and Smith to enter the colt in the Derby.

When the morning line was announced, Shirreffs was surprised at the lack of respect given the California horses. Santa Anita Derby winner Buzzards Bay was 20-1, as was Wilko, who had finished third in the Santa Anita Derby. Don't Get Mad, despite shipping to Kentucky and romping in the Derby Trial Stakes by seven lengths, was 30-1, and Giacomo had the dubious honor of being the longest price in the field at 50-1.

"How can the Santa Anita Derby winner be 20-1?" Shirreffs asked. "How often do people think a race is bad, then a horse wins coming out of that race, and suddenly, they're all good horses? And how often do California horses come out here and kick a little butt? All I know is that Giacomo is doing really well, and he's so good now mentally. He always runs his heart out, goes to sleep that night, and the next day it's, 'OK, what do you want to do today?'"

The day before the Derby, Smith was interviewed on TVG and was asked what a Derby victory would mean to him, considering he'd won just about every other big race in country. Smith went right to his gut for the answer. "You know what, for me, my career just wouldn't be complete if I never win the Derby," he said. "I just don't believe I belong in the Hall of Fame if I don't win this. I would feel like a failure. I realize there are great riders in the Hall of Fame that never won the Derby, but they haven't had the number of opportunities I've had to win it. I've ridden some serious horses in the Derby, but it just wasn't my turn."

Derby Day dawned with clear skies, as 156,435, the second-largest crowd in Derby history, packed the historic track. Giacomo was sent off at his morning line odds of 50-1, but there actually were six others at higher odds, including the longest-priced horse in the field, Closing Argument, at 71-1.

In the paddock, Jerry Moss presented Smith with a $200 win ticket on Giacomo, which the jockey slipped into his boot. After saddling

Giacomo, Shirreffs, wearing a dark sport jacket and his signature Mill Ridge Farm baseball cap, took up a position by the rail, along with exercise rider Frank Herrate.

The start was uneventful, as Giacomo quickly dropped back and had only two of the twenty horses behind him as they passed the stands for the first time. Smith found himself sandwiched between Greeley's Galaxy and Don't Get Mad and decided to get Giacomo in the clear. He swung him to the outside but got fanned six wide going into the first turn.

Spanish Chestnut, meanwhile, was doing his job, cutting out a blistering pace, with an opening quarter in :22 1/5 and a half in :45 1/5. Going Wild also showed speed, with Bellamy Road and Flower Alley getting sucked up in the suicidal fractions.

Down the backstretch Giacomo still had only two horses behind him, but Smith liked what he felt under him. "I got carried out on the first turn, and once I got back off horses' heels I was able to steer him back to the inside," he said. "We were backed up pretty far, but he was on cruise control. In the middle of the backstretch, I started passing horses real easy and thought, 'Man, he's gonna run huge. It's just a matter of whether I get there in time or not.'"

Shirreffs, who likes to stay as close to the track as possible, watched on the infield screen and was able to follow Giacomo going into the first turn. He saw him go wide and then cut over, but after that he lost him and had no idea where he was the entire run down the backstretch and around the far turn.

Spanish Chestnut was still winging out there on the lead as Bellamy Road and High Fly began to close in, with Buzzards Bay making a huge run on the far outside. But after three-quarters in a scorching 1:09 2/5, it was unlikely that any horse within a half-dozen lengths of the lead would be around at the finish. Closing Argument was holding tough, looking for an opening, while Jeremy Rose had Afleet Alex on the move and was making up ground along the inside.

Giacomo had moved up to mid-pack but was surrounded by horses, and it was obvious he would need some holes to open for him. As they hit the quarter pole, High Fly and Bellamy Road stuck their heads in front of Spanish Chestnut, who was beginning his retreat, as expected. Buzzards Bay, on the outside, looked to be the main danger, but after turning for home it was Closing Argument and Afleet Alex who kicked into gear. The pace finally took its toll on Bellamy Road, and he and High Fly gave way to Closing Argument and Afleet Alex.

Giacomo seemed to have clear sailing, right behind Buzzards Bay, and Shirreffs finally was able to spot his shadow roll and the Mosses' green silks. Greeley's Galaxy and Don't Get Mad came flying on the far outside. With a cavalry charge outside him, Smith steered Giacomo to the inside looking for an opening and found himself behind a wall of horses. As the field began to fan out, Wilko came out into Giacomo, forcing him back toward the outside. Smith looked up and, lo and behold, there was nothing but open spaces in front of him. Wilko had knocked him into the perfect spot.

For Smith, it was as if the pearly gates had opened for him and he could smell his first Derby roses. He went to a series of left-handed whips, and Giacomo kept grinding his way toward the wire. Only Closing Argument and Afleet Alex stood between him and the roses. As they passed Shirreffs, there was still a sixteenth of a mile to go, and the trainer thought his horse could get third.

But inside the final sixteenth, it was obvious that Giacomo was the strongest horse. He surged to the front in the final yards, winning by a half-length over Closing Argument, with Afleet Alex another half-length back in third. Don't Get Mad, Buzzards Bay, and Wilko finished fourth, fifth, and sixth, respectively, meaning the much-maligned Santa Anita Derby had produced four of the top six finishers.

Because of the bad angle Shirreffs wasn't even sure Giacomo had won. "I wear glasses, because my eyes aren't worth a damn," he said.

"As they crossed the finish line, Frankie grabbed me and said, 'We won, boss; we won,' and he started jumping up and down."

For most everyone at Churchill Downs and those watching on TV, the result of Kentucky Derby 131 was a shocker; one of the greatest upsets in Derby history. How could a 50-1 shot who had won only one race in his career defeat such an illustrious field, and with a 71-1 shot finishing second? They might have gotten their answer had they taken a good look at Mike Smith returning to the winner's circle aboard a son of Holy Bull and seen the smile on the faces of the Derby gods. When it comes to the Run for the Roses, things often make a lot more sense after they have occurred.

But the bottom line is that Giacomo had become the longest-priced Derby winner since Donerail in 1913 and the second longest-priced winner in Derby history.

Shirreffs made his way on to the track as if in a daze, not knowing what to do next. Jerry Moss went over and hugged him. "That was an amazing thing you did," Moss said. "Just an amazing thing."

Smith returned to a hero's welcome. He took off his helmet and raised it over his head to salute the crowd, which gave him a rousing reception. As the roses were being draped over Giacomo's withers, Smith was greeted by Shirreffs and tried to put his feelings into words, but was unable to finish his first few sentences: "I'm tellin' you, man ... I got to tell you ... I never in my life ... I was so confident all the way around. Even when they took me out and I ducked back in, I just kept talkin' to him. I said, 'You're gonna get it boy,' and he kept talkin' back, 'I got 'em; I got 'em.'"

Shirreffs, still unsure what to do, started walking back to the test barn with Giacomo following the winner's circle celebration, not realizing that NBC had sent out a search party to find him so they could begin the trophy presentations. Shirreffs and Giacomo began heading back on the turf course until Shirreffs was directed to an opening to the

Kentucky Derby
Purse: $2,000,000 Added

Churchill Downs - May 7, 2005. One hundred thirty-first running Kentucky Derby.
Purse $2,000,000 added. Three-year-olds. 1 1-4 Miles. Main Track. Track: Fast.
Value of race $2,399,600. Net value to winner, $1,639,600 and gold trophy; second, $400,000; third, $200,000; fourth,
$100,000; fifth $60,000.

Horse	A	Wgt	Eqp	Odds	PP	1/4	1/2	3/4	1	Str	Fin	Jockey
Giacomo	3	126		50.30	10	18^{x}	18^{2x}	18^{1x}	11^{hd}	6^{x}	1^{x}	M Smith
Closing Argument	3	126		71.60	18	5^{hd}	6^{x}	6^{hd}	4^{hd}	1^{x}	2^{x}	C Velasquez
Afleet Alex	3	126	f	4.50	12	11^{hd}	11^{2x}	9^{x}	6^{1x}	2^{1}	3^{2x}	J Rose
Don't Get Mad	3	126		29.20	17	19^{6}	19^{3x}	19^{3x}	10^{hd}	7^{x}	4^{2x}	T Baze
Buzzards Bay	3	126	f	46.30	20	10^{x}	10^{hd}	7^{x}	5^{x}	5^{hd}	5^{x}	M Guidry
Wilko	3	126		21.70	14	13^{x}	14^{hd}	16^{2x}	13^{1x}	10^{x}	6no	C Nakatani
Bellamy Road	3	126		2.60	16	3^{x}	5^{2}	5^{2}	2^{hd}	3^{hd}	7^{x}	J Castellano
Andromeda's Hero	3	126		57.30	2	16^{hd}	15^{2}	13^{hd}	16^{2}	14^{1x}	8no	R Bejerano
Flower Alley	3	126	b	41.30	7	4^{hd}	3^{hd}	2^{hd}	7^{1x}	8^{1}	9^{hd}	J Chavez
High Fly	3	126		7.10	11	6^{1}	4^{1}	3^{hd}	1^{hd}	4^{1}	10^{nk}	J Bailey
Greeley's Galaxy	3	126		21.00	9	17^{1}	16^{x}	14^{hd}	8^{hd}	12^{2x}	11^{2x}	K Desormeaux
Coin Silver	3	126		38.60	5	14^{x}	12^{hd}	12^{1x}	9^{x}	11^{1}	12^{1x}	P Valenzuela
Greater Good	3	126		58.40	8	20	20	20	17^{x}	15^{4}	13^{x}	J McKee
Noble Causeway	3	126		12.30	4	12^{2}	13^{2x}	15^{hd}	12^{hd}	13^{x}	14^{2x}	G Stevens
Sun King	3	126		15.70	3	9^{x}	9^{hd}	8^{hd}	15^{1x}	16^{4}	15^{4}	E Prado
Spanish Chestnut	3	126		71.00	13	1^{x}	1^{1x}	1^{1x}	3^{hd}	9^{hd}	16^{7}	J Bravo
Sort It Out	3	126		61.90	1	15^{x}	17^{hd}	17^{hd}	18^{4}	17^{2x}	17^{3x}	B Blanc
Going Wild	3	126	b	59.50	19	2^{1}	2^{1}	4^{x}	14^{hd}	18^{5x}	18^{3x}	J Valdivia Jr
Bandini	3	126		6.80	15	7^{hd}	8^{2}	11^{1x}	20	19^{3}	19^{12}	J Velazquez
High Limit	3	126		22.50	6	8^{2}	7^{hd}	10^{3x}	19^{hd}	20	20	R Dominguez

Off Time: 6:11　　Time Of Race: :22½　:45½　1:09¾　1:35½　2:02¾
Start: Good For All　　Track: Fast
Equipment: b for blinkers; f for front bandages

Mutuel Payoffs

10	Giacomo	$102.60	$45.80	$19.80
18	Closing Argument		70.00	24.80
12	Afleet Alex			4.60

Winner: Giacomo, gr/ro. c. by Holy Bull—Set Them Free, by Stop the Music (Trained by John A. Shirreffs).
　　　 Bred by Mr. and Mrs. J.S. Moss in Kentucky.

GIACOMO, in a bit tight between horses at the start, was unhurried while five wide between rivals during the early stages, continued five wide along the backstretch, worked his way forward between horses six wide on the far turn, was in behind a wall of horses entering the upper stretch, was alertly angled eight abreast to secure racing room at the furlong grounds, then closed determinedly under extreme left-handed urging to prevail in the final seventy yards. CLOSING ARGUMENT bobbled slightly while drifting out for a stride at the break, angled a forward position while nine wide during the opening quarter, angled inward to be four wide on the first turn and along the backstretch, inched up between foes four wide entering the far turn, angled five wide while going between horses at the top of the stretch, gained a narrow advantage leaving the three-sixteenth pole, was joined by the winner from the outside about the sixteenth pole and held on tenaciously to save the place. AFLEET ALEX, nicely placed under light rating from early on while between foes four or five wide, rallied near the inside around the far turn, came out and split rivals while four wide when straightened into the stretch, gained on even terms for the lead in deep stretch and wasn't quite good enough. DON'T GET MAD raced four wide on the backstretch, was asked for his best nearing the three-eighths pole while circling foes eight wide, came to the exteme outside to be ten wide entering the stretch, offered a serious bid entering the final furlong but couldn't sustain the needed momentum. BUZZARDS BAY gained a striking position early while maneuvering in six wide, edged closer nearing the end of the backstretch, commenced a sweeping bid seven wide to reach contention approaching the final quarter, loomed menacingly in upper stretch but came up empty. WILKO came out between horses six wide for the drive, checked in tight quarters leaving the three-sixteenths pole, gained a slight advantage between calls when straightened into the stretch, remained a factor into upper stretch, then weakened. ANDROMEDA'S HERO, unhurried to the far turn and racing near the inside, came out six or seven wide entering the stretch and produced a mild gain. FLOWER ALLEY, leaned in early bumping with HIGH LIMIT, and forced that one in on NOBLE CAUSEWAY, moved inside, continued forwardly placed along the backstretch, was steadied approaching the five-sixteenths pole, dropped back nearing the quarter pole and weakened soon after. HIGH FLY, nicely placed while working his way near the inside between foes, continued between horses while going after SPANISH CHESTNUT approaching the stretch, put a head in front near the final quarter, battled heads apart into upper stretch, but couldn't sustain the needed momentum. GREELEY'S GALAXY was pinched back in tight after a tardy start, quickly was angled in to race four abreast, came a bit wider on the far turn to commence a sweeping bid, reached contention when straightened for the drive and lacked a further account. COIN SILVER, eased back early after being forced to steady behind NOBLE CAUSEWAY, made a run four or five wide around the far turn, was joined for the drive but was unable to continue his bid. GREATER GOOD, void of early speed and outrun to the stretch, came out ten wide for the drive and failed to menace while improving his postition. SUN KING, in contention near the inside for seven furlongs, made a brief move in close quarters approaching the far turn then gradually weakened. GOING WILD angled in early to press front-running SPANISH CHESTNUT four wide, was asked for more leaving the backstretch, failed to keep the pace and faded. BANDINI, in contention while racing in mid-pack between rivals, was finished entering the far turn.

Owners: (1) Mr & Mrs Jerome S Moss; (2) Philip & Marcia Cohen; (3) Cash is King LLC; (4) B Wayne Hughes; (5) Fog City Stable; (6) J Paul Reddam & Susan Roy; (7) Kinsman Stable; (8) Robert V LaPenta; (9) Melnyk Racing Stables, Inc; (10) Live Oak Plantation; (11) B Wayne Hughes; (12) Peachtree Stable; (13) Lewis G Lakin; (14) My Meadowview Farm; (15) Tracy Farmer; (16) Derrick Smith & Michael Tabor; (17) Stonerside Stable & Preferred Pals Stable; (18) Robert & Beverly Lewis; (19) Derrick Smith & Michael Tabor; (20) Gary L & Mary E West

©EQUIBASE

dirt track. "I just want to make sure he gets back okay," Shirreffs said.

After trying to decide whether to follow Giacomo back to the barn or go to the trophy presentation, he reluctantly backed away from the horse when told he'd be wanted for the presentation. "I've never run in this race before," he said. "I don't know the routine." Just then, an NBC producer came running over to him. "You're killin' me, John," he said. "You're killin' me."

In the jocks' room, there was no doubt this was one of the most popular Derby victories ever. "Good for Mike," Jerry Bailey said. "Yeah, I wish it could have been me, but good for him," said Buzzards Bay's rider Mark Guidry.

Gary Stevens, who had won three Kentucky Derbys, was noticeably choked up. "I'm as excited right now as I would be had it been me that won," he said. "He's wanted this for so long. And I would say the Mosses are the most loyal owners I've ever ridden for. And John is just a blue-collar kind of guy, but one of the best horsemen around and very humble."

Smith echoed Stevens' words. "John and Dottie and the Mosses are the greatest people I've ever met," he said. "They've done so much for my life it's amazing."

Smith couldn't wait to go off to a quiet corner of the jocks' room and call his father, George, who galloped horses at Philadelphia Park in the mornings and parked cars in the afternoons. George watched the Derby by himself at his home in Croyden, Pennsylvania, about fifteen minutes from Philadelphia Park

"It was unbelievable," the elder Smith said later that night. "I started shaking and then began jumping up and down. I'm sure they heard me all the way down the street. I really couldn't say much when we spoke, I was so emotional. Mike is such a good guy, and I'm so proud of him. It's just hitting me now. I'm sure I won't be able to go to sleep tonight."

Back at the barn Shirreffs rewarded Giacomo with a smoothie, into which the colt promptly buried his head, emerging with a thick orange coat around his mouth, much like a child gulping down a milkshake.

The Mosses arrived and couldn't take their eyes off Giacomo. "I'm going to have to watch the replay ten or twelve times before it sinks in," said Jerry, who then called Robbie Harris to congratulate him.

Harris recalled the "gangly teenager" he had broken two years earlier. "He was a very smart colt and did everything right, but I'm not going to sit here and tell you I thought he was going to win the Kentucky Derby," Harris said. "It was John who loved him from day one. He picked him out of the whole group of homebreds and purchases. He's just done a super job with him. This couldn't happen to nicer people."

Shirreffs and Dottie flew back to California with the Mosses that night and about a week later attended a Derby celebration/birthday party for Jerry, with famed chef Wolfgang Puck preparing the food. "They had a huge tent set up in a big grass field next to the Mosses' home, with a giant quartz crystal globe all lit up," Shirreffs said. "Ann always had visions of Giacomo grazing in that field. They brought in Sergio Mendez to sing and they had a lot of the A&M people there. They also flew Mike Smith in and flew him right back the next day before the races. And, of course, they showed the replay of the Derby."

Kentucky Derby 131 had found its place in the history books. Holy Bull and Mike Smith had been redeemed, and the often-maligned Giacomo finally was getting the respect Shirreffs and the Mosses felt he deserved.

As Moss said while staring at Giacomo after the race, "It's amazing how much more respect you get when you win the Kentucky Derby."

By Steve Haskin

Photo Credits

Page 1: Elwood (Kinetic Corporation/Churchill Downs Inc.); Boots Durnell and John Gates (Keeneland-Cook); Donerail (Kinetic Corporation/Churchill Downs Inc.); T.P. Hayes (Blood-Horse Library)

Page 2: Exterminator and Sun Briar (Keeneland-Cook); Exterminator (Blood-Horse Library)

Page 3: Bold Venture (Kinetic Corporation/Churchill Downs Inc.); Mr. and Mrs. Morton Schwartz (Morgan Photo Service); Brevity (Joe Fleischer)

Page 4: Gallahadion's Derby finish (J.A. Estes); trophy presentation (H.C. Ashby); Gallahadion (H.C. Ashby); Bimelech (H. Rhodenbaugh)

Page 5: Dark Star in Derby turn (Blood-Horse Library); Derby finish (Kinetic Corporation/Churchill Downs Inc.); winner's circle (*Courier-Journal and Louisville Times*); Native Dancer (Bert Morgan)

Pages 6-7: Gen. Duke's Florida Derby (Jim Raftery/Turfotos); Bold Ruler and Gallant Man (Mike Sirico/NYRA); Iron Liege's Derby finish (Bud Kamenish/*Courier-Journal and Louisville Times*); winner's circle (Skeets Meadors); Iron Liege returning to barn (Skeets Meadors)

Pages 8-9: Canonero II in stretch, galloping out, and winner's circle (Kinetic Corporation/Churchill Downs Inc.)

Pages 10-11: Genuine Risk in Derby turn (Lexington *Herald-Leader*); Rockhill Native (Milt Toby); Genuine Risk winning Derby (Lexington *Herald-Leader*); Derby winner's circle (Milt Toby); Plugged Nickle (NYRA Photo)

Page 12: Lil E. Tee winning Derby (Skip Dickstein); trophy presentation (Skip Dickstein); Arazi (Barbara D. Livingston)

Pages 13-14: Timber Country (Barbara D. Livingston); Thunder Gulch winning Derby (Skip Dickstein); Serena's Song (Barbara D. Livingston); Thunder Gulch (Barbara D. Livingston); trophy presentation (Skip Dickstein)

Pages 15-16: Bellamy Road (Anne M. Eberhardt); Afleet Alex (Barbara D. Livingston); Giacomo winning Derby (Barbara D. Livingston); Giacomo's win payoff (Barbara D. Livingston); John Shirreffs with Giacomo (Dave Harmon); winner's circle (Anne M. Eberhardt)

About the Authors

RENA BAER is an assistant editor with Eclipse Press, the book division of Blood-Horse Publications. She also writes freelance for magazines, including *Keeneland*. Baer lives in Lexington, Kentucky.

EDWARD L. BOWEN is an award-winning author of eighteen books, including biographies of Man o' War and War Admiral, the two-volume set on the great breeders titled *Legacies of the Turf*, and a book on the great trainers of the early twentieth century, *Masters of the Turf*. Bowen resides in Versailles, Kentucky.

TIMOTHY T. CAPPS is the author of the Thoroughbred Legends books on Secretariat, Spectacular Bid, and Affirmed and Alydar. He has served as executive director of the Maryland Jockey Club and as editor and publisher of *MidAtlantic Thoroughbred*. Capps lives in Columbia, Maryland.

JOHN EISENBERG, a sports columnist for the *Baltimore Sun*, is the author of biographies on Native Dancer and Lil E. Tee as well as *The Great Match Race: When North Met South in America's First Sports Spectacle*, published in 2006, and other sports books.

STEVE HASKIN is an award-winning senior correspondent for *The Blood-Horse* and author of several books, including *Horse Racing's Holy Grail: The Epic Quest for the Kentucky Derby* and biographies on John Henry, Dr. Fager, and Kelso for the Thoroughbred Legends series. Haskin lives in Hamilton Square, New Jersey.

AVALYN HUNTER is a mental health care professional and Thoroughbred pedigree researcher. She is the author of *The Kingmaker: How Northern Dancer Founded a Racing Dynasty* and *American Classic Pedigrees*, as well as *The Gold Rush*, a biography of Mr. Prospector to be published in 2007. She lives in Lake City, Florida.

MICHELE MACDONALD began reporting on Thoroughbred racing in the mid-1980s after cultivating a virtually lifelong passion for horses and the sport. She has earned multiple awards for her writing, and her work has been published in a number of periodicals in the United States, Britain, and Dubai. When not at her computer, she spends much of her time with her two retired racehorses. She lives in Lexington, Kentucky.

ELIZA R.L. MCGRAW is a freelance writer living in Washington, D.C. Her work has appeared in *The Blood-Horse*, *EQUUS*, and the *Washington Post*, and she contributed to the book *Horse Racing's Top 100 Moments*. Her book, *Everyday Horsemanship*, was published in 2003.

GARY MCMILLEN is assistant director of human resources at Louisiana State University Health Sciences Center in New Orleans. As a freelance writer, he is a racing correspondent for *The Blood-Horse* and *Louisiana Horse* magazines. Living in New Orleans, he has been a "regular" at Fair Grounds since 1970.

GARY WEST is a sportswriter and horse racing columnist for the Fort Worth (Texas) *Star-Telegram* and is author of *Razoo at the Races*, a humorous look at horse racing and handicappers.